# ACKNOWLEDGEMENTS

The Government Statistical Service gratefully acknowledges the major work undertaken by the Institute for Employment Research at the University of Warwick, under the direction of Dr Peter Elias, in the development and compilation of this classification.

The work was strongly supported through a Steering Group comprising staff from the Office of Population Censuses and Surveys, the Employment Department Group, the Central Statistical Office, and the Department of Applied Economics at the University of Cambridge.

The preparation of this publication was also made possible with the considerable help and co-operation of a large number of organisations and individuals who supplied information, commented on consultative documents, tested the classification, and offered numerous constructive suggestions.

Employment Department Group
Office of Population Censuses and Surveys

# Standard Occupational Classification
# Volume 1

First edition February 1990

## Structure and Definition of Major, Minor and Unit Groups

LONDON : HMSO

© Crown copyright 1990
First published 1990

ISBN 0 11 691284 7

**British Library Cataloguing in Publication Data**
Standard occupational classification.
Vol. 1. Structure and definition of major, minor
and unit groups
1. Great Britain. Occupations
I. Great Britain. Office of Population Censuses and
Surveys II. Employment Department Group
331.7'00941

# CONTENTS

**Standard Occupational Classification Volume 1**

# LIST OF TABLES

# PREFACE

Accurate and comprehensive occupational classification is essential for identifying occupational trends and developments in the labour market to enable the effective planning and implementation of relevant employment and training programmes. This is all the more important as the pace of technological progress increases and occupational skills change.

The Standard Occupational Classification (SOC) has been developed as a single, standard classification which will replace a number of incompatible classifications systems. It is intended that the main occupational data series compiled by Government Departments will be converted onto SOC during the early 1990s.

SOC uses a structured approach to occupational classification. Occupations are identified and aggregated with reference to the similarity of qualifications, training, skills and experience commonly associated with the competent performance of constituent tasks. Variations in the tasks performed occur between one place of employment and another and consequently not all definitions can be expected to coincide exactly with specific jobs in a particular establishment or in a given locality.

The definitions of occupations should not be regarded as setting any standard or relative level in respect of pay, hours of work or related subjects. The classification does not refer directly to level of authority or status in employment.

No single classification system can completely satisfy the requirements of every potential user, but it is hoped that the straightforward and structured approach adopted by SOC, and its broad compatibility with international classifications, will ensure its wide use by providers and users of occupational data.

# INTRODUCTION

## 1. General background and introduction

The Standard Occupational Classification (SOC) has been developed in collaboration by the Employment Department Group (EDG)[1] and the Office of Population Censuses and Surveys (OPCS).

SOC replaces both the Classification of Occupations and Directory of Occupational Titles (CODOT) and the 1980 version of the OPCS Classification of Occupations (CO80). CODOT was published in 1972 by a predecessor of EDG and has been used and supported since by EDG both in client-oriented applications (e.g. job placement, vocational guidance) and as a basis for labour market statistics. CO80 was developed from a series of earlier classifications used in OPCS to code occupational information on census of population forms and in many other applications.

In developing CO80 a partial harmonisation for statistical purposes was made between it and CODOT. This gave rise to the classification known as Condensed Key Occupations for Statistical Purposes (Condensed KOS). By the mid-nineteen eighties CO80, CODOT and Condensed KOS all needed extensive revision and a decision was accordingly made to update and replace them by developing the Standard Occupational Classification.[2]

It happened that the 1968 version of the International Standard Classification of Occupations (ISCO), developed and promulgated by the International Labour Office, was also simultaneously up for revision. The joint IER/OPCS SOC development team took the opportunity to consult and liaise with the ISCO revision team at ILO in order to achieve the closest feasible harmonisation between SOC and the new International Standard (ISCO 88).

Technical development work was carried out on contract to EDG by the Institute for Employment Research of the University of Warwick (IER). A development team at IER worked closely with a team from OPCS, consulting with users in the employment field within and outside EDG as development proceeded. OPCS also consulted users of the occupational and occupation-based statistics and data which it provides through censuses and surveys.

## 2. The SOC Manual

The present manual is being published to enable operational users in both research/statistical and client-oriented applications to use SOC in as consistent a way as possible; and to enable users of SOC-based occupational statistics to understand the classificatory principles and coding practices according to which those statistics are produced. The manual is published as three volumes —Volumes 1 and 2 together, followed later by Volume 3.

The remainder of Volume 1 comprises the following sections. Section 3 gives a brief account of some important principles, concepts and conventions according to which SOC has been developed. Section 4 explains the treatment in SOC of some technical problems in the classification of occupations. Section 5 sets out the detailed SOC structure of Unit,

---

[1] Consists of: the Department of Employment, Employment Service and Training Agency.

[2] For further background information see R. Thomas and P. Elias 'The development of the Standard Occupational Classification', Population Trends No. 55 Spring 1989.

Minor, Sub-major and Major Groups. Section 6 gives a description of each of the groups distinguished and lists job tasks which persons classified to the group typically carry out and common job titles which are classified to the group.

Volume 2 mainly consists of a detailed alphabetical index of job titles, giving the SOC Unit Group to which each is assigned. This is designed for use in coding occupations. To assist consistent coding some guidance notes are provided on the way in which the index has been compiled and organised and on how to locate exactly the right index entry, given the kind of description of the job typically provided by informants. These notes form the introductory sections to Volume 2.

Volume 3 (to be published later) covers several different topics. The first part describes in detail how summary socio-economic classifications derived from information on occupation and employment are formed using data coded to SOC (plus certain ancillary information). The second part provides information on the degree and nature of discontinuities between SOC and its predecessor CO80. The third part contains some remarks on issues arising in implementing the classification and coding of occupations and in the use of socio-economic classifications derived from information on occupation.

## 3.   Principles and concepts

### 3.1  Types of economic activity classification

In classifying jobs and persons by reference to their economic activity four distinct concepts are generally recognised and separately measured in standard statistical sources. These are:

1. Economic activity status

2. Occupation

3. Status in employment

4. Industry

Economic activity status defines whether the person is or is not at some reference time a member of the workforce. In practice those in paid employment and those currently looking for or available for paid employment are classified as economically active and the remainder as economically inactive. Many economically inactive persons (e.g. most of those wholly retired from employment) have, of course, had an occupation at some time in the past.

Occupation is most often determined by reference to a person's main job at the reference time, but for persons not currently employed may be determined by reference to the most recent, or most recent main, job. The SOC principles used in classifying occupations are discussed below.

Status in employment refers to the relationship of a person doing a job to the means of production (i.e. proprietor or self-employed versus employee); and, for an employee, to his or her position in the seniority structure of the workplace (e.g. apprentice/trainee, foreman/supervisor, manager, other employee). Not all these status distinctions are made in every data source and there have been differences over time and between different classificatory schemes as to whether certain distinctions should be built into the classification of occupations or introduced separately. For their treatment in SOC see Sections 3.2 and 4.2 below.

Industry refers to the economic sector to which the work done in a particular job contributes. It is usually defined by reference to the main product made or service performed at the workplace at or from which a job is carried on. Thus the job of a person who is occupationally a carpenter will be classified industrially to building, if employed by a building firm, but to brewing, if employed by a brewing firm. Most occupational groups include jobs located in many different industrial sectors; but there are some cases of occupations which in practice are associated almost entirely with one particular industry. In general, classification of occupations to SOC takes no account of information on industry, but for certain exceptions to this see Section 4.3 below and the Notes on coding included in Volume 2 of the SOC Manual.

## 3.2 Objects to be classified and criteria of classification

SOC has been designed as a classification applicable to all paid jobs currently done by economically active persons in Great Britain. Any given job is assumed to involve a set of typical work activities and to be an instance of one particular occupation. The object has then been to group together occupations (basically by reference to job titles) which are deemed to be similar, taking simultaneous account of two main criteria. These criteria are: the level of skill and/or experience and/or formal qualification which is required to carry out competently the work activities typically involved in the occupation; and the nature of those work activities. These same criteria are applied as principles of aggregation at different levels within SOC (see Section 3.3 below).

These criteria are not new and have been implicitly or explicitly invoked in previous schemes of occupational classification. However, in the case of SOC a thorough-going attempt has been made to apply them in a consistent manner throughout the classification.

The first criterion —skill level —is applied where possible by reference to the level of formal qualifications currently required in order for a person to be recognised as fully competent in the occupation concerned; but in other cases by reference to the duration of training andor experience recognised in the field of employment concerned as being normally required to pursue the occupation competently.

The second criterion —nature of work activities —may refer to any or all of a number of aspects of the work, including the materials handled, the type of tools and equipment used and so on. However, it focusses specifically in all cases on work activities, rather than on other aspects of the job such as, for example, whether the worker has trainee or supervisory status, or what industrial function the job serves. These are ignored by SOC —so that, for example, a 'carpenter', an 'apprentice or trainee carpenter' and a 'foreman carpenter' are all assigned to exactly the same occupational group. (For limited exceptions in the case of managerial occupations see Section 4.3 below.)

In this respect the SOC unit group classification differs from the classificatory scheme of CO80, where some groups are distinguished by reference to whether or not the job-holder had the status of a foreman or supervisor.

Other criteria which have been significant in the development of the SOC are:

3

- to ensure that the classification bridges past and future usage —i.e. that a balance is struck between the need to provide an up-to-date classification which will be used for some time into the future and the need to retain a reasonable degree of continuity with previous classifications;

- to reduce the usage of 'not elsewhere classified' categories which appeared in previous classifications;

- to identify additional occupational categories in areas of work where women predominate and which lacked differentiation in previous classifications;

- to recognise significant developments in the structure of occupations over recent years and take account of the modern usage of job titles;

- to distinguish occupations in ways which can be reliably classified using responses to the Census of Population, the Labour Force Survey and the New Earnings Survey;

- to align as far as possible with ISCO 88.


Further information on the application of these criteria is given in Section 4.1 below.

## 3.3  Structure of the classification

Unlike CO80, but like CODOT and ISCO 88, SOC has an explicitly hierarchical structure. At the most detailed level of classification 374 unit groups are distinguished.  Each occupation unit group is allocated to a minor group (two-digit), of which there are 77 and a major group (one-digit), of which there are nine.

The major group structure is a set of broad occupational categories which are designed to be useful in bringing together unit groups which are similar in terms of the qualifications, training, skills and experience commonly associated with the competent performance of work tasks.  The divisions between major groups also reflect the important aim of aligning SOC as far as possible with the international classification ISCO 88, in which major groups are distinguished on similar criteria.

Table 1 shows the nine major groups of SOC, defined in terms of the general nature of the qualifications, training and experience associated with competent performance of tasks in the occupations classified within each major group.

**Table 1:  General Nature of Qualifications, Training and Experience for Occupations in SOC Major Groups**

| Major Group | General Nature of Qualifications, Training and Experience for Occupations in the Major Group |
| --- | --- |
| Managers and Administrators | A significant amount of knowledge and experience of the production processes, administrative procedures or service requirements associated with the efficient functioning of organisations and businesses. |
| Professional Occupations | A degree or equivalent qualification, with some occupations requiring post graduate qualifications and/or a formal period of experience-related training. |
| Associate Professional and Technical Occupations | An associated high-level vocational qualification, often involving a substantial period of full-time training or further study.  Some additional task-related training is usually provided through a formal period of induction |
| Clerical and Secretarial Occupations | A good standard of general education. Certain occupations will require further additional vocational training to a well defined standard (e.g. typing or shorthand). |
| Craft and Related Occupations | A substantial period of training, often provided by means of a work-based training programme. |
| Personal and Protective Service Occupations | A good standard of general education. Certain occupations will require further additional vocational training, often provided by means of a work-based training programme. |
| Sales Occupations | A general education and a programme of work-based training related to sales procedures.  Some occupations require additional specific technical knowledge but are included in this major group because the primary task involves selling. |
| Plant and Machine Operatives | The knowledge and experience necessary to operate vehicles and other mobile and stationary machinery, to operate and monitor industrial plant and equipment, to assemble products from component parts according to strict rules and procedures and subject assembled parts to routine tests. Most occupations in this major group will specify a minimum standard of competence that must be attained for satisfactory performance of the associated tasks and will have an associated period of formal experience-related training. |
| Other Occupations | The knowledge and experience necessary to perform mostly simple and routine tasks involving the use of hand-held tools and in some cases, requiring a degree of physical effort. Most occupations in the major group require no formal educational qualifications but will usually have an associated short period of formal experience-related training.  All non-managerial agricultural occupations are also included in this major group, primarily because of the difficulty of distinguishing between those occupations which require only a limited knowledge of agricultural techniques, animal husbandry, etc. from those which require specific training and experience in these areas. These occupations are defined in a separate minor group. |

Minor groups in SOC are distinguished mainly by reference to the type of work performed or the area of occupational specialism which characterises the constituent unit groups.

Each Unit Group is identified by a three-digit number, which indexes its position in the SOC structure as shown in the following example.

Town Planners     SOC Unit Group 261

The first digit references the major group, the second digit references the minor group, the third digit references the unit group, as follows:

| Major group 2 | Minor group 26 | Unit group 261 |
|---|---|---|
| (Professional Occupations) | (Architects, town planners and surveyors) | (Town planners) |

Within each level of the classification the digit '9' is reserved for occupations 'not elsewhere classified' at each level of the structured classification.

Following the lead of ISCO, it was acknowledged that some analysts may feel the need for a classification more detailed than SOC Major Groups, but less detailed than Minor Groups. In order to meet this need a further level between Major and Minor levels is defined, known as Sub-major Groups. The 22 Sub-major Groups are defined in Table 2 which follows and may be formed by aggregating Minor Groups, but the Sub-major Group level of classification is not indexed in the numbering system.

The sub-major groups are particularly useful in that they distinguish between some of the broad groups of occupations which, because of the nature of their associated qualifications, training or work experience, are aggregated into the same major group. Thus, for example, important distinctions are made in Major Group 1: Managers and Administrators, between managers of small businesses and other managers; in Major Group 2: Professional Occupations, between science and engineering, health and education professions; in Major Group 3 between science and engineering on the one hand and health occupations on the other in Associate Professional and Technical Occupations. Major Group 4 distinguishes clerical from secretarial occupations at the level of sub-major groups. In Major Group 5: Craft and Related Occupations, skilled construction and skilled engineering trades are separately identified because of their numerical importance in this major group and their distinctive training requirements. In Major Group 6: Personal and Protective Service Occupations, protective service occupations (armed forces, fire, police, prison, security occupations) are identified separately at the level of sub-major group. Major Group 7: Sales Occupations, separates buyers, brokers and sales representatives from other sales occupations at the level of sub-major group. In major Group 8: Plant and Machine Operatives, drivers and other mobile machine operators are distinguished from other plant and machine operators and assembly workers. Major Group 9: Other Occupations distinguishes between the agricultural group of occupations and other elementary occupations at the level of sub-major group, recognising the special treatment of agricultural occupations in the Standard Occupational Classification (see Section 4.4).

**Table 2: The Definition of Sub-Major Groups and Constituent Minor Groups**

| Major Group | Sub-major Groups | Constituent Minor Groups |
|---|---|---|
| 1 Managers and Administrators | a) Corporate Managers and Administrators | 10, 11, 12, 13, 14, 15, 19 |
| | b) Managers / Proprietors in Agriculture and Services | 16, 17 |
| 2 Professional Occupations | a) Science and Engineering Professionals | 20, 21 |
| | b) Health Professionals | 22 |
| | c) Teaching Professionals | 23 |
| | d) Other Professional Occupations | 24, 25, 26, 27, 29 |
| 3 Associate Professional and Technical Occupations | a) Science and Engineering Associate Professionals | 30, 31, 32 |
| | b) Health Associate Professionals | 34 |
| | c) Other Associate Professional Occupations | 33, 35, 36, 37, 38, 39 |
| 4 Clerical and Secretarial Occupations | a) Clerical Occupations | 40, 41, 42, 43, 44, 49 |
| | b) Secretarial Occupations | 45, 46 |
| 5 Craft and Related Occupations | a) Skilled Construction Trades | 50 |
| | b) Skilled Engineering Trades | 51, 52 |
| | c) Other Skilled Trades | 53, 54, 55, 56, 57, 58, 59 |
| 6 Personal and Protective Service Occupations | a) Protective Service Occupations | 60, 61 |
| | b) Personal Service Occupations | 62, 63, 64, 65, 66, 67, 69 |
| 7 Sales Occupations | a) Buyers, Brokers and Sales Reps. | 70, 71 |
| | b) Other Sales Occupations | 72, 73, 79 |
| 8 Plant and Machine Operatives | a) Industrial Plant and Machine Operators, Assemblers | 80, 81, 82, 83, 84, 85, 86, 89 |
| | b) Drivers and Mobile Machine Operators | 87, 88 |
| 9 Other Occupations | a) Other Occupations in Agriculture, Forestry and Fishing | 90 |
| | b) Other Elementary Occupations | 91, 92, 93, 94, 95, 99 |

# 4 Approach to certain technical problems in the classification of occupations

## 4.1 Continuity versus up-to-dateness

The development of SOC has inevitably required compromise between, on the one hand, the need for a classification which adequately and usefully reflects the current structure of occupations; and, on the other hand, the need for a reasonable degree of continuity in the classifications used in producing statistics, as a basis for comparisons over time.

In pursuing the first of these goals a strong effort was made to move where necessary towards more consistent use of the two criteria described at 3.2 above in drawing distinctions between groups.

A further major effort was concentrated on the 'not elsewhere classified' (n.e.c.) groups which appeared at various places in CODOT, KOS and CO80. These groups contained a number of well-identified types of job which were neither common enough to justify being given a separate occupational group of their own, nor had enough in common with existing occupational groups to be included in any of them. They thus had something of a 'rag-bag' character and were not very useful for analytic purposes. In developing SOC the aim was to adjust group definitions in a way which ensured that as many as possible of the jobs previously assigned to n.e.c. groups could be more usefully classified. As a result, the proportion of jobs allocated to n.e.c. groups is much reduced in SOC.

A third aim in developing SOC was to reconsider the occupational groups to which high proportions of jobs done by women were allocated. It was felt that previous classifications might for historical reasons have a bias towards finer classification of traditionally male than of traditionally female occupations. Special attention was given to the treatment of clerical, teaching, nursing and child care occupations, for example, and in each of these cases it was found possible to introduce a finer classification.

A fourth aim in developing SOC was to take account of changes in the structure of occupations which had manifested themselves since 1980. Such changes had become apparent to users of CO80, CODOT and KOS and many were naturally in areas of rapid technological development, such as computing. A particular problem with 'new' jobs is that job-title terminology, on which occupational classification depends, may not have settled into a consistent pattern. Efforts were nevertheless made to take account of 'new' or greatly expanded occupations and areas of employment by adjusting group boundaries and, where justified, creating new occupational groups.

Other changes, such as the convergence of existing occupational groups through automation and 'de-skilling', are also certainly taking place, but are much harder to identify unambiguously. It is therefore likely that in this respect SOC, like its predecessors, tends to be conservative in recognising old distinctions which are embedded in job-title terminology.

The result of efforts in these four directions clearly had to be a degree of discontinuity for statistical purposes with both CO80 and KOS. It is hard to define summary measures of discontinuity which would not be misleading in some contexts. A section dealing with this topic is therefore included in Volume 3 of the SOC Manual.

## 4.2 Information base for SOC coding

SOC has been developed for application to raw data collected in surveys in broadly the same way as in the national Census of Population. Recent censuses have contained two questions addressed to occupation, the first asking for the title of the person's job and the second for a brief description of the main job activities. The questions are answered in the census by a household form filler who may or may not consult other members of the household.

The 1991 Census will include questions on industry and on higher qualifications and in certain situations the answers to these may be used to improve the accuracy of occupational coding to SOC. However, it is intended that SOC should permit reasonably accurate coding on the basis of answers to questions on job title and job activities, without recourse to such ancillary information.

It is anticipated that many data sources to which SOC is applied will be broadly comparable to the census, others better and some worse. Better occupational information may be obtained by trained interviewers who are able to speak directly to job holders, or by persons experienced in job placement who are able to speak directly to job applicants or employers. It should, however, be noted that fuller information about jobs is not necessarily better information for SOC coding purposes. Coding is likely to be most accurate and reliable where the information recorded is succinct but directly relevant to the distinctions which SOC aims to make.

## 4.3 Treatment of managerial occupations

An area where nature of activities, type of skill and status in employment may be difficult to separate conceptually is management. The SOC approach is to treat jobs where the main activity is, 'management above the level of a first-line supervisor or foreman', as requiring a special class of skills and thus needing to be classified separately from the jobs of the workers managed.

Thus in allocating jobs to occupational groups SOC takes account, in appropriate and defined cases, of the designation 'manager' and also of indications that the person is the proprietor of a business. These are treated as indications that the job involves activities and skills typical of managers. On the same principle there are a few cases (indicated in the SOC index) where allocation to an occupational group may be assisted by a knowledge of whether or not the person has self-employed status. In these limited respects information on status in employment is taken into account in SOC.

## 4.4 Treatment of agricultural, forestry and fishing occupations

Occupations which are specifically agricultural, forestry and fishing, but not managerial, in nature are allocated to Minor Group 90 of SOC and its constituent unit groups. This solution is a compromise. This group of occupations is sufficiently distinct from other occupations to require their own small set of minor groups and might therefore claim their own major group. However, one criterion for distinguishing major groups was that each should contain a substantial proportion of all occupations; and the proportion of the labour force of Great Britain currently engaged in agriculture, forestry and fishing is now so small that major group status was judged not to be appropriate.

## 4.5 Treatment of labouring and similar unskilled occupations

Jobs having the title 'Labourer' are in general classified, along with other jobs requiring relatively little skill, qualification or experience, to Major Group 9 of SOC. Because of the unspecific terms in which many such jobs are reported in practice it is necessary to invoke a quasi-industrial principle for classifying below major group level. This gives rise to minor group headings such as: '91 Other occupations in mining and manufacturing'; '92 Other occupations in construction'; and so on. Each of these contains unit group titles which convey some useful information about the jobs classified to them.

The ultimate recourse is to Minor Group 99 and Unit Group 990, which is a catch-all for 'All other labourers and related workers'. The practical implications of this are tending to diminish as the number of generalised unskilled jobs in the economy continues to decline.

## 4.6 Treatment of Armed Forces occupations

Members of the Armed Forces may in certain cases have jobs which are unique to that sector of the economy. SOC makes provision for military occupations specified in terms of ranks (e.g. 'Lieutenant Commander', 'Sergeant' etc.) in Minor Groups 15 (Commissioned Officers) and 60 (NCOs and Other Ranks).

In other cases job titles, if given, may equate to those of civilian jobs (e.g. vehicle mechanic, radio operator etc.), though of course the persons concerned all hold military ranks also. Here the basic classificatory assumption is that both Armed Forces and civilian jobs will be coded to the same groups without any distinction being made between them.

In practice, however, this assumption is somewhat academic, since members of the Armed Forces are normally under orders for security reasons to give only a minimum amount of information about their job titles and activities when responding to censuses and surveys. In the coding of the 1991 Census it is likely that most members of the Armed Forces will identify themselves by rank only and be classified to Unit Groups 150, 151, 600 and 601 as appropriate.

# 5   Updating of SOC

Changes occur in work organisation as a result of technological developments, use of new materials, improved methods of production or delivery of services etc.  New occupations arise either because tasks are enlarged, contracted or combined within and between existing occupations or because new, different tasks are introduced into the organisation of work. Such new occupations may become sufficiently important to warrant their recognition and inclusion in the classification.  Additionally, new index entries for Volume 2 may be required.

The Occupation Information Unit, which has been set up within the Office of Population Censuses and Surveys to support SOC, would welcome information on such changes. This will be taken into account in the periodical updating of SOC.

Please contact,

> Occupation Information Unit,
> Office of Population, Censuses and Surveys,
> Segensworth Road,
> Titchfield,
> Fareham,
> Hants,
> PO15 5RR
>
> Telephone    Titchfield (0329) 42511

# STRUCTURE OF THE CLASSIFICATION

The Standard Occupational Classification consists of the following major groups:

1 Managers and Administrators

2 Professional Occupations

3 Associate Professional and Technical Occupations

4 Clerical and Secretarial Occupations

5 Craft and Related Occupations

6 Personal and Protective Service Occupations

7 Sales Occupations

8 Plant and Machine Operatives

9 Other Occupations

The minor group and unit group structure of these major groups is defined as follows:

# MAJOR GROUP 1
# MANAGERS AND ADMINISTRATORS

Minor Groups

**10  GENERAL MANAGERS AND ADMINISTRATORS IN NATIONAL AND LOCAL GOVERNMENT, LARGE COMPANIES AND ORGANISATIONS**

**11  PRODUCTION MANAGERS IN MANUFACTURING, CONSTRUCTION, MINING AND ENERGY INDUSTRIES**

**12  SPECIALIST MANAGERS**

**13  FINANCIAL INSTITUTION AND OFFICE MANAGERS, CIVIL SERVICE EXECUTIVE OFFICERS**

**14  MANAGERS IN TRANSPORT AND STORING**

**15  PROTECTIVE SERVICE OFFICERS**

**16  MANAGERS IN FARMING, HORTICULTURE, FORESTRY AND FISHING**

**17  MANAGERS AND PROPRIETORS IN SERVICE INDUSTRIES**

**19  MANAGERS AND ADMINISTRATORS NEC**

Unit Groups within Minor Groups

**10  GENERAL MANAGERS AND ADMINISTRATORS IN NATIONAL AND LOCAL GOVERNMENT, LARGE COMPANIES AND ORGANISATIONS**

100   General administrators; national government (Assistant Secretary/Grade 5 and above)

101   General managers; large companies and organisations

102   Local government officers (administrative and executive functions)

103   General administrators; national government (HEO to Senior Principal/Grade 6)

**11  PRODUCTION MANAGERS IN MANUFACTURING, CONSTRUCTION, MINING AND ENERGY INDUSTRIES**

110   Production, works and maintenance managers

111   Managers in building and contracting

112   Clerks of works

113   Managers in mining and energy industries

## 12 SPECIALIST MANAGERS

120  Treasurers and company financial managers
121  Marketing and sales managers
122  Purchasing managers
123  Advertising and public relations managers
124  Personnel, training and industrial relations managers
125  Organisation and methods and work study managers
126  Computer systems and data processing managers
127  Company secretaries

## 13 FINANCIAL INSTITUTION AND OFFICE MANAGERS, CIVIL SERVICE EXECUTIVE OFFICERS

130  Credit controllers
131  Bank, Building Society and Post Office managers (except self-employed)
132  Civil Service executive officers
139  Other financial institution and office managers n.e.c.

## 14 MANAGERS IN TRANSPORT AND STORING

140  Transport managers
141  Stores controllers
142  Managers in warehousing and other materials handling

## 15 PROTECTIVE SERVICE OFFICERS

150  Officers in UK armed forces
151  Officers in foreign and Commonwealth armed forces
152  Police officers (inspector and above)
153  Fire service officers (station officer and above)
154  Prison officers (principal officer and above)
155  Customs and excise, immigration service officers

       (customs: chief preventive officer and above;

       excise: surveyor and above)

## 16 MANAGERS IN FARMING, HORTICULTURE, FORESTRY AND FISHING

160  Farm owners and managers, horticulturists
169  Other managers in farming, horticulture, forestry and fishing n.e.c.

## 17 MANAGERS AND PROPRIETORS IN SERVICE INDUSTRIES

## 19 MANAGERS AND ADMINISTRATORS NEC

# MAJOR GROUP 2
# PROFESSIONAL OCCUPATIONS

Minor Groups

**20  NATURAL SCIENTISTS**

**21  ENGINEERS AND TECHNOLOGISTS**

**22  HEALTH PROFESSIONALS**

**23  TEACHING PROFESSIONALS**

**24  LEGAL PROFESSIONALS**

**25  BUSINESS AND FINANCIAL PROFESSIONALS**

**26  ARCHITECTS, TOWN PLANNERS AND SURVEYORS**

**27  LIBRARIANS AND RELATED PROFESSIONALS**

**29  PROFESSIONAL OCCUPATIONS NEC**


Unit Groups within Minor Groups

## 20  NATURAL SCIENTISTS

200  Chemists
201  Biological scientists and biochemists
202  Physicists, geologists and meteorologists
209  Other natural scientists n.e.c.

## 21  ENGINEERS AND TECHNOLOGISTS

210  Civil, structural, municipal, mining and quarrying engineers
211  Mechanical engineers
212  Electrical engineers
213  Electronic engineers
214  Software engineers
215  Chemical engineers
216  Design and development engineers
217  Process and production engineers
218  Planning and quality control engineers
219  Other engineers and technologists n.e.c.

## 22 HEALTH PROFESSIONALS

220 Medical practitioners
221 Pharmacists/pharmacologists
222 Ophthalmic opticians
223 Dental practitioners
224 Veterinarians

## 23 TEACHING PROFESSIONALS

230 University and polytechnic teaching professionals
231 Higher and further education teaching professionals
232 Education officers, school inspectors
233 Secondary (and middle school deemed secondary) education teaching professionals
234 Primary (and middle school deemed primary) and nursery education teaching professionals
235 Special education teaching professionals
239 Other teaching professionals n.e.c.

## 24 LEGAL PROFESSIONALS

240 Judges and officers of the Court
241 Barristers and advocates
242 Solicitors

## 25 BUSINESS AND FINANCIAL PROFESSIONALS

250 Chartered and certified accountants
251 Management accountants
252 Actuaries, economists and statisticians
253 Management consultants, business analysts

## 26 ARCHITECTS, TOWN PLANNERS AND SURVEYORS

260 Architects
261 Town planners
262 Building, land, mining and 'general practice' surveyors

## 27 LIBRARIANS AND RELATED PROFESSIONALS

270 Librarians
271 Archivists and curators

## 29 PROFESSIONAL OCCUPATIONS NEC

290 Psychologists
291 Other social and behavioural scientists
292 Clergy
293 Social workers, probation officers

# MAJOR GROUP 3
## ASSOCIATE PROFESSIONAL AND TECHNICAL OCCUPATIONS

Minor Groups

**30 SCIENTIFIC TECHNICIANS**

**31 DRAUGHTSPERSONS, QUANTITY AND OTHER SURVEYORS**

**32 COMPUTER ANALYST/PROGRAMMERS**

**33 SHIP AND AIRCRAFT OFFICERS, AIR TRAFFIC PLANNERS AND CONTROLLERS**

**34 HEALTH ASSOCIATE PROFESSIONALS**

**35 LEGAL ASSOCIATE PROFESSIONALS**

**36 BUSINESS AND FINANCIAL ASSOCIATE PROFESSIONALS**

**37 SOCIAL WELFARE ASSOCIATE PROFESSIONALS**

**38 LITERARY, ARTISTIC AND SPORTS PROFESSIONALS**

**39 ASSOCIATE PROFESSIONAL AND TECHNICAL OCCUPATIONS NEC**

Unit Groups within Minor Groups

**30 SCIENTIFIC TECHNICIANS**

300 Laboratory technicians
301 Engineering technicians
302 Electrical/electronic technicians
303 Architectural and town planning technicians
304 Building and civil engineering technicians
309 Other scientific technicians n.e.c.

**31 DRAUGHTSPERSONS, QUANTITY AND OTHER SURVEYORS**

310 Draughtspersons
311 Building inspectors
312 Quantity surveyors
313 Marine, insurance and other surveyors

## 32 COMPUTER ANALYST/PROGRAMMERS

320 Computer analyst/programmers

## 33 SHIP AND AIRCRAFT OFFICERS, AIR TRAFFIC PLANNERS AND CONTROLLERS

330 Air traffic planners and controllers

331 Aircraft flight deck officers

332 Ship and hovercraft officers

## 34 HEALTH ASSOCIATE PROFESSIONALS

340 Nurses

341 Midwives

342 Medical radiographers

343 Physiotherapists

344 Chiropodists

345 Dispensing opticians

346 Medical technicians, dental auxiliaries

347 Occupational and speech therapists, psychotherapists, therapists n.e.c.

348 Environmental health officers

349 Other health associate professionals n.e.c.

## 35 LEGAL ASSOCIATE PROFESSIONALS

350 Legal service and related occupations

## 36 BUSINESS AND FINANCIAL ASSOCIATE PROFESSIONALS

360 Estimators, valuers

361 Underwriters, claims assessors, brokers, investment analysts

362 Taxation experts

363 Personnel and industrial relations officers

364 Organisation and methods and work study officers

## 37 SOCIAL WELFARE ASSOCIATE PROFESSIONALS

370 Matrons, houseparents

371 Welfare, community and youth workers

## 38 LITERARY, ARTISTIC AND SPORTS PROFESSIONALS

380 Authors, writers, journalists

381 Artists, commercial artists, graphic designers

382 Industrial designers

383 Clothing designers

384 Actors, entertainers, stage managers, producers and directors

385 Musicians

386 Photographers, camera, sound and video equipment operators

387 Professional athletes, sports officials

## 39 ASSOCIATE PROFESSIONAL AND TECHNICAL OCCUPATIONS NEC

390 Information officers

391 Vocational and industrial trainers

392 Careers advisers and vocational guidance specialists

393 Driving instructors (excluding HGV)

394 Inspectors of factories, utilities and trading standards

395 Other statutory and similar inspectors n.e.c.

396 Occupational hygienists and safety officers (health and safety)

399 Other associate professional and technical occupations n.e.c.

# MAJOR GROUP 4
# CLERICAL AND SECRETARIAL OCCUPATIONS

Minor Groups

**40    ADMINISTRATIVE/CLERICAL OFFICERS AND
         ASSISTANTS IN CIVIL SERVICE AND
         LOCAL GOVERNMENT**

**41    NUMERICAL CLERKS AND CASHIERS**

**42    FILING AND RECORDS CLERKS**

**43    CLERKS (NOT OTHERWISE SPECIFIED)**

**44    STORES AND DESPATCH CLERKS, STOREKEEPERS**

**45    SECRETARIES, PERSONAL ASSISTANTS, TYPISTS, WORD
         PROCESSOR OPERATORS**

**46    RECEPTIONISTS, TELEPHONISTS AND RELATED
         OCCUPATIONS**

**49    CLERICAL AND SECRETARIAL OCCUPATIONS NEC**

Unit Groups within Minor Groups

**40    ADMINISTRATIVE/CLERICAL OFFICERS AND
         ASSISTANTS IN CIVIL SERVICE
         AND LOCAL GOVERNMENT**

400    Civil Service administrative officers and assistants
401    Local government clerical officers and assistants

**41    NUMERICAL CLERKS AND CASHIERS**

410    Accounts and wages clerks, book-keepers, other financial clerks
411    Counter clerks and cashiers
412    Debt, rent and other cash collectors

**42    FILING AND RECORDS CLERKS**

420    Filing, computer and other records clerks (inc. legal conveyancing)
421    Library assistants/clerks

## 43 CLERKS (NOT OTHERWISE SPECIFIED)

430    Clerks (n.o.s.)


## 44 STORES AND DESPATCH CLERKS, STOREKEEPERS

440    Stores, despatch and production control clerks
441    Storekeepers and warehousemen/women


## 45 SECRETARIES, PERSONAL ASSISTANTS, TYPISTS, WORD PROCESSOR OPERATORS

450    Medical secretaries
451    Legal secretaries
452    Typists and word processor operators
459    Other secretaries, personal assistants, typists, word processor
          operators n.e.c.


## 46 RECEPTIONISTS, TELEPHONISTS AND RELATED OCCUPATIONS

460    Receptionists
461    Receptionist/telephonists
462    Telephone operators
463    Radio and telegraph operators, other office communication system operators


## 49 CLERICAL AND SECRETARIAL OCCUPATIONS NEC

490    Computer operators, data processing operators, other office machine operators
491    Tracers, drawing office assistants

# MAJOR GROUP 5
# CRAFT AND RELATED OCCUPATIONS

Minor Groups

**50   CONSTRUCTION TRADES**

**51   METAL MACHINING, FITTING AND INSTRUMENT MAKING TRADES**

**52   ELECTRICAL/ELECTRONIC TRADES**

**53   METAL FORMING, WELDING AND RELATED TRADES**

**54   VEHICLE TRADES**

**55   TEXTILES, GARMENTS AND RELATED TRADES**

**56   PRINTING AND RELATED TRADES**

**57   WOODWORKING TRADES**

**58   FOOD PREPARATION TRADES**

**59   OTHER CRAFT AND RELATED OCCUPATIONS NEC**

Unit Groups within Minor Groups

**50   CONSTRUCTION TRADES**

500   Bricklayers, masons
501   Roofers, slaters, tilers, sheeters, cladders
502   Plasterers
503   Glaziers
504   Builders, building contractors
505   Scaffolders, stagers, steeplejacks, riggers
506   Floorers, floor coverers, carpet fitters and planners, floor and wall tilers
507   Painters and decorators
509   Other construction trades n.e.c.

**51   METAL MACHINING, FITTING AND INSTRUMENT MAKING TRADES**

510   Centre, capstan, turret and other lathe setters and setter-operators
511   Boring and drilling machine setters and setter-operators
512   Grinding machine setters and setter-operators
513   Milling machine setters and setter-operators
514   Press setters and setter-operators
515   Tool makers, tool fitters and markers-out

516 Metal working production and maintenance fitters

517 Precision instrument makers and repairers

518 Goldsmiths, silversmiths, precious stone workers

519 Other machine tool setters and setter-operators n.e.c
     (including CNC setter-operators)

## 52  ELECTRICAL/ELECTRONIC TRADES

520 Production fitters (electrical/electronic)

521 Electricians, electrical maintenance fitters

522 Electrical engineers (not professional)

523 Telephone fitters

524 Cable jointers, lines repairers

525 Radio, TV and video engineers

526 Computer engineers, installation and maintenance

529 Other electrical/electronic trades n.e.c.

## 53  METAL FORMING, WELDING AND RELATED TRADES

530 Smiths and forge workers

531 Moulders, core makers, die casters

532 Plumbers, heating and ventilating engineers and related trades

533 Sheet metal workers

534 Metal plate workers, shipwrights, riveters

535 Steel erectors

536 Barbenders, steel fixers

537 Welding trades

## 54  VEHICLE TRADES

540 Motor mechanics, auto engineers (inc. road patrol engineers)

541 Coach and vehicle body builders

542 Vehicle body repairers, panel beaters

543 Auto electricians

544 Tyre and exhaust fitters

## 55  TEXTILES, GARMENTS AND RELATED TRADES

550 Weavers
551 Knitters
552 Warp preparers, bleachers, dyers and finishers
553 Sewing machinists, menders, darners and embroiderers

554   Coach trimmers, upholsterers and mattress makers

555   Shoe repairers, leather cutters and sewers, footwear lasters,
        makers and finishers, other leather making and repairing

556   Tailors and dressmakers

557   Clothing cutters, milliners, furriers

559   Other textiles, garments and related trades n.e.c.

## 56   PRINTING AND RELATED TRADES

560   Originators, compositors and print preparers

561   Printers

562   Bookbinders and print finishers

563   Screen printers

569   Other printing and related trades n.e.c.

## 57   WOODWORKING TRADES

570   Carpenters and joiners

571   Cabinet makers

572   Case and box makers

573   Pattern makers (moulds)

579   Other woodworking trades n.e.c.

## 58   FOOD PREPARATION TRADES

580   Bakers, flour confectioners

581   Butchers, meat cutters

582   Fishmongers, poultry dressers

## 59   OTHER CRAFT AND RELATED OCCUPATIONS NEC

590   Glass product and ceramics makers

591   Glass product and ceramics finishers and decorators

592   Dental technicians

593   Musical instrument makers, piano tuners

594   Gardeners, groundsmen/groundswomen

595   Horticultural trades

596   Coach painters, other spray painters

597   Face trained coalmining workers, shotfirers and deputies

598   Office machinery mechanics

599   Other craft and related occupations n.e.c.

# MAJOR GROUP 6
# PERSONAL AND PROTECTIVE SERVICE
# OCCUPATIONS

Minor Groups

**60  NCOs AND OTHER RANKS, ARMED FORCES**

**61  SECURITY AND PROTECTIVE SERVICE OCCUPATIONS**

**62  CATERING OCCUPATIONS**

**63  TRAVEL ATTENDANTS AND RELATED OCCUPATIONS**

**64  HEALTH AND RELATED OCCUPATIONS**

**65  CHILDCARE AND RELATED OCCUPATIONS**

**66  HAIRDRESSERS, BEAUTICIANS AND RELATED
     OCCUPATIONS**

**67  DOMESTIC STAFF AND RELATED OCCUPATIONS**

**69  PERSONAL AND PROTECTIVE SERVICE OCCUPATIONS
     NEC**

Unit Groups within Minor Groups

**60  NCOs AND OTHER RANKS, ARMED FORCES**

600  NCOs and other ranks, UK armed forces
601  NCOs and other ranks, foreign and Commonwealth armed forces

**61  SECURITY AND PROTECTIVE SERVICE OCCUPATIONS**

610  Police officers (sergeant and below)
611  Fire service officers (leading fire officer and below)
612  Prison service officers (below principal officer)
613  Customs and excise officers, immigration officers
         (customs: below chief preventive officer; excise: below surveyor)
614  Traffic wardens
615  Security guards and related occupations
619  Other security and protective service occupations n.e.c.

**62  CATERING OCCUPATIONS**

620  Chefs, cooks
621  Waiters, waitresses
622  Bar staff

## 63 TRAVEL ATTENDANTS AND RELATED OCCUPATIONS

630 Travel and flight attendants
631 Railway station staff

## 64 HEALTH AND RELATED OCCUPATIONS

640 Assistant nurses, nursing auxiliaries
641 Hospital ward assistants
642 Ambulance staff
643 Dental nurses
644 Care assistants and attendants

## 65 CHILDCARE AND RELATED OCCUPATIONS

650 Nursery nurses
651 Playgroup leaders
652 Educational assistants
659 Other childcare and related occupations n.e.c.

## 66 HAIRDRESSERS, BEAUTICIANS AND RELATED OCCUPATIONS

660 Hairdressers, barbers
661 Beauticians and related occupations

## 67 DOMESTIC STAFF AND RELATED OCCUPATIONS

670 Domestic housekeepers and related occupations
671 Housekeepers (non-domestic)
672 Caretakers
673 Launderers, dry cleaners, pressers

## 69 PERSONAL AND PROTECTIVE SERVICE OCCUPATIONS NEC

690 Undertakers
691 Bookmakers
699 Other personal and protective service occupations n.e.c.

# MAJOR GROUP 7
# SALES OCCUPATIONS

Minor Groups

**70  BUYERS, BROKERS AND RELATED AGENTS**

**71  SALES REPRESENTATIVES**

**72  SALES ASSISTANTS AND CHECK-OUT OPERATORS**

**73  MOBILE, MARKET AND DOOR-TO-DOOR SALESPERSONS AND AGENTS**

**79  SALES OCCUPATIONS NEC**

Unit Groups within Minor Groups

**70  BUYERS, BROKERS AND RELATED AGENTS**

700  Buyers (retail trade)
701  Buyers and purchasing officers (not retail)
702  Importers and exporters
703  Air, commodity and ship brokers

**71  SALES REPRESENTATIVES**

710  Technical and wholesale sales representatives
719  Other sales representatives n.e.c.

**72  SALES ASSISTANTS AND CHECK-OUT OPERATORS**

720  Sales assistants
721  Retail cash desk and check-out operators
722  Petrol pump forecourt attendants

**73  MOBILE, MARKET AND DOOR-TO-DOOR SALESPERSONS AND AGENTS**

730  Collector salespersons and credit agents
731  Roundsmen/women and van salespersons
732  Market and street traders and assistants
733  Scrap dealers, scrap metal merchants

## 79   SALES OCCUPATIONS NEC

790   Merchandisers
791   Window dressers, floral arrangers
792   Telephone salespersons

# MAJOR GROUP 8
# PLANT AND MACHINE OPERATIVES

Minor Groups

**80   FOOD, DRINK AND TOBACCO PROCESS OPERATIVES**

**81   TEXTILES AND TANNERY PROCESS OPERATIVES**

**82   CHEMICALS, PAPER, PLASTICS AND RELATED PROCESS OPERATIVES**

**83   METAL MAKING AND TREATING PROCESS OPERATIVES**

**84   METAL WORKING PROCESS OPERATIVES**

**85   ASSEMBLERS/LINEWORKERS**

**86   OTHER ROUTINE PROCESS OPERATIVES**

**87   ROAD TRANSPORT OPERATIVES**

**88   OTHER TRANSPORT AND MACHINERY OPERATIVES**

**89   PLANT AND MACHINE OPERATIVES NEC**

Unit Groups within Minor Groups

## 80   FOOD, DRINK AND TOBACCO PROCESS OPERATIVES

800   Bakery and confectionery process operatives
801   Brewery and vinery process operatives
802   Tobacco process operatives
809   Other food, drink and tobacco process operatives n.e.c.

## 81   TEXTILES AND TANNERY PROCESS OPERATIVES

810   Tannery production operatives
811   Preparatory fibre processors
812   Spinners, doublers, twisters
813   Winders, reelers
814   Other textiles processing operatives

## 82 CHEMICALS, PAPER, PLASTICS AND RELATED PROCESS OPERATIVES

820 Chemical, gas and petroleum process plant operatives

821 Paper, wood and related process plant operatives

822 Cutting and slitting machine operatives (paper products etc.)

823 Glass and ceramics furnace operatives, kilnsetters

824 Rubber process operatives, moulding machine operatives, tyre builders

825 Plastics process operatives, moulders and extruders

826 Synthetic fibre makers

829 Other chemicals, paper, plastics and related process operatives n.e.c.

## 83 METAL MAKING AND TREATING PROCESS OPERATIVES

830 Furnace operatives (metal)

831 Metal drawers

832 Rollers

833 Annealers, hardeners, temperers (metal)

834 Electroplaters, galvanisers, colour coaters

839 Other metal making and treating process operatives n.e.c.

## 84 METAL WORKING PROCESS OPERATIVES

840 Machine tool operatives (inc CNC machine tool operatives)

841 Press stamping and automatic machine operatives

842 Metal polishers

843 Metal dressing operatives

844 Shot blasters

## 85 ASSEMBLERS/LINEWORKERS

850 Assemblers/lineworkers (electrical/electronic goods)

851 Assemblers/lineworkers (vehicles and other metal goods)

859 Other assemblers/lineworkers n.e.c.

## 86 OTHER ROUTINE PROCESS OPERATIVES

860 Inspectors, viewers and testers (metal and electrical goods)
861 Inspectors, viewers, testers and examiners (other manufactured goods)
862 Packers, bottlers, canners, fillers
863 Weighers, graders, sorters
864 Routine laboratory testers
869 Other routine process operatives n.e.c.

## 87 ROAD TRANSPORT OPERATIVES

870 Bus inspectors
871 Road transport depot inspectors and related occupations
872 Drivers of road goods vehicles
873 Bus and coach drivers
874 Taxi, cab drivers and chauffeurs
875 Bus conductors

## 88 OTHER TRANSPORT AND MACHINERY OPERATIVES

880 Seafarers (merchant navy); barge, lighter and boat operatives
881 Rail transport inspectors, supervisors and guards
882 Rail engine drivers and assistants
883 Rail signal operatives and crossing keepers
884 Shunters and points operatives
885 Mechanical plant drivers and operatives (earth moving and civil engineering)
886 Crane drivers
887 Fork lift and mechanical truck drivers
889 Other transport and machinery operatives n.e.c.

## 89 PLANT AND MACHINE OPERATIVES NEC

890 Washers, screeners and crushers in mines and quarries
891 Printing machine minders and assistants
892 Water and sewerage plant attendants
893 Electrical, energy, boiler and related plant operatives and attendants
894 Oilers, greasers, lubricators
895 Mains and service pipe layers, pipe jointers
896 Construction and related operatives
897 Woodworking machine operatives
898 Mine (excluding coal) and quarry workers
899 Other plant and machine operatives n.e.c.

# MAJOR GROUP 9
# OTHER OCCUPATIONS

Minor Groups

**90 OTHER OCCUPATIONS IN AGRICULTURE, FORESTRY AND FISHING**

**91 OTHER OCCUPATIONS IN MINING AND MANUFACTURING**

**92 OTHER OCCUPATIONS IN CONSTRUCTION**

**93 OTHER OCCUPATIONS IN TRANSPORT**

**94 OTHER OCCUPATIONS IN COMMUNICATION**

**95 OTHER OCCUPATIONS IN SALES AND SERVICES**

**99 OTHER OCCUPATIONS NEC**


Unit Groups within Minor Groups

**90 OTHER OCCUPATIONS IN AGRICULTURE, FORESTRY AND FISHING**

900   Farm workers
901   Agricultural machinery drivers and operatives
902   All other occupations in farming and related
903   Fishing and related workers
904   Forestry workers


**91 OTHER OCCUPATIONS IN MINING AND MANUFACTURING**

910   Coal mine labourers
911   Labourers in foundries
912   Labourers in engineering and allied trades
913   Mates to metal/electrical and related fitters
919   Other labourers in making and processing industries n.e.c.


**92 OTHER OCCUPATIONS IN CONSTRUCTION**

920   Mates to woodworking trades workers
921   Mates to building trades workers
922   Rail construction and maintenance workers
923   Road construction and maintenance workers
924   Paviors, kerb layers
929   Other building and civil engineering labourers n.e.c.

## 93 OTHER OCCUPATIONS IN TRANSPORT

930 Stevedores, dockers
931 Goods porters
932 Slingers
933 Refuse and salvage collectors
934 Driver's mates

## 94 OTHER OCCUPATIONS IN COMMUNICATION

940 Postal workers, mail sorters
941 Messengers, couriers

## 95 OTHER OCCUPATIONS IN SALES AND SERVICES

950 Hospital porters
951 Hotel porters
952 Kitchen porters, hands
953 Counterhands, catering assistants
954 Shelf fillers
955 Lift and car park attendants
956 Window cleaners
957 Road sweepers
958 Cleaners, domestics
959 Other occupations in sales and services n.e.c.

## 99 OTHER OCCUPATIONS NEC

990 All other labourers and related workers
999 All others in miscellaneous occupations n.e.c.

# DEFINITION OF THE MAJOR, MINOR AND UNIT GROUPS OF THE STANDARD OCCUPATIONAL CLASSIFICATION

# MAJOR GROUP 1

## MANAGERS AND ADMINISTRATORS

# MAJOR GROUP 1
# MANAGERS AND ADMINISTRATORS

This major group covers occupations whose main tasks consist of the direction and co-ordination of the functioning of organisations and businesses, including internal departments and sections, often with the help of subordinate managers and supervisors. Working proprietors in small businesses are included, although allocated to separate minor groups within the major group.

Most occupations in this major group will require a significant amount of knowledge and experience of the production processes, administrative procedures or service requirements associated with the efficient functioning of organisations and businesses.

Occupations in this major group are classified into the following minor groups:

10 GENERAL MANAGERS AND ADMINISTRATORS IN NATIONAL AND LOCAL GOVERNMENT, LARGE COMPANIES AND ORGANISATIONS

11 PRODUCTION MANAGERS IN MANUFACTURING, CONSTRUCTION, MINING AND ENERGY INDUSTRIES

12 SPECIALIST MANAGERS

13 FINANCIAL INSTITUTION AND OFFICE MANAGERS, CIVIL SERVICE EXECUTIVE OFFICERS

14 MANAGERS IN TRANSPORT AND STORING

15 PROTECTIVE SERVICE OFFICERS

16 MANAGERS IN FARMING, HORTICULTURE, FORESTRY AND FISHING

17 MANAGERS AND PROPRIETORS IN SERVICE INDUSTRIES

19 MANAGERS AND ADMINISTRATORS NEC

# MINOR GROUP 10
# GENERAL MANAGERS AND ADMINISTRATORS IN NATIONAL AND LOCAL GOVERNMENT, LARGE COMPANIES AND ORGANISATIONS

Workers in this unit group formulate national and local government policy; plan, organise and direct government departments and plan and organise (usually with other managers) the operations of large companies and organisations employing over 500 people.

Occupations in this minor group are classified into the following unit groups:

**100 GENERAL ADMINISTRATORS; NATIONAL GOVERNMENT (ASSISTANT SECRETARY/GRADE 5 AND ABOVE)**

**101 GENERAL MANAGERS; LARGE COMPANIES AND ORGANISATIONS**

**102 LOCAL GOVERNMENT OFFICERS (ADMINISTRATIVE AND EXECUTIVE FUNCTIONS)**

**103 GENERAL ADMINISTRATORS; NATIONAL GOVERNMENT (HEO TO SENIOR PRINCIPAL/GRADE 6)**

## 100 GENERAL ADMINISTRATORS; NATIONAL GOVERNMENT (ASSISTANT SECRETARY/ GRADE 5 AND ABOVE)

Workers in this unit group formulate and ratify legislation and government policy, act as elected representatives of parliamentary or local government constituencies and as representatives of the government, direct the diplomatic and administrative operations of government departments and hold grade 5 level or equivalent rank and above in the Civil Service.

### TYPICAL ENTRY ROUTES AND ASSOCIATED QUALIFICATIONS

Entry is either by appointment, election or internal promotion.

### TASKS

- evaluates departmental activities, discusses problems with government officials and administrators, notes national and international opinion and formulates departmental policy;

- recommends or reviews potential policy or legislation and offers advice and opinions on current policy;

- investigates matters of concern to the general public or particular groups and recommends government action where appropriate;

- advises on interpretation and implementation of policy decisions, acts and regulations;

- tables questions to ministers, introduces proposals for government action and otherwise serves public and electoral interest;

- co-ordinates operations in fields of activity not elsewhere classified, including the armed forces.

### RELATED JOB TITLES

Assistant secretary/Grade 5
Diplomat
Member of European Parliament
Member of Parliament
Permanent secretary (*government*)

44

## 101  GENERAL MANAGERS; LARGE COMPANIES AND ORGANISATIONS

Workers in this unit group head large enterprises and organisations employing over 500 people. They plan, direct and co-ordinate, with other managers, the resources necessary for operations such as processing, production, construction, maintenance, transport, storage, handling and warehousing, the resources of offices performing clerical and related functions and the specialist activities of enterprises and organisations not elsewhere classified.

### TYPICAL ENTRY ROUTES AND ASSOCIATED QUALIFICATIONS

Entry is either by appointment, election or internal promotion.

### TASKS

- analyses economic, social, legal and other data and plans, formulates and directs the operation of a company or organisation;

- consults with subordinates to formulate, implement and review company policy;

- prepares, or arranges for the preparation of reports, budgets, forecasts or other information;

- plans and controls the allocation of resources and the selection of senior staff;

- authorises funding for policy implementation programmes and institutes reporting, auditing and control systems.

### RELATED JOB TITLES

Chief executive (*large organisations*)
Company director (*large organisations*)
Director (*large organisations*)
General manager (*large organisations*)
Managing director (*large organisations*)

## 102  LOCAL GOVERNMENT OFFICERS (ADMINISTRATIVE AND EXECUTIVE FUNCTIONS)

Workers in this unit group participate in the formulation and implementation of local government policies, ensure that legal, statutory and other provisions concerning the running of a local authority are observed, organise local authority office work and resources and undertake registration of all births, deaths and marriages within a local authority area.

### TYPICAL ENTRY ROUTES AND ASSOCIATED QUALIFICATIONS

There are no pre-set entry requirements. Candidates are recruited with a variety of academic qualifications or with relevant experience. Entry is also possible by internal promotion.

### TASKS

- evaluates departmental performance, discusses problems with other officials and formulates departmental policies;

- arranges local council meetings and draws up and circulates agenda and other documents;

- studies any legislation that may affect the local authority and represents the authority in its dealings with other authorities;

- institutes legal proceedings under Acts of Parliament and bye-laws as necessary;

- advises on the interpretation and implementation of local government policy;

- co-ordinates clerical, secretarial, accounting and other office functions;

- examines and assesses housing applications, advises on rent levels, investigates complaints, maintains estate's amenities and liaises with tenants' association and social workers to resolve any family problems;

- registers and maintains records of all births, deaths and marriages in local authority area, issues appropriate certificates and reports any suspicious causes of death to the coroner.

## RELATED JOB TITLES

Chief executive (*local government*)
Housing manager (*local authority*)
Registrar (*births, deaths and marriages*)
Town clerk

## 103 GENERAL ADMINISTRATORS; NATIONAL GOVERNMENT (HEO TO SENIOR PRINCIPAL/GRADE 6)

Workers in this unit group undertake general administrative and executive functions in national government and plan and direct the resources and activities of local offices of national government departments.

### TYPICAL ENTRY ROUTES AND ASSOCIATED QUALIFICATIONS

Candidates are recruited with a variety of academic qualifications or with relevant experience. Entry is frequently by internal promotion.

### TASKS

- advise on interpretation and implementation of policy decisions, acts and regulations;

- co-ordinates activities of office staff, assigns tasks and responsibilities and makes changes in procedures to deal with variations in workload;

- arranges for the acceptance and recording of vacancy details, the selection of suitable applicants and the provision of vocational training;

- authorises the payment of social security benefits, arranges for domiciliary visits to assess the financial circumstances of claimants and investigates any state insurance contribution problems;

- advises public or companies on general tax problems and arranges for the issue, receipt and examination of tax forms, assessment of P.A.Y.E codes and the computation of tax arrears and rebates.

### RELATED JOB TITLES

Higher executive officer (*national government*)
Principal/Grade 7
Senior executive officer (*national government*)
Senior principal/Grade 6

# MINOR GROUP 11
# PRODUCTION MANAGERS IN MANUFACTURING, CONSTRUCTION, MINING AND ENERGY INDUSTRIES

Workers in this minor group plan, organise, direct and co-ordinate all activities and resources involved with production, processing, maintenance and construction operations in industry.

Occupations in this minor group are classified into the following unit groups:

**110 PRODUCTION, WORKS AND MAINTENANCE MANAGERS**
**111 MANAGERS IN BUILDING AND CONTRACTING**
**112 CLERKS OF WORKS**
**113 MANAGERS IN MINING AND ENERGY INDUSTRIES**

## 110 PRODUCTION, WORKS AND MAINTENANCE MANAGERS

Production, works and maintenance managers plan, organise, direct and co-ordinate the activities and resources necessary for production in manufacturing industries and the maintenance of engineering items, equipment and machinery.

### TYPICAL ENTRY ROUTES AND ASSOCIATED QUALIFICATIONS

There are no pre-set entry standards. Entry is possible with either a degree or equivalent qualification, relevant experience or without academic qualifications. On-the-job training is provided and professional qualifications are available.

### TASKS

- liaises with other managers to plan overall production activity and daily manufacturing and maintenance activity;

- manages production, production control, purchasing and other departments;

- monitors production and production costs and undertakes or arranges for the preparation of reports and records;

- arranges for regular inspections of plant, machinery and equipment to detect wear or deterioration;

- establishes causes of breakdowns, arranges for any necessary repairs, keeps records of faults and checks completed maintenance work for compliance with statutory regulations.

### RELATED JOB TITLES

Production controller
Production manager
Service manager
Works engineer
Works manager

## 111 MANAGERS IN BUILDING AND CONTRACTING

Managers in building and contracting plan, organise, direct and co-ordinate the construction and maintenance of civil and structural engineering works including houses, flats, factories, roads and runways, bridges, tunnels and railway works, harbour, dock and marine works and water supply, drainage and sewage works.

There are no pre-set entry standards. Entry is possible with either a degree or equivalent qualification, relevant experience or without academic qualifications. On-the-job training is provided and professional qualifications are available.

## TASKS

- receives invitations to tender, arranges for estimates and liaises with client, architect and engineers to prepare contract documents;

- plans site layout and access routes, attends site meetings to represent contractor and ensures that there are no deviations from agreed plans without client's consent;

- examines designs, drawings and specifications and lays down building lines, levels, etc. and checks work in progress to ensure that materials and construction methods meet with specifications and statutory requirements;

- advises on technical problems and staffing, oversees implementation of site security and safety procedures and prepares progress reports;

- arranges for regular inspections to detect any construction faults and organises maintenance and remedial work as necessary;

- checks completed work for compliance with specifications, safety and other statutory requirements;

- plans, directs and co-ordinates the construction and maintenance of civil and structural engineering works not elsewhere classified, including demolition contracts, opencast mining works and pipeline and piling contracts.

## RELATED JOB TITLES

Contracts manager (*building*)
Site agent
Site engineer
Site manager

## 112 CLERKS OF WORKS

Clerks of works represent architects on building projects to ensure compliance with design specifications and material and construction standards.

There are no pre-set entry standards. Entry is possible with either a degree or equivalent qualification, relevant experience or without academic qualifications. On-the-job training is provided and professional qualifications are available.

## TASKS

- confirms programme of building work with contractors and engineers and checks building lines, etc.;

- inspects work as building proceeds to ensure compliance with design specifications and required material and construction standards;

- keeps records of all excavations, foundations and other work that will be hidden by subsequent construction;

- reports to, and consults with, architect to discuss progress and standards of building work;

- instructs contractors concerning any remedial work required and advises on any design problems;

- records details of all agreed deviations from contract.

## RELATED JOB TITLES

Clerk of works
Senior clerk of works

## 113 MANAGERS IN MINING AND ENERGY INDUSTRIES

Managers in mining and energy industries plan, organise, direct and co-ordinate the activities and resources necessary for the extraction of minerals and other natural deposits and the production, storage and provision of gas, water and electricity supplies.

## TYPICAL ENTRY ROUTES AND ASSOCIATED QUALIFICATIONS

There are no pre-set entry standards. Entry is possible with either GCSE/SCE S-grades or A-levels/H-grades, with a degree/BTEC/SCOTVEC

or with relevant experience. Some apprenticeships are available. Off- and on-the-job training is
available and may last up to 5 years and lead to
professional qualifications.

## TASKS

- determines staffing, material and other needs;

- co-ordinates all surface and underground activities in mines, quarries and drilling operations;

- ensures that all haulage, storage, purification and
  distribution work is performed in compliance
  with statutory and other regulations;

- negotiates with public utility authorities for the
  provision of gas, water and electricity supplies;

- arranges for water storage, treatment and other
  facilities to be made available and for the drawing of bulk supplies from and discharge into
  rivers and reservoirs.

## RELATED JOB TITLES

Operations manager (*mining*)
Overman/woman (*mining*)
Quarry manager

# MINOR GROUP 12
# SPECIALIST MANAGERS

Specialist managers plan, organise and advise on specialist functions or fields of activity in an organisation. They formulate and administer policies concerning the legal, financial, marketing, sales, purchasing, work methods, public relations, personnel and computing operations of an organisation.

Occupations in this minor group are classified into the following unit groups:

120    TREASURERS AND COMPANY FINANCIAL MANAGERS

121    MARKETING AND SALES MANAGERS

122    PURCHASING MANAGERS

123    ADVERTISING AND PUBLIC RELATIONS MANAGERS

124    PERSONNEL, TRAINING AND INDUSTRIAL RELATIONS
         MANAGERS

125    ORGANISATION AND METHODS AND WORK STUDY
         MANAGERS

126    COMPUTER SYSTEMS AND DATA PROCESSING MANAGERS

127    COMPANY SECRETARIES

## 120  TREASURERS AND COMPANY FINANCIAL MANAGERS

Treasurers and company financial managers plan, organise, direct and co-ordinate the work of accountants, advise on company financial policy, administer the estates of deceased persons and other trusts and act as trustees in marriage or other monetary settlements.

### TYPICAL ENTRY ROUTES AND ASSOCIATED QUALIFICATIONS

Entry is possible with either GCSE/SCE S-grades, A-levels/H-grades, a BTEC/SCOTVEC award or a degree or equivalent qualification. Professional qualifications are available and are required for certain posts.

### TASKS

- liaises with other managers to determine company financial policy and staffing levels appropriate for accounting activities;

- advises on financial matters, plans external and internal audit programmes and arranges for the collection and analysis of accounting, budgetary and related information;

- co-ordinates the development, implementation and monitoring of manual and computerised accounting systems;

- arranges for valuations of the assets and liabilities of the estate being administered;

- ensures that terms of will are observed, all bequests are settled and all taxes and duties are paid;

- prepares, or arranges for the preparation of executors and trustees accounts, maintains records of all action taken and acts as trustee in marriage or other monetary settlement.

### RELATED JOB TITLES

Company treasurer
Finance manager
Financial controller

Financial director
Merchant banker
Trust officer

## 121 MARKETING AND SALES MANAGERS

Marketing and sales managers plan, organise, direct and undertake market research and formulate and implement an organisation's marketing and sales policies.

### TYPICAL ENTRY ROUTES AND ASSOCIATED QUALIFICATIONS

Entry is most common with a BTEC/SCOTVEC award or a degree or equivalent qualification but is possible with other qualifications and/or relevant experience. Professional qualifications are available.

### TASKS

- liaises with other managers/staff to determine the range of goods or services to be sold;

- discusses employer's or client's requirements, plans surveys and analyses customers' reactions to product, packaging, price, etc.;

- examines and analyses sales figures and prepares proposals for marketing campaigns and promotional activities;

- controls the recruitment and training of sales staff;

- produces reports and recommendations concerning marketing and sales strategies.

### RELATED JOB TITLES

Analyst (*market research*)
Commercial manager
Export manager
Marketing director
Marketing manager
Product manager
Sales consultant
Sales director
Sales executive
Sales manager

## 122 PURCHASING MANAGERS

Purchasing managers (not retail) plan, organise, direct and co-ordinate the purchasing policies and activities of industrial, commercial and other establishments.

### TYPICAL ENTRY ROUTES AND ASSOCIATED QUALIFICATIONS

Entry is most common with GCSE/SCE S-grades and A-levels/H-grades but is possible with other academic qualifications and/or relevant experience.

### TASKS

- determines staffing, financial and other short and long term needs;

- assesses the type, quality, quantity and price of items and dates when they must be available;

- decides on whether orders should be put out to tender and evaluates suppliers' quotes;

- negotiates contract with supplier and draws up contract documents;

- arranges for quality checks of incoming goods;

- interviews suppliers' representatives and visits trade fairs.

### RELATED JOB TITLES

Purchasing director
Purchasing manager

## 123 ADVERTISING AND PUBLIC RELATIONS MANAGERS

Advertising and public relations managers plan, organise, direct and co-ordinate the advertising, public relations and public information activities of an organisation.

### TYPICAL ENTRY ROUTES AND ASSOCIATED QUALIFICATIONS

Entry is most common with a degree or equivalent qualification but is possible with professional qualifications or relevant experience.

**TASKS**

- determines staffing, financial and other short and long term needs;

- liaises with client to discuss product/service to be marketed, defines target group and assesses the suitability of various media;

- conceives advertising campaign to impart the desired product image in an effective and economical way;

- reviews and revises campaign in light of sales figures, surveys, etc.;

- stays abreast of changes in media, readership or viewing figures and advertising rates;

- arranges conferences, exhibitions, seminars, etc. and promotes company's image.

**RELATED JOB TITLES**

Account executive (*advertising*)
Advertising executive
Advertising manager
Media director
Public relations manager
Publicity manager

# 124 PERSONNEL, TRAINING AND INDUSTRIAL RELATIONS MANAGERS

Personnel, training and industrial relations managers plan, organise, direct and co-ordinate the personnel, training and industrial relations policies and activities of an organisation.

## TYPICAL ENTRY ROUTES AND ASSOCIATED QUALIFICATIONS

Entry is possible with GCSE/SCE S-grades but is more common with A-levels/H-grades. Graduate entry is also possible. Up to 2 years off- and on-the-job training is provided and professional qualifications are available.

## TASKS

- determines staffing, financial and other short and long term needs;

- prepares job descriptions, drafts advertisements and interviews candidates;

- identifies training needs and develops or arranges training courses;

- undertakes industrial relations negotiations with employees representatives or trade unions;

- develops and administers salary, health and safety and promotion policies;

- undertakes staff appraisals and discusses career plan with employees.

**RELATED JOB TITLES**

Industrial relations manager
Personnel and training manager
Personnel manager
Training manager

# 125 ORGANISATION AND METHODS AND WORK STUDY MANAGERS

Workers in this unit group advise on resource allocation and utilisation problems, measure the effectiveness of an organisation's systems, methods and procedures and advise on, plan and implement procedures to improve utilisation of labour, equipment and materials.

## TYPICAL ENTRY ROUTES AND ASSOCIATED QUALIFICATIONS

Entry is most common with relevant experience but is possible with academic qualifications up to degree level. Off- and on-the-job training is provided and professional qualifications are available.

## TASKS

- agrees terms of reference for work study or organisation and methods project with client;

- examines company and departmental structures, chains of command, information flows, etc. and evaluates efficiency of existing operations;

- considers alternative work procedures to improve productivity or make more efficient use of labour, plant, materials or space;

- assesses and evaluates work involved in and time taken for a particular task/operation;

- collects other data and prepares and presents reports and recommendations to client.

## RELATED JOB TITLES

Organisation and methods manager
Work study manager

## 126 COMPUTER SYSTEMS AND DATA PROCESSING MANAGERS

Workers in this unit group plan, organise, direct and co-ordinate the clerical, operative and other work necessary to operate computer equipment and develop procedures and prepare programs for automatic data processing.

## TYPICAL ENTRY ROUTES AND ASSOCIATED QUALIFICATIONS

Entry will usually require GCSE/SCE A-levels/H-grades but is possible with other academic qualifications and/or relevant experience.

## TASKS

- determines staffing, financial and other short and long term needs, plans work schedules and assigns responsibilities and tasks;

- advises on the uses and capabilities of computers and integrates new and existing projects into the system;

- co-ordinates and controls the work of systems analysts and programmers;

- plans and organises data reception, data library, standard operating procedures and maintenance work.

## RELATED JOB TITLES

Computer manager
Computer operations manager
Data processing manager
Systems manager

## 127 COMPANY SECRETARIES

Company secretaries organise and direct the work associated with meetings of directors and shareholders, act as company representatives, control share registration work in Local Authority and commercial enterprises, advise on company law and ensure that all statutory and other regulations concerning the running of a company are observed.

## TYPICAL ENTRY ROUTES AND ASSOCIATED QUALIFICATIONS

There are no fixed requirements for entry but candidates usually possess a degree or equivalent qualification in law, accountancy or a related subject. Professional qualifications are available.

## TASKS

- arranges board and shareholders meetings and draws up and circulates agenda and other relevant documents;

- attends meetings and records, or arranges for the recording of, minutes and advises board on company law or practice as required;

- ensures that minutes are agreed, signed and circulated and communicates board decisions to relevant staff;

- calls meetings of shareholders in accordance with the requirements of the company's articles of association;

- signs documents and correspondence requiring signature on behalf of company and receives company's correspondence;

- ensures that company's articles and memorandum of association are adhered to at all times;

- maintains share registers in accordance with the Companies Act and deals with all matters relating to the sale, transfer and purchase of shares.

## RELATED JOB TITLES

Company registrar
Company secretary

# MINOR GROUP 13
# FINANCIAL INSTITUTION AND OFFICE MANAGERS, CIVIL SERVICE EXECUTIVE OFFICERS

Workers in this minor group supervise and co-ordinate clerical work in government offices and plan, organise and direct the day-to-day running of banks, Building Societies, Post Offices and other offices performing clerical and related tasks.

Occupations in this minor group are classified into the following unit groups:

130    CREDIT CONTROLLERS

131    BANK, BUILDING SOCIETY AND POST OFFICE MANAGERS (EXCEPT SELF-EMPLOYED)

132    CIVIL SERVICE EXECUTIVE OFFICERS

139    OTHER FINANCIAL INSTITUTION AND OFFICE MANAGERS NEC

## 130 CREDIT CONTROLLERS

Credit controllers plan, organise, direct and co-ordinate the activities and resources of an office or department responsible for credit control and debt collection.

### TYPICAL ENTRY ROUTES AND ASSOCIATED QUALIFICATIONS

Entry is most common with GCSE/SCE S-grades but is possible with other academic qualifications. Holders of a degree (or equivalent) may be exempt from parts of the professional examinations that are available and required for some posts.

### TASKS

- plans work schedules, assigns tasks and delegates responsibilities;

- arranges for investigations of the credit worthiness of individuals or companies;

- deals with any enquiries or difficulties concerning the acceptance or rejection of credit applications;

- checks that accounting, recording and statutory procedures are adhered to for all credit transactions;

- arranges for the collection of arrears of payment.

### RELATED JOB TITLES

Credit control manager
Credit controller
Credit manager

## 131 BANK, BUILDING SOCIETY AND POST OFFICE MANAGERS (EXCEPT SELF-EMPLOYED)

Workers in this unit group plan, organise, direct and co-ordinate the activities and resources of bank, Building Society and Post Office branch offices.

### TYPICAL ENTRY ROUTES AND ASSOCIATED QUALIFICATIONS

Candidates require GCSE/SCE S-grades, but A-level/H-grade or degree holders usually obtain accelerated training. Internal promotion to management is possible. On-the-job training is provided. Professional qualifications are available and often mandatory.

### TASKS

- plans work schedules, assigns tasks and delegates responsibilities;

- verifies that accounting, recording and information storage and retrieval procedures are adhered to;

- advises clients on all financial matters including the raising of loan, overdraft and mortgage facilities;

- authorises loans and mortgages in accordance with bank or Building Society policy;

- promotes bank or Building Society services, establishes contact with the local business community and professional firms and helps administer the National Giro service.

## RELATED JOB TITLES

Bank manager
Branch manager (*banking*)
Building society manager
Postal executive, grades A and B
Sub-postmaster

## 132 CIVIL SERVICE EXECUTIVE OFFICERS

Workers in this unit group plan, organise, direct and co-ordinate the work and resources of government offices and departments carrying out clerical and related functions.

### TYPICAL ENTRY ROUTES AND ASSOCIATED QUALIFICATIONS

Entry is most common with GCSE/SCE S-grades and A-levels/H-grades or a degree/BTEC/SCOT-VEC. Candidates should be between seventeen and a half and fifty years of age.

### TASKS

- plans work schedules and assigns duties;

- undertakes random or regular checks of work to assess output and its quality;

- ensures that accounting, verifying, recording and other prescribed procedures are adhered to;

- prepares policy and budget proposals and advises on the purchase of office equipment and supplies;

- directly supervises the activities of clerical staff;

- provides analyses, reports, statistics and other information for senior officers.

## RELATED JOB TITLES

Executive officer (*Civil service*)

## 139 OTHER FINANCIAL INSTITUTION AND OFFICE MANAGERS NEC

Workers in this unit group perform a variety of managerial tasks in financial institutions and offices not elsewhere classified in MINOR GROUP 13: Financial Institution and Office Managers, Civil Service Executive Officers.

### TYPICAL ENTRY ROUTES AND ASSOCIATED QUALIFICATIONS

Entry will usually require GCSE/SCE S-grades but is possible with other academic qualifications and/or relevant experience. Professional qualifications are available in some occupations.

### TASKS

- plans work schedules, assigns tasks and delegates responsibilities;

- advises on the handling of all correspondence and enquiries relating to accounts, sales, statistical and vacancy records;

- determines most economical and efficient freight routes and decides most efficient method of processing bills of loading and customs and excise documentation;

- ensures that procedures for considering, issuing, amending and endorsing insurance policies are adhered to;

- plans installation and maintenance work necessary for the provision of a local telephone, radio, telegraph or teleprinter service;

- analyses faults with radio, telegraph, teleprinter and telephone services and advises users accordingly;

- plans, organises, directs and co-ordinates the activities and resources of other offices not elsewhere classified including box offices, other ticket offices and accommodation offices.

## RELATED JOB TITLES

Accounts manager
Area telephone manager
Insurance office manager
Medical records officer
Office manager
Shipping manager

# MINOR GROUP 14
# MANAGERS IN TRANSPORT AND STORING

Managers in transport and storing plan, organise, direct and co-ordinate the activities and resources necessary for the efficient, convenient and economic transportation of passengers and freight and the loading, unloading, storage and distribution of goods and materials.

Occupations in this minor group are classified into the following unit groups:

**140 TRANSPORT MANAGERS**

**141 STORES CONTROLLERS**

**142 MANAGERS IN WAREHOUSING AND OTHER MATERIALS HANDLING**

## 140 TRANSPORT MANAGERS

Transport managers plan, organise, direct and co-ordinate the activities and resources necessary for the safe, efficient and economic movement of passengers and freight by road, rail, sea and air transport.

### TYPICAL ENTRY ROUTES AND ASSOCIATED QUALIFICATIONS

Entry is possible without academic qualifications but some employers require GCSE/SCE S-grades or A-levels/H-grades. Transport managers in the hire and reward sector will require the Certificate of Professional Competence issued by the RSA and the Operator's Licence. Entry to Harbour Master will require sea-going experience and candidates should hold the Department of Trade and Industry Certificate of Competence. Entry to Station Manager/Master is by internal promotion only from Railwayman/woman.

### TASKS

- plans optimum utilisation of all operating equipment and co-ordinates maintenance activities to ensure least possible disruption to services;

- examines traffic reports, load patterns, traffic receipts and other data and revises transport services or freight rates accordingly;

- supervises day-to-day activities in a railway station;

- ensures that regulations regarding hours of work, the licensing of crews and transport equipment, the operational safety and efficiency of equipment, the insurance of vehicles and other statutory regulations are complied with;

- ensures that harbour channels are clear, maintains buoys and lighting and arranges for the navigation of vessels to and from berths;

- liaises with ship owners, crew, customs officials, dock and harbour staff to arrange entry, berthing and servicing of ships;

- arranges for maintenance of airport runways and buildings, liaises with fuel and catering crews to ensure adequate supplies and resolves any complaints and problems raised by airport users.

### RELATED JOB TITLES

Harbour master
Station master
Traffic controller
Transport manager

## 141 STORES CONTROLLERS

Stores controllers plan, organise, direct and co-ordinate the receipt, issue and storage of materials and the procedures and resources necessary for maintaining stocks at an optimum level.

## TYPICAL ENTRY ROUTES AND ASSOCIATED QUALIFICATIONS

Academic qualifications may be required for some posts and entry is also possible with relevant experience.

## TASKS

- liaises with production, maintenance, sales and other departments to determine the materials and other items required for current and future production schedules and sales commitments;

- develops and implements stock control policies to maximise use of space, money, labour and other resources;

- arranges for regular inspections of stock to detect deterioration or damage;

- advises purchasing department on type, quality and quantity of goods required and dates by which they must be available;

- prepares reports on expenditure and advises on materials and parts standardisation, future stores and stock control policies.

## RELATED JOB TITLES

Materials controller
Parts manager
Stock control manager
Stock controller
Stores manager

# 142 MANAGERS IN WAREHOUSING AND OTHER MATERIALS HANDLING

Workers in this unit group plan, organise, direct and co-ordinate the receipt, storage and warehousing, handling, despatch and transport of goods and the loading and unloading of cargo and/or the embarkation and disembarkation of ships' and aircraft passengers.

## TYPICAL ENTRY ROUTES AND ASSOCIATED QUALIFICATIONS

Academic qualifications may be required for some posts, and entry is also possible with relevant experience.

## TASKS

- advises on product planning, packaging, materials handling and suitable handling equipment;

- decides on storage conditions for particular items, allocates warehouse space and arranges for regular stock inspections to detect deterioration or damage;

- plans and supervises loading and unloading of goods and maintains statutory and other records of all items handled;

- arranges for the issue of boarding cards and other documentation and co-ordinates the disembarkation of passengers and their transport from dock, quayside or airport;

- reviews space utilisation, staffing and distribution expenditure and determines future warehousing and distribution policies.

## RELATED JOB TITLES

Cargo superintendant
Despatch manager
Distribution manager
Warehouse manager

# MINOR GROUP 15
# PROTECTIVE SERVICE OFFICERS

Protective service officers manage the operations of police stations, fire stations and prisons, supervise customs, excise and immigration staff and assist with inspections of goods and persons entering or leaving the country and serve as commissioned officers in Her Majesty's armed forces and in foreign and Commonwealth armed forces.

Occupations in this minor group are classified into the following unit groups:

> 150 OFFICERS IN UK ARMED FORCES
>
> 151 OFFICERS IN FOREIGN AND COMMONWEALTH ARMED FORCES
>
> 152 POLICE OFFICERS (INSPECTOR AND ABOVE)
>
> 153 FIRE SERVICE OFFICERS (STATION OFFICER AND ABOVE)
>
> 154 PRISON OFFICERS (PRINCIPAL OFFICER AND ABOVE)
>
> 155 CUSTOMS AND EXCISE, IMMIGRATION SERVICE OFFICERS (CUSTOMS: CHIEF PREVENTIVE OFFICER AND ABOVE; EXCISE: SURVEYOR AND ABOVE)

## 150 OFFICERS IN UK ARMED FORCES

Workers in this unit group serve as commissioned officers in Her Majesty's armed forces, plan, direct, organise and administer military operations and perform duties for which there is no civilian equivalent.

### TYPICAL ENTRY ROUTES AND ASSOCIATED QUALIFICATIONS

Entry is possible with GCSE/SCE S-grades, A-levels/H-grades or with higher academic qualifications or by promotion from NCO or other rank. Each arm of the forces has different upper and lower age limits. Candidates must pass a medical examination and an interview.

### TASKS

- advises and provides information on military aspects of defence policy;

- plans, directs and co-ordinates training and military manoeuvres;

- supervises the operation of military units and monitors the activities of junior officers, NCOs and other ranks;

- plans, directs and administers aid to civilian authorities as requested or when faced with civil disorder, natural disaster or other emergency;

- monitors record keeping systems and prepares reports and expenditure estimates.

### RELATED JOB TITLES

Captain
Flight Lieutenant
Lieutenant
Lieutenant Commander
Major
Officer (armed forces)
Squadron Leader

## 151 OFFICERS IN FOREIGN AND COMMONWEALTH ARMED FORCES

Workers in this unit group serve as commissioned officers in foreign and Commonwealth armed forces, plan, direct, organise and administer military operations and perform duties for which there is no civilian equivalent.

## TYPICAL ENTRY ROUTES AND ASSOCIATED QUALIFICATIONS

Entry requirements depend upon which branch of the armed forces the person is serving.

## TASKS

- advises and provides information on military aspects of defence policy;

- plans, directs and co-ordinates training and military manoeuvres;

- supervises the operation of military units and monitors the activities of junior officers, NCOs and other ranks;

- plans, directs and administers aid to civilian authorities as requested or when faced with civil disorder, natural disaster or other emergency;

- monitors record keeping systems and prepares reports and expenditure estimates.

## RELATED JOB TITLES

Captain
Flight Lieutenant
Lieutenant
Lieutenant Commander
Major
Officer (*armed forces*)
Squadron Leader

## 152 POLICE OFFICERS (INSPECTOR AND ABOVE)

Police officers plan, organise, direct and co-ordinate the resources and activities of a specific geographical or functional area of generalised or specialised police work.

## TYPICAL ENTRY ROUTES AND ASSOCIATED QUALIFICATIONS

Entry is only possible by internal promotion from sergeant. Degree or equivalent qualification holders may obtain accelerated promotion. All police forces have height, age and eyesight requirements.

## TASKS

- liaises with senior officers to determine staff, financial and other short and long term needs;

- plans, directs and co-ordinates general policing for an area or functional unit;

- directs and monitors the work of subordinate officers;

- establishes contacts and sources of information concerning crimes planned or committed;

- directs and co-ordinates the operation of record keeping systems and the preparation of reports.

## RELATED JOB TITLES

Assistant chief constable
Chief constable
Chief inspector
Chief superintendent
Deputy chief constable

## 153 FIRE SERVICE OFFICERS (STATION OFFICER AND ABOVE)

Workers in this unit group plan, organise, direct and co-ordinate the activities and resources of a specific physical or functional area of a statutory or private fire brigade and the resources necessary for the protection of property at fires within a salvage corps area.

## TYPICAL ENTRY ROUTES AND ASSOCIATED QUALIFICATIONS

Entry is only possible by internal promotion from Fireman, Leading fireman or Sub-officer.

## TASKS

- liaises with senior officers to determine staffing, financial and other short and long term needs;

- plans, directs and co-ordinates an operational plan for a physical or functional area;

- controls one or more fire stations and monitors subordinate officers;

- attends fires and other emergencies and co-operates with other emergency services to minimise damage to property;

- arranges for the salvaging of goods, materials, etc. from fire damaged premises, organises immediate temporary repairs and arranges for security patrols as necessary;

- prepares reports for insurance companies.

## RELATED JOB TITLES

Area controller (*fire service*)
Chief officer (*fire service*)
Divisional officer (*fire service*)
Senior controller (*fire service*)
Station officer (*fire service*)

## 154 PRISON OFFICERS (PRINCIPAL OFFICER AND ABOVE)

Prison officers (grade 6 and above) plan, organise, direct, and co-ordinate the activities and resources necessary for the running of a prison, remand or detention centre.

### TYPICAL ENTRY ROUTES AND ASSOCIATED QUALIFICATIONS

Entry is either by internal promotion or open competition for which no academic qualifications are required. There is a lower age limit of 21 years of age (24 in Scotland) and candidates must be at least 5'6" (men) or 5'3" (women).

### TASKS

- liaises with the Home Office or Scottish Home and Health Department to determine staffing, financial and other short and long terms needs;

- advises on the recruitment, training and monitoring of staff;

- interviews prisoners on arrival and discharge/departure;

- receives reports on disciplinary problems and decides on appropriate action;

- makes periodic checks on internal and external security;

- prepares necessary reports for the Home Office, Scottish Home and Health Department and other bodies.

## RELATED JOB TITLES

Chief officer (*prison service*)
Prison governor

## 155 CUSTOMS AND EXCISE, IMMIGRATION SERVICE OFFICERS (CUSTOMS: CHIEF PREVENTIVE OFFICER AND ABOVE; EXCISE: SURVEYOR AND ABOVE)

Workers in this unit group plan and direct the work of customs, excise and immigration staff and assist with inspections of goods and persons crossing national borders to ensure compliance with acts, orders and regulations concerning payment of customs and excise duties and the entry of aliens and Commonwealth citizens into the United Kingdom.

### TYPICAL ENTRY ROUTES AND ASSOCIATED QUALIFICATIONS

Entry is most common by internal promotion but some open competitions occur which require no academic qualifications.

### TASKS

- liaises with senior officers to determine staffing, financial and other short and long term needs;

- advises organisations and the general public on the proper interpretation of laws and regulations concerning taxes, duties and immigration requirements;

- questions passengers and crews, arranges for searches of aircraft and vessels and seizes or detains undeclared items;

- monitors duty-free stores and sales at air and sea ports;

- maintains revenue control at premises where dutiable goods are manufactured, processed or stored;

- examines goods entering the country, ensures that correct duty is paid and controls the movement of goods into and out of bonded warehouses;

- checks the travel documents of those crossing national borders to ensure that they have any necessary authorisations;

- prepares reports and gives evidence in court as necessary.

## RELATED JOB TITLES

Chief immigration officer
Chief preventive officer
Surveyor (*customs and excise*)

# MINOR GROUP 16
# MANAGERS IN FARMING, HORTICULTURE, FORESTRY AND FISHING

Workers in this minor group plan, organise, direct, and control the activities and resources of agricultural and similar establishments.

Occupations in this minor group are classified into the following unit groups:

**160 FARM OWNERS AND MANAGERS, HORTICULTURISTS**
**169 OTHER MANAGERS IN FARMING, HORTICULTURE, FORESTRY AND FISHING NEC**

## 160 FARM OWNERS AND MANAGERS, HORTICULTURISTS

Workers in this unit group plan, organise and co-ordinate the activities and resources of farming establishments cultivating arable crops, fruits, trees and shrubs and raising cattle, sheep, pigs and poultry.

### TYPICAL ENTRY ROUTES AND ASSOCIATED QUALIFICATIONS

No qualifications are required to become an independent or tenant farmer, or market gardener, but experience and/or qualifications are an advantage. Most farm and horticultural managers have a vocational agricultural qualification. These range from City and Guilds to post graduate awards. Candidates must normally have had practical experience before starting a course.

### TASKS

- determines staffing, financial, and other long and short term needs and keeps records of production, finance and breeding;

- decides or advises on the types of crops to be grown or livestock raised;

- plans intensity and sequence of farm operations and orders seed, fertilizer, farming equipment and other supplies;

- plants, propagates, sprays, fertilizes and harvests field crops and horticultural produce;

- controls or personally performs farming operations such as preparing land for cultivation, raising livestock, milking, collecting eggs, etc.;

- selects and pairs animals for breeding purposes, allocates cattle to pastures, treats minor ailments and injuries and calls vet if necessary;

- arranges for sale of crops, livestock and other farm produce;

- maintains, cleans and disinfects farm buildings, sheds, pens and equipment.

### RELATED JOB TITLES

Farm manager
Farmer
Horticulturist (*market gardening*)
Market gardener
Poultry farmer

## 169 OTHER MANAGERS IN FARMING, HORTICULTURE, FORESTRY AND FISHING NEC

Workers in this unit group perform a variety of managerial tasks in farming, horticulture, forestry and fishing not elsewhere classified in MINOR GROUP 16: Managers in Farming, Horticulture, Forestry and Fishing.

## TYPICAL ENTRY ROUTES AND ASSOCIATED QUALIFICATIONS

Entry requirements range from no qualifications to degree level or equivalent awards depending on the occupation. Skippers of fishing vessels larger than 16.5 metres must obtain a Department of Transport Certificate of Competence. Trainers of racehorses and racing greyhounds must meet the requirements of the Jockey Club and National Greyhound Racing Club respectively to obtain a licence.

## TASKS

- determines staffing, financial and other long and short term needs and keeps records on finance, production and breeding;

- decides, or advises on, type of animal to be bred and/or trained and selects, buys and trains animals accordingly;

- plans and directs the establishment of forest nurseries, assumes responsibility for a particular area of forest/woodland and regularly inspects forest work;

- commands and navigates fishing vessels, ensuring that vessel is properly equipped and complying with all fishing and navigation laws and regulations;

- selects suitable breeding grounds for shellfish, sea and freshwater fish and purchases stock;

- advises farmers and horticulturists on cropping requirements, cultivation problems and gardening and grounds keeping;

- plans, organises, directs and co-ordinates the activities and resources of farming, fishing, forestry and related establishments not elsewhere classified, including tree felling and related services and agricultural contracting services.

## RELATED JOB TITLES

Fish farmer
Forestry officer
Greyhound trainer
Horse trainer
Kennel manager
Race horse trainer
Skipper (*fishing*)
Stable manager
Tree surgeon

# MINOR GROUP 17
# MANAGERS AND PROPRIETORS IN SERVICE INDUSTRIES

Workers in this minor group plan, organise, direct and co-ordinate (usually with the help of other managers) the activities and resources of offices, wholesale and retail establishments, hotels, public houses and similar establishments, recreation and entertainment establishments and a variety of other business and personal service offices and establishments not elsewhere classified.

Occupations in this minor group are classified into the following unit groups:

170 PROPERTY AND ESTATE MANAGERS

171 GARAGE MANAGERS AND PROPRIETORS

172 HAIRDRESSERS' AND BARBERS' MANAGERS AND PROPRIETORS

173 HOTEL AND ACCOMMODATION MANAGERS

174 RESTAURANT AND CATERING MANAGERS

175 PUBLICANS, INNKEEPERS AND CLUB STEWARDS

176 ENTERTAINMENT AND SPORTS MANAGERS

177 TRAVEL AGENCY MANAGERS

178 MANAGERS AND PROPRIETORS OF BUTCHERS AND FISHMONGERS

179 MANAGERS AND PROPRIETORS IN SERVICE INDUSTRIES NEC

## 170 PROPERTY AND ESTATE MANAGERS

Property and estate managers manage estates and arrange for the sale, purchase, rental and leasing of property on behalf of clients and employers.

### TYPICAL ENTRY ROUTES AND ASSOCIATED QUALIFICATIONS

Entry is most common with membership of either the Royal Institute of Chartered Surveyors or the Incorporated Society of Valuers and Auctioneers but is possible with academic qualifications and/or relevant experience.

### TASKS

- discusses client's requirements and may advise client on the purchase of property and land for investment and other purposes;

- conducts or arranges for structural surveys of properties and undertakes any necessary valuations of property or agricultural land;

- negotiates land or property purchases and sales or leases and tenancy agreements and arranges legal formalities with solicitors, building societies and other parties;

- maintains or arranges for the maintenance of estate accounts and records;

- acts as arbiter in disputes between landlord and tenant and ensures that both fulfill their legal obligations.

**RELATED JOB TITLES**

Estate agent
Land agent
Property manager

## 171 GARAGE MANAGERS AND PROPRIETORS

Garage managers and proprietors plan, organise, direct and co-ordinate the day-to-day running of garages and filling stations.

**TYPICAL ENTRY ROUTES AND ASSOCIATED QUALIFICATIONS**

Academic qualifications may be required. Relevant experience may be required by some employers.

**TASKS**

- determines staffing, financial and other short and long term requirements;

- ensures that necessary spare parts, materials and equipment are available or obtainable at short notice;

- arranges for maintenance staff to perform necessary maintenance and repair work on vehicles or motorcycles;

- checks completed work for compliance with safety and other statutory regulations;

- maintains records of repair work to detect recurrent faults;

- provides information about garage merchandise for staff and customers.

**RELATED JOB TITLES**

Garage manager
Garage owner
Garage proprietor

## 172 HAIRDRESSERS' AND BARBERS' MANAGERS AND PROPRIETORS

Workers in this unit group plan, organise, direct and co-ordinate the activities and resources of hairdressing, beauty treatment and similar establishments.

**TYPICAL ENTRY ROUTES AND ASSOCIATED QUALIFICATIONS**

Academic qualifications may be required. Relevant experience is required by some employers.

**TASKS**

- determines staffing, financial, material and other short and long term needs;

- controls the allocation, training and remuneration of hairdressing and beauty treatment staff;

- provides clients with information and resolves any complaints or problems;

- undertakes and/or directs hair or beauty treatments;

- prepares estimates, financial statements and other reports.

**RELATED JOB TITLES**

Hairdressing manager
Manager (*beauty treatment*)
Manager (*hairdressers*)

## 173 HOTEL AND ACCOMMODATION MANAGERS

Workers in this unit group plan, organise, direct and co-ordinate the activities and resources of hotels, hostels, lodging homes, holiday camps and holiday flats and chalets and organise the domestic, catering, and entertainment facilities on a passenger ship.

**TYPICAL ENTRY ROUTES AND ASSOCIATED QUALIFICATIONS**

Entry is possible with a variety of academic qualifications and/or relevant experience. Knowledge of a foreign language is advantageous. Professional qualifications are available and required for some posts. In particular, candidates for hotel management schemes may need either a degree, a BTEC/SCOTVEC national or higher national award or membership qualifications of the Hotel, Catering and Institutional Management Association.

**TASKS**

- determines staffing, financial, material and other short and long term needs;

- analyses demand and decides on type, standard and cost of services to be offered;

- ensures physical comfort of residents or passengers and makes special arrangements for children, the elderly and the infirm if required;

- approves and arranges shipboard entertainments and shore trips and liaises with ship's agent to ensure that ship is adequately provisioned;

- arranges for payment of bills, keeps accounts and adheres to licensing and other statutory regulations.

**RELATED JOB TITLES**

Caravan site manager
Guest house proprietor
Hotel manager
Hotel proprietor
Hotelier
Purser
Warden (*hostel*)

## 174 RESTAURANT AND CATERING MANAGERS

Restaurant and catering managers plan, direct and co-ordinate the catering services and resources of hotels, hospitals, schools, clubs and restaurants.

**TYPICAL ENTRY ROUTES AND ASSOCIATED QUALIFICATIONS**

Entry is possible with a variety of academic qualifications and/or relevant experience. Knowledge of a foreign language is advantageous. Professional qualifications are available and required for some posts. In particular, candidates for catering management schemes may need either a degree, a BTEC/SCOTVEC national or higher national award or membership qualifications of the Hotel, Catering and Institutional Management Association.

**TASKS**

- plans catering services and directs junior staff;

- decides on range and quality of meals and beverages to be provided or discusses customer's requirements for special occasions;

- purchases or directs the purchasing of supplies and arranges for preparation of accounts;

- verifies that quality of food, beverages and waiting service are as required and that kitchen and dining areas are kept clean in compliance with statutory requirements;

- plans and arranges food preparation in collaboration with other staff and organises the provision of waiting or counter staff;

- checks that supplies are properly used and accounted for to prevent wastage and loss and to keep within budget limit.

**RELATED JOB TITLES**

Canteen manager
Caterer
Catering manager
Restaurant manager
Restaurateur

## 175 PUBLICANS, INNKEEPERS AND CLUB STEWARDS

Publicans, innkeepers and club stewards plan, organise, direct and co-ordinate the activities and resources of non-residential and residential public houses and the bar and catering facilities at non-residential clubs.

**TYPICAL ENTRY ROUTES AND ASSOCIATED QUALIFICATIONS**

No academic qualifications are required. Relevant experience is advantageous and candidates must be over 18 years of age. Off- and on-the-job training is provided.

**TASKS**

- determines staffing, financial, material and other short and long term needs;

- arranges purchase of alcoholic and other beverages, bar snacks, cigarettes and other items and ensures that stocks are stored in proper conditions;

- supervises bar, kitchen and cleaning staff and, if necessary, assists with the serving of drinks;

- observes licensing laws and other statutory regulations and regulates behaviour of customers as necessary.

## RELATED JOB TITLES

Club steward
Innkeeper
Licensed house manager
Licensee
Publican

## 176 ENTERTAINMENT AND SPORTS MANAGERS

Entertainment and sports managers plan, organise, direct and co-ordinate the activities and resources required for the provision of sporting, artistic, theatrical and other recreational and amenity services.

### TYPICAL ENTRY ROUTES AND ASSOCIATED QUALIFICATIONS

Both graduate and non-graduate entry is possible. Some employers do not require candidates to have any academic qualifications. Relevant experience is advantageous and off- and on-the-job training is provided.

### TASKS

- determines staffing, financial, material and other short and long term requirements;

- recruits and trains box office staff, cashiers, gardeners, coaches, groundsmen/women, etc.;

- ensures that facilities are kept clean and in good condition;

- keeps abreast of new trends and developments in the creative arts and arranges exhibitions, theatrical productions, bands, orchestras, etc.;

- advises on the facilities available and promotes publicity in relation to shows, games, races, new theme parks, etc.;

- checks and keeps custody of all cash receipts and makes regular stock checks of items sold.

## RELATED JOB TITLES

Bingo club manager
Casino manager
Cinema manager
Manager (*entertainment/sports establishment*)
Manager (*horse riding school*)
Showman/woman
Sports centre manager

## 177 TRAVEL AGENCY MANAGERS

Travel agency managers plan, organise, direct and co-ordinate the resources and activities of travel agencies and booking offices.

### TYPICAL ENTRY ROUTES AND ASSOCIATED QUALIFICATIONS

Entry is most common with GCSE/SCE S-grades but is possible with other academic qualifications and/or relevant experience.

### TASKS

- plans work schedules and assigns tasks and responsibilities;

- co-ordinates the activities of clerical, secretarial and other staff;

- discusses client's requirements and advises on road, rail, air and sea travel and accommodation;

- makes and confirms travel and accommodation bookings and arranges group holidays and tours and individual itineraries;

- advises on currency and passport/visa regulations and any necessary health precautions needed.

## RELATED JOB TITLES

Travel agency manager
Travel agent

## 178 MANAGERS AND PROPRIETORS OF BUTCHERS AND FISHMONGERS

Workers in this unit group plan, organise, direct and co-ordinate the operations of a retail establishment selling meat or fish.

### TYPICAL ENTRY ROUTES AND ASSOCIATED QUALIFICATIONS

Entry requirements vary from company to company. Some companies do not require candidates to have academic qualifications but others require a degree or equivalent qualification. Off- and on-the-job training is provided.

### TASKS

- determines staffing, financial, material and other short and long term requirements;

- advertises, displays and sells meat and fish;

- provides information about merchandise to staff and customers;

- ensures that adequate stocks are held and stored correctly;

- deals with customer complaints and authorises refunds for returned meat or fish;

- maintains financial and other records and controls security arrangements for the premises.

### RELATED JOB TITLES

Butchers' shop manager
Fishmonger's manager
Retail butcher

## 179 MANAGERS AND PROPRIETORS IN SERVICE INDUSTRIES NEC

Workers in this unit group perform a variety of managerial tasks in wholesale and retail establishments not elsewhere classified in MINOR GROUP 17: Managers and Proprietors in Service Industries.

### TYPICAL ENTRY ROUTES AND ASSOCIATED QUALIFICATIONS

Entry requirements vary from company to company. Some companies do not require candidates to have academic qualifications but others require a degree or equivalent qualification. Off- and on-the-job training is provided.

### TASKS

- determines staffing, financial, material and other short and long term requirements;

- ensures that adequate reserves of merchandise are held and that stock keeping is carried out efficiently;

- authorises payment for supplies received and decides on vending price and credit terms;

- examines quality of merchandise and ensures that effective use is made of advertising and display facilities;

- controls store security, deals with customer complaints, arranges for refunds for returned merchandise and interviews suspected shoplifters;

- directs and co-ordinates the operation of retail trading establishments not elsewhere classified including florists, dry cleaning shops and receiving agencies, launderettes, mail order establishments, pawnbrokers, fuel merchants and horse and livestock dealers.

### RELATED JOB TITLES

Antiques dealer
Greengrocer
Grocer
Newsagent
Shopkeeper
Store manager (*retail trade*)

69

# MINOR GROUP 19
# MANAGERS AND ADMINISTRATORS NEC

Workers in this minor group perform a variety of managerial and administrative tasks not elsewhere classified in MAJOR GROUP 1: Managers and Administrators.

Occupations in this minor group are classified into the following unit groups:

**190 OFFICIALS OF TRADE ASSOCIATIONS, TRADE UNIONS, PROFESSIONAL BODIES AND CHARITIES**

**191 REGISTRARS AND ADMINISTRATORS OF EDUCATIONAL ESTABLISHMENTS**

**199 OTHER MANAGERS AND ADMINISTRATORS NEC**

## 190 OFFICIALS OF TRADE ASSOCIATIONS, TRADE UNIONS, PROFESSIONAL BODIES AND CHARITIES

Workers in this unit group ensure that legal, statutory and other regulations concerning the running of trade associations, employers associations, learned societies, trade unions, charitable organisations and similar bodies are observed and act as representatives of the organisation concerned.

### TYPICAL ENTRY ROUTES AND ASSOCIATED QUALIFICATIONS

Entry is most common by election, internal promotion or direct appointment and is usually based on relevant experience although some employers also require candidates to have academic qualifications.

### TASKS

- arranges for meetings and conferences and draws up and circulates agenda and other relevant material;

- represents union, association or organisation in consultation or negotiation with other bodies;

- maintains records of membership details, subscription fees, mailing lists, etc.;

- stimulates public interest by providing publicity, giving lectures and interviews and organising appeals for a variety of causes;

- directs or undertakes the preparation, publication and dissemination of reports and other information of interest to members and other interested parties.

### RELATED JOB TITLES

Area secretary (*trade union*)
General secretary (*trade union*)
National organiser (*trade union*)
Party agent
Trade union official

## 191 REGISTRARS AND ADMINISTRATORS OF EDUCATIONAL ESTABLISHMENTS

Workers in this unit group plan, organise, direct and co-ordinate the administrative work and financial resources of a university, college or other educational establishment.

### TYPICAL ENTRY ROUTES AND ASSOCIATED QUALIFICATIONS

Entry will require a degree or equivalent qualification and (for some posts) relevant experience.

## TASKS

- considers staffing, financial, material and other short and long term needs;

- arranges for evaluation of management, accounting, information storage and retrieval and other facilities;

- controls administrative aspects of student registration and admission;

- acts as secretary to statutory and other bodies/committees associated with the educational establishment;

- organises examinations, necessary invigilations and any security procedures required;

- arranges for the preparation, publication and despatch of syllabuses and other official documents.

## RELATED JOB TITLES

Bursar
Registrar (*educational services*)

## 199 OTHER MANAGERS AND ADMINISTRATORS NEC

Workers in this unit group perform a variety of managerial and administrative tasks not elsewhere classified in MINOR GROUP 19: Managers and Administrators n.e.c.

## TYPICAL ENTRY ROUTES AND ASSOCIATED QUALIFICATIONS

There are no pre-set entry requirements. Candidates are recruited with a variety of academic qualifications or with relevant experience.

## RELATED JOB TITLES

Hospital administrator
Manager (*cleaning, refuse disposal*)
Manager (*plant hire*)
Manager (*sewage works*)
Security manager
Station officer (*ambulance service*)
Superintendant (*cemetery*)

# MAJOR GROUP 2

## PROFESSIONAL OCCUPATIONS

# MAJOR GROUP 2
# PROFESSIONAL OCCUPATIONS

This major group covers occupations whose main tasks require a high level of knowledge and experience in the natural sciences, engineering, life sciences, social sciences, humanities and related fields. The main tasks consist of the practical application of an extensive body of theoretical knowledge, increasing the stock of knowledge by means of research and communicating such knowledge by teaching methods and other means.

Most occupations in this major group will require a degree or equivalent qualification, with some occupations requiring post graduate qualifications and/or a formal period of experience-related training.

Occupations in this major group are classified into the following minor groups:

20  NATURAL SCIENTISTS

21  ENGINEERS AND TECHNOLOGISTS

22  HEALTH PROFESSIONALS

23  TEACHING PROFESSIONALS

24  LEGAL PROFESSIONALS

25  BUSINESS AND FINANCIAL PROFESSIONALS

26  ARCHITECTS, TOWN PLANNERS AND SURVEYORS

27  LIBRARIANS AND RELATED PROFESSIONALS

29  PROFESSIONAL OCCUPATIONS NEC

# MINOR GROUP 20
# NATURAL SCIENTISTS

Natural scientists are involved in planning, directing and undertaking research and development, providing technical advisory and consultancy services and related work in the fields of natural phenomena and mathematics for industrial, medical, agricultural, military, mining and similar applications.

Occupations in this minor group are classified into the following unit groups:

- 200   CHEMISTS
- 201   BIOLOGICAL SCIENTISTS AND BIOCHEMISTS
- 202   PHYSICISTS, GEOLOGISTS AND METEOROLOGISTS
- 209   OTHER NATURAL SCIENTISTS NEC

## 200 CHEMISTS

Chemists analyse and research physical aspects of chemical structure and change within substances and develop chemical techniques used in the manufacture or modification of natural substances and processed products.

### TYPICAL ENTRY ROUTES AND ASSOCIATED QUALIFICATIONS

Entry will usually require a chemistry degree but is possible with BTEC Higher National awards followed by study for professional qualifications.

### TASKS

- develops experimental procedures, instruments and recording and testing systems;

- conducts experiments to identify chemical composition, energy and chemical changes in natural substances and processed materials;

- analyses results and experimental data;

- tests techniques and processes for reliability under a variety of conditions;

- develops procedures for quality control of manufactured products.

### RELATED JOB TITLES

Analytical chemist
Chemist
Development chemist
Industrial chemist
Physical chemist
Research chemist

## 201 BIOLOGICAL SCIENTISTS AND BIOCHEMISTS

Biological scientists and biochemists examine and investigate the morphology, structure, chemistry and physical characteristics of living organisms, including their inter-relationships, environments and diseases.

### TYPICAL ENTRY ROUTES AND ASSOCIATED QUALIFICATIONS

Entry is most common with a degree or equivalent qualification, but is possible with other academic qualifications and/or professional training.

### TASKS

- studies the physical and chemical form, structure, composition and function of organs and tissues;

- identifies and studies the chemical substances, including microbial infections, involved in physiological processes and the progress of disease;

- performs blood tests to study physiological and pathological characteristics within blood cells;

- researches the effects of internal and external environmental factors on the life processes and other functions of living organisms;

- observes the structure of communities of organisms in the laboratory and in their natural environment;

- advises farmers, medical staff and others, on the nature of field crops, livestock and produce and on the treatment and prevention of disease.

## RELATED JOB TITLES

Biochemist
Biologist
Botanist
Clinical biochemist
Medical laboratory scientific officer
Microbiologist
Pathologist
Zoologist

## 202 PHYSICISTS, GEOLOGISTS AND METEOROLOGISTS

Physicists, geologists and meteorologists study relationships between matter, energy and other physical phenomena, the nature, composition and structure of the Earth and other planetary bodies and forecast weather conditions and electrical, magnetic, seismic and thermal activity.

### TYPICAL ENTRY ROUTES AND ASSOCIATED QUALIFICATIONS

Entry is most common with a degree or equivalent qualification, but is possible with other academic qualifications and/or professional training.

### TASKS

- conducts experiments and tests and uses mathematical models and theories to investigate the structure and properties of matter, transformations and propagations of energy, the behaviour of macro-molecules and living cells and their interaction with various forms of energy;

- uses surveys, seismology and other methods to determine the earth's mantle, crust, rock structure and type and investigates evidence of similar structures in other planetary bodies;

- observes, records and collates data on atmospheric conditions to plot and forecast weather conditions;

- applies models and techniques to industrial functions and seeks out new applications.

## RELATED JOB TITLES

Geologist
Geophysicist
Mathematician
Meteorologist
Physicist
Seismologist

## 209 OTHER NATURAL SCIENTISTS NEC

Workers in this unit group perform a variety of natural science occupations not elsewhere classified in MINOR GROUP 20: Natural Scientists.

### TYPICAL ENTRY ROUTES AND ASSOCIATED QUALIFICATIONS

Entry is most common with a degree or equivalent qualification, but is possible with other academic qualifications and/or professional training.

### TASKS

- plans, directs and undertakes research into natural phenomena;

- applies scientific method and mathematical simulation techniques to the study and analysis of complex management problems;

- provides technical advisory and consulting services;

- designs tests and experiments to isolate problems and find solutions;

- applies models and techniques to medical, industrial, agricultural, military and similar applications.

**RELATED JOB TITLES**

Natural scientist
Scientific officer

# MINOR GROUP 21
# ENGINEERS AND TECHNOLOGISTS

Engineers and engineering technologists plan, organise and technically supervise the construction, testing, installation and maintenance of mechanical, structural, chemical, electrical and electronic systems and equipment. They also undertake research and consultancy work in their specialist fields.

Occupations in this minor group are classified into the following unit groups:

210 CIVIL, STRUCTURAL, MUNICIPAL, MINING
    AND QUARRYING ENGINEERS
211 MECHANICAL ENGINEERS
212 ELECTRICAL ENGINEERS
213 ELECTRONIC ENGINEERS
214 SOFTWARE ENGINEERS
215 CHEMICAL ENGINEERS
216 DESIGN AND DEVELOPMENT ENGINEERS
217 PROCESS AND PRODUCTION ENGINEERS
218 PLANNING AND QUALITY CONTROL ENGINEERS
219 OTHER ENGINEERS AND TECHNOLOGISTS NEC

## 210 CIVIL, STRUCTURAL, MUNICIPAL, MINING AND QUARRYING ENGINEERS

Civil, structural, municipal, mining and quarrying engineers undertake research and design, direct construction and manage the operation and maintenance of civil and mining engineering structures.

### TYPICAL ENTRY ROUTES AND ASSOCIATED QUALIFICATIONS

Most entrants have an engineering degree accredited by the relevant professional body. To become a Chartered Engineer graduates also need to complete an approved period of training and experience with an employer. Non-graduate entrants can qualify by taking professional examinations. For this route engineers need A-levels/H-grades or BTEC/SCOTVEC awards. BTEC/SCOTVEC Higher National awards may give some examination exemptions.

### TASKS

- undertakes research and advises on mineral deposits, soil mechanics, concrete technology, hydraulics, water and waste water treatment processes and other civil engineering matters;

- determines and specifies construction methods, materials, quality and safety standards and ensures that equipment operation and maintenance comply with design specifications;

- designs structures such as roads, dams, bridges, railways, hydraulic systems, sewerage systems, industrial and other buildings and plans the layout of tunnels, wells and construction shafts;

- organises and plans projects, arranges work schedules, carries out inspection work and plans maintenance control;

- organises and establishes control systems to monitor operational efficiency and performance of materials and systems.

Chartered civil engineer
Chartered structural engineer
City engineer
Civil engineer
Drainage engineer
Irrigation engineer
Mining engineer
Municipal engineer
Petroleum engineer
Structural engineer

# 211 MECHANICAL ENGINEERS

Mechanical engineers undertake research and design, direct construction and manage the operation and maintenance of engines, machines, aircraft, vehicle and ships' structures and other mechanical items.

## TYPICAL ENTRY ROUTES AND ASSOCIATED QUALIFICATIONS

Most entrants have an engineering degree accredited by the relevant professional body. To become a Chartered Engineer graduates also need to complete an approved period of training and experience with an employer. Non-graduate entrants can qualify by passing professional examinations. For this route candidates need A-levels/H-grades or BTEC/SCOTVEC awards. BTEC/SCOTVEC Engineering Higher National awards may give some examination exemptions.

## TASKS

- undertakes research and advises on energy use, materials handling, thermodynamic processes, fluid mechanics, vehicles and environmental controls;

- determines materials, equipment, piping, capacities, layout of plant or system and specification for manufacture;

- designs mechanical equipment, such as steam, internal combustion and other non-electrical motors for railway locomotives, road vehicles, aeroplanes and other machinery;

- ensures that equipment, operation and maintenance comply with design specifications and safety standards;

- organises and establishes control systems to monitor operational efficiency and performance of materials and systems.

## RELATED JOB TITLES

Aeronautical engineer
Automobile engineer
Hydraulic engineer
Marine engineer
Mechanical engineer
Welding engineer

# 212 ELECTRICAL ENGINEERS

Electrical engineers undertake research and design, direct construction and manage the operation and maintenance of electrical equipment, power stations and other electrical products and systems.

## TYPICAL ENTRY ROUTES AND ASSOCIATED QUALIFICATIONS

Most entrants have an engineering degree accredited by the relevant professional body. To become a Chartered Engineer entrants also need to complete an approved period of training and experience with an employer. Non-graduate entrants can qualify by passing professional examinations. For this route candidates need A-levels/H-grades or BTEC/SCOTVEC awards. BTEC/SCOTVEC Engineering Higher National awards may give some examination exemptions.

## TASKS

- undertakes research and advises on all aspects of power generation, transmission and distribution systems, control, instrumentation and other electrical systems;

- determines and specifies manufacturing methods, quality and safety standards;

- ensures that manufacture, operation and maintenance comply with design specifications and contractual arrangements;

- organises and establishes control systems to monitor performance and safety standards.

## RELATED JOB TITLES

Electrical engineer (*professional*)
Generating engineer (*electricity board*)
Power engineer
Power transmission engineer

## 213 ELECTRONIC ENGINEERS

Electronic engineers undertake research and design, direct construction and manage the operation and maintenance of electronic motors, communications systems, microwave systems, and other electronic electronic equipment.

### TYPICAL ENTRY ROUTES AND ASSOCIATED QUALIFICATIONS

Most entrants have an engineering degree accredited by the relevant professional body. To become a Chartered Engineer graduates also need to complete an approved period of training and experience with an employer. Non-graduate entrants can qualify by passing professional qualifications. For this route candidates need A-levels/H-grades or BTEC/SCOTVEC awards. BTEC/SCOTVEC Engineering Higher National awards may give some examination exemptions.

### TASKS

- undertakes research and advises on all aspects of telecommunications equipment, radar, telemetry and remote control systems, data processing equipment, microwaves and other electronic equipment;

- determines and specifies appropriate production and/or installation methods and quality and safety standards;

- ensures that production, installation and maintenance comply with specifications and safety standards;

- organises and establishes control systems to monitor performance and evaluate designs.

### RELATED JOB TITLES

Broadcasting engineer
Electronic engineer
Microwave engineer
Radar research engineer
Radio engineer (*professional*)

## 214 SOFTWARE ENGINEERS

Software engineers are responsible for all aspects of production and support of software for computer-based systems.

### TYPICAL ENTRY ROUTES AND ASSOCIATED QUALIFICATIONS

Most entrants have a degree in a subject related to computer work and accredited by a relevant professional organisation (e.g. the British Computer Society, the Institution of Electrical Engineers). Some have post-graduate qualifications. Post-recruitment training includes attending specialised courses in particular development methods and management/planning.

### TASKS

- liaises with client to discuss user requirements and estimates resources needed to achieve desired functionality;

- designs and develops the software needed to achieve specified functionality within stated constraints;

- creates and applies tests to demonstrate that specified software achieves required effects;

- writes reports, specifications, codes of practice and instruction manuals;

- plans the process of software development and monitors progress with respect to the plan;

- may develop new methods or techniques for any of the above with appropriate formal notations and software tools.

### RELATED JOB TITLES

Project leader (*computing*)
Software engineer
Systems designer (*computing*)

## 215 CHEMICAL ENGINEERS

Chemical engineers undertake research on commercial scale chemical processes and processed products, design and provide specifications and direct the construction, operation, maintenance and repair of chemical plants and control systems.

## TYPICAL ENTRY ROUTES AND ASSOCIATED QUALIFICATIONS

Most entrants have an engineering degree accredited by the relevant professional body. To become a Chartered Engineer graduates also need to complete an approved period of training and experience with an employer. Non-graduate entrants can qualify by taking professional examinations. For this route candidates need A-levels/H-grades or BTEC/SCOTVEC awards. BTEC/SCOTVEC Engineering Higher National awards may give some examination exemptions.

## TASKS

- undertakes research and develops processes to achieve physical and/or chemical change for oil, pharmaceutical, synthetic, plastic, food and other products;

- designs, controls and constructs process plants to manufacture products;

- ensures that production methods, materials and quality standards conform to specifications and safety requirements;

- manages the safe and efficient operation, maintenance and control of processing plant;

- prepares reports, feasibility studies and costings for major investments in processing facilities for increased capacity and novel product manufacture.

## RELATED JOB TITLES

Chemical engineer
Plastics engineer

## 216  DESIGN AND DEVELOPMENT ENGINEERS

Design and development engineers conceive engineering designs from product ideas or requirements in mechanical, electrical and electronic engineering.

## TYPICAL ENTRY ROUTES AND ASSOCIATED QUALIFICATIONS

Most entrants have an engineering degree accredited by the relevant professional body. To become

a Chartered Engineer graduates also need to complete an approved period of training and experience with an employer. Non-graduate entrants can also qualify by taking professional examinations. For this route candidates need A-levels/H-grades or BTEC/SCOTVEC awards. BTEC/SCOTVEC engineering Higher National awards may give some examination exemptions.

## TASKS

- assesses product requirements, including costs, manufacturing feasibility and market requirements;

- prepares working designs for steam, aero, turbine, marine, electrical and electronic engines, mechanical instruments, aircraft and missile structures, vehicle and ship structures, plant and machinery equipment, domestic electrical appliances and electronic computing and telecommunications equipment;

- arranges construction and testing of model or prototype and modifies design if necessary;

- produces final design information for use in preparation of layouts, parts lists, etc.;

- prepares specifications for materials and other components.

## RELATED JOB TITLES

Computer engineer (*design*)
Design engineer
Development engineer

## 217  PROCESS AND PRODUCTION ENGINEERS

Process and production engineers advise on and direct technical aspects of production programmes to ensure cost-effectiveness and efficiency.

## TYPICAL ENTRY ROUTES AND ASSOCIATED QUALIFICATIONS

Most entrants have an engineering degree accredited by the relevant professional body. To become a Chartered Engineer graduates also need to complete an approved period of training and experience with an employer. Non-graduate entrants can also qualify by passing professional examinations For this route candidates need A-levels/H-grades or BTEC/SCOTVEC awards. BTEC/SCOTVEC Engineering Higher National awards may give some examination exemptions.

## TASKS

- Studies existing and alternative production methods, regarding work flow, plant layout, types of machinery and cost;

- recommends optimum equipment and layout and prepares drawings and specifications;

- devises production control methods to monitor operational efficiency;

- investigates and eliminates potential hazards and bottlenecks in production;

- advises management on new production methods, techniques and equipment;

- liaises with materials buying, storing and controlling departments to ensure a steady flow of supplies.

### RELATED JOB TITLES

Process engineer
Production engineer

## 218 PLANNING AND QUALITY CONTROL ENGINEERS

Planning and quality control engineers plan production schedules, work sequences and manufacturing and processing procedures to ensure accuracy, quality and reliability.

### TYPICAL ENTRY ROUTES AND ASSOCIATED QUALIFICATIONS

Most entrants have an engineering degree accredited by the relevant professional body. To become a Chartered Engineer graduates also need to complete an approved period of training and experience with an employer. Non-graduate entrants can qualify by passing professional examinations. For this route candidates need A-levels/H-grades or BTEC/SCOTVEC awards. BTEC/SCOTVEC Engineering Higher National awards may give some examination exemptions.

## TASKS

- analyses plans, drawings, specifications and safety, quality, accuracy reliability and contractual requirements;

- prepares plan of sequence of operations and completion dates for each phase of production or processing;

- advises on existing plant machinery/layout and any modifications required;

- devises inspection, testing and evaluation methods for bought-in materials, components, semi-finished and finished products;

- ensures accuracy of machines, jigs, fixtures, gauges and other manufacturing and testing equipment;

- prepares work flow charts for individual departments and compiles detailed instructions on processes, work methods and quality and safety standards for workers.

### RELATED JOB TITLES

Industrial engineer
Planning engineer
Production planner
Quality control engineer
Quality engineer

## 219 OTHER ENGINEERS AND TECHNOLOGISTS NEC

Other engineers and technologists n.e.c. perform a variety of engineering and technology occupations not elsewhere classified in MINOR GROUP 21: Engineers and Technologists.

### TYPICAL ENTRY ROUTES AND ASSOCIATED QUALIFICATIONS

Most entrants have an engineering degree accredited by the relevant professional body. To become a Chartered Engineer graduates also need to complete an approved period of training and experience with an employer. Non-graduate entrants can qualify by passing professional examinations. For this route candidates need A-levels/H-grades or BTEC/SCOTVEC awards. BTEC/SCOTVEC Engineering Higher National awards may give some examination exemptions.

## TASKS

- researches into problem areas to advance basic knowledge, evaluate new theories and techniques and to solve specific problems;

- establishes principles and techniques to improve the quality, durability and performance of materials such as textiles, glass, rubber, plastics, ceramics, metals and alloys;

- designs new systems and equipment with regard to cost, market requirements and feasibility of manufacture;

- devises and implements control systems to monitor operational efficiency and performance of system and materials;

- prepare sketches, drawings and specifications showing materials to be used, construction and finishing methods and other details;

- examines and advises on patent applications;

- provides technical consultancy services.

## RELATED JOB TITLES

Agricultural engineer
Brewing technologist
Ceramics engineer/technologist
Fuel engineer/technologist
Glass technologist
Materials scientist/technologist
Metallurgist
Nuclear engineer
Patent agent
Plastics technologist
Project engineer
Rubber technologist
Traffic engineer

# MINOR GROUP 22
# HEALTH PROFESSIONALS

Health practice professionals diagnose mental and physical injuries, disorders and diseases, provide treatment with drugs, surgery, therapy and corrective devices, carry out routine medical tests and recommend preventative action to patients, conduct research into treatments and drugs and dispense pharmaceutical compounds.

Occupations in this minor group are classified into the following unit groups:

**220 MEDICAL PRACTITIONERS**
**221 PHARMACISTS/PHARMACOLOGISTS**
**222 OPHTHALMIC OPTICIANS**
**223 DENTAL PRACTITIONERS**
**224 VETERINARIANS**

## 220 MEDICAL PRACTITIONERS

Medical practitioners diagnose mental and physical injuries, disorders and diseases, prescribe and give treatment, recommend preventative action and where necessary, refer the patient to a specialist.

### TYPICAL ENTRY ROUTES AND ASSOCIATED QUALIFICATIONS

Entry will require a University degree or equivalent qualification, followed by an internship of a year or more in a hospital. Specialist fields will require further study and training.

### TASKS

- examines patient, arranges for any necessary x-rays or other tests and interprets results;

- diagnoses condition and prescribes and/or administers appropriate treatment/surgery;

- administers routine medical tests and inoculations against communicable diseases;

- supervises patient's progress and advises on diet, exercise and other preventative action;

- refers patient to specialist where necessary and liaises with specialist.

### RELATED JOB TITLES

Anaesthetist
General practitioner
Medical consultant
Medical doctor
Physician
Psychiatrist
Psycho-analyst
Registrar (*hospital service*)
Specialist consultant
Surgeon

## 221 PHARMACISTS/ PHARMACOLOGISTS

Pharmacists/pharmacologists advise and participate in the development and testing of new drugs and compound and dispense drugs and medicaments in hospitals and pharmacies.

### TYPICAL ENTRY ROUTES AND ASSOCIATED QUALIFICATIONS

Entry will require a University degree or equivalent qualification.

### TASKS

- prepares or directs the preparation of prescribed medicaments in liquid, powder, tablet, ointment or other form;

- checks that recommended doses are not being exceeded and that instructions are understood by patients;

- maintains prescription files and records issue of narcotics, poisons and other habit-forming drugs;

- liaises with other professionals regarding the development, manufacturing and testing of drugs;

- tests and analyses drugs to determine their identity, purity and strength

- ensures that drugs and medicaments are in good supply and are stored properly.

## RELATED JOB TITLES

Chemist (*pharmaceutical / retail*)
Druggist
Pharmaceutical chemist
Pharmacist
Pharmacologist

# 222 OPHTHALMIC OPTICIANS

Ophthalmic opticians test patient's vision, diagnose defects and disorders and prescribe glasses or contact lenses as required.

## TYPICAL ENTRY ROUTES AND ASSOCIATED QUALIFICATIONS

Entry will require a University degree or equivalent qualification.

## TASKS

- examines eyes and tests vision of patient;

- prescribes, supplies and fits appropriate spectacle lenses, contact lenses or other aids;

- advises patient on proper use of glasses, contact lenses and other aids, and on appropriate lighting conditions for reading and working;

- refers patient to a specialist, where necessary;

- carries out research with glass and lens manufacturers.

## RELATED JOB TITLES

Ophthalmic optician
Optometrist

# 223 DENTAL PRACTITIONERS

Dental practitioners diagnose dental and oral diseases, injuries and disorders, prescribe and administer treatment, recommend preventative action and, where necessary, refer the patient to a specialist.

## TYPICAL ENTRY ROUTES AND ASSOCIATED QUALIFICATIONS

Entry will require a University degree or equivalent qualification. Specialist fields will require further study and training.

## TASKS

- examines patient's teeth, gums and jaw, using dental and x-ray equipment;

- administers local or general anaesthetics;

- drills, prepares and fills cavities in teeth;

- constructs and fits braces, inlays, dentures and other appliances;

- supervises patient's progress and advises on preventative action;

- refers patient to specialist, where necessary.

## RELATED JOB TITLES

Dental surgeon
Dentist
Orthodontist
Periodontist

# 224 VETERINARIANS

Veterinarians diagnose and treat animal injuries, diseases and disorders, and advise on preventative action.

## TYPICAL ENTRY ROUTES AND ASSOCIATED QUALIFICATIONS

Entry will require a University degree in veterinary science.

## TASKS

- examines animal and arranges or undertakes any necessary x-ray or other tests;

- diagnoses condition and prescribes and administers appropriate drugs, dressings, etc.;

- performs routine medical tests and inoculates animals against communicable diseases;

- administers local or general anaesthetics and performs surgery;

- investigates outbreaks of animal diseases and advises owners on feeding, breeding and general care.

## RELATED JOB TITLES

Veterinarian
Veterinary officer
Veterinary surgeon

# MINOR GROUP 23
# TEACHING PROFESSIONALS

Teaching professionals plan, organise, control, advise on and provide instruction in academic, technical, vocational, diversionary and other subjects and inspect schools and training establishments.

Occupations in this minor group are classified into the following unit groups:

230 UNIVERSITY AND POLYTECHNIC TEACHING PROFESSIONALS

231 HIGHER AND FURTHER EDUCATION TEACHING PROFESSIONALS

232 EDUCATION OFFICERS, SCHOOL INSPECTORS

233 SECONDARY (AND MIDDLE SCHOOL DEEMED SECONDARY) EDUCATION TEACHING PROFESSIONALS

234 PRIMARY (AND MIDDLE SCHOOL DEEMED PRIMARY) AND NURSERY EDUCATION TEACHING PROFESSIONALS

235 SPECIAL EDUCATION TEACHING PROFESSIONALS

239 OTHER TEACHING PROFESSIONALS NEC

## 230 UNIVERSITY AND POLYTECHNIC TEACHING PROFESSIONALS

University and polytechnic teaching professionals deliver lectures and teach students to at least first degree level, undertake research and write journal articles and books in their chosen field of study.

### TYPICAL ENTRY ROUTES AND ASSOCIATED QUALIFICATIONS

Entry will require a good initial degree plus higher degree including research. For vocational subjects, practical experience is also required.

### TASKS

- prepares, delivers and directs lectures, seminars and tutorials;

- prepares, administers and marks examinations, essays and other assignments;

- advises students on academic matters and encourages independent research;

- participates in decision making processes regarding curricula, budgetary, departmental and other matters;

- directs the work of post-graduate students;

- undertakes research, writes articles and books and attends conferences and other meetings.

### RELATED JOB TITLES

Lecturer
Polytechnic lecturer
Professor
Reader
Senior lecturer
University lecturer

## 231 HIGHER AND FURTHER EDUCATION TEACHING PROFESSIONALS

Higher and further education teaching professionals supervise and teach trade, technical, commercial, adult education, secondary and post-secondary courses to students beyond minimum school leaving age.

Entry will require a degree or equivalent qualification and often a post-graduate qualification. As some HE/FE courses are vocational, work experience may also be required.

## TASKS

- prepares, delivers and directs lectures, seminars and tutorials;

- prepares, administers and marks examinations, essays and other assignments;

- arranges instructional visits and periods of employment experience for students;

- assists with the administration of teaching and the arranging of timetables;

- liaises with other professional and commercial organisations to review course content.

## RELATED JOB TITLES

College lecturer
Lecturer (*college of education*)
Principal lecturer
Senior lecturer (*college of education*)
Teacher (*further education*)

## 232 EDUCATION OFFICERS, SCHOOL INSPECTORS

Education officers plan, organise and direct the educational activities and resources in a local authority education area. HM Inspectors of Schools undertake inspections of schools and other training establishments excluding universities.

## TYPICAL ENTRY ROUTES AND ASSOCIATED QUALIFICATIONS

Entry is most common with an education-related degree and ten or more years relevant experience in the field of education.

## TASKS

- advises on all aspects of education and ensures that all statutory educational requirements are being met;

- plans and advises on the provision of special schools for the physically and mentally handicapped;

- appoints and controls teaching staff;

- verifies that school buildings are adequately maintained;

- arranges for the provision of school medical and meals services;

- observes teaching, assesses learning level and discusses any apparent faults with teachers, heads of department and head teachers;

- prepares reports on schools concerning teaching standards, the role of the school in the forward planning of the education system, etc.

## RELATED JOB TITLES

Chief education officer
Curriculum development officer
Director of education
Education inspector
Education officer
HM Inspector of Schools

## 233 SECONDARY (AND MIDDLE SCHOOL DEEMED SECONDARY) EDUCATION TEACHING PROFESSIONALS

Secondary (and middle school deemed secondary) education teaching professionals plan, organise and provide instruction in one or more subjects, including physical education and diversionary activities, within a prescribed curriculum in a secondary or secondary/middle school.

## TYPICAL ENTRY ROUTES AND ASSOCIATED QUALIFICATIONS

Entry is only possible with a Bachelor of Education or other relevant degree followed by a Post Graduate Certificate of Education which includes 15–17 weeks of on-the-job training. Further and higher professional qualifications are required for some teaching posts.

## TASKS

- prepares courses in accordance with curriculum requirements and teaches one or more subjects;

- prepares, assigns and corrects exercises and examinations to record and evaluate students' progress;

- supervises any practical work and maintains classroom discipline;

- discusses progress with student, parents and/or other education professionals;

- assists with or plans and develops curriculum and rota of teaching duties.

## RELATED JOB TITLES

Head teacher (*secondary school*)
PE teacher (*secondary school*)
Secondary school teacher
Teacher (*secondary school*)

## 234 PRIMARY (AND MIDDLE SCHOOL DEEMED PRIMARY) AND NURSERY EDUCATION TEACHING PROFESSIONALS

Primary (and middle school deemed primary) and nursery education teaching professionals plan, organise and provide instruction to children at all levels up to the age of entry into secondary education.

## TYPICAL ENTRY ROUTES AND ASSOCIATED QUALIFICATIONS

Entry is only possible with a Bachelor of Education or other relevant degree followed by a Post Graduate Certificate of Education which includes 15–17 weeks on-the-job training. Further and higher professional qualifications are available and are required for certain posts.

## TASKS

- prepares courses and teaches a range of subjects;

- prepares, assigns and corrects exercises to record and evaluate students progress;

- supervises students in classroom and maintains discipline;

- teaches simple songs and rhymes and reads stories to promote language development;

- discusses progress with student, parents and/or other education professionals.

## RELATED JOB TITLES

Head teacher (*primary/middle school*)
Infant teacher
Junior school teacher
Nursery school teacher
Primary school teacher

## 235 SPECIAL EDUCATION TEACHING PROFESSIONALS

Special education teaching professionals organise and provide instruction at a variety of different levels to children who are partially blind, deaf, physically or mentally handicapped, epileptic or suffering from speech defects or other learning difficulties.

## TYPICAL ENTRY ROUTES AND ASSOCIATED QUALIFICATIONS

Entry is possible with a Bachelor of Education or other relevant degree followed by a Post Graduate Certificate of Education which includes 15–17 weeks on-the-job training. Further training lasting between one and four years is also mandatory.

## TASKS

- assesses student's abilities and needs and devises curriculum and rota of teaching duties accordingly;

- gives instruction, using techniques appropriate to the student's handicap;

- encourages the student to develop self-help skills to circumvent the limitations imposed by their disability;

- prepares, assigns and corrects exercises to record and evaluate students progress;

- supervises students in classroom and maintains discipline;

- discusses student's progress with parents and other staff.

**RELATED JOB TITLES**

Head teacher (*special school*)
Teacher (*blind school*)
Teacher (*deaf children*)
Teacher (*lip reading*)
Teacher (*mentally handicapped*)
Teacher (*physically handicapped children*)

## 239 OTHER TEACHING PROFESSIONALS NEC

Workers in this unit group perform a variety of other education and teaching occupations not elsewhere classified in MINOR GROUP 23: Teaching Professionals.

**TYPICAL ENTRY ROUTES AND ASSOCIATED QUALIFICATIONS**

Entry is most common with a Bachelor of Education or other relevant degree, a Post Graduate Certificate of Education or a Scottish Teaching qualification, but is possible with other academic qualifications.

**TASKS**

- inspects and advises on the work of training and similar establishments;

- teaches dancing, musical instruments and/or theory and academic subjects privately to individuals or groups;

- teaches general interest diversionary activities such as cookery, car maintenance, photography and decorating at evening schools and other establishments;

- guides and co-ordinates the educational or training work carried out by an establishment.

**RELATED JOB TITLES**

Dance teacher (*dancing school*)
Music teacher
Piano teacher
Principal (*dancing/evening school*)
Teacher (*diversionary activities*)

# MINOR GROUP 24
# LEGAL PROFESSIONALS

Legal practice professionals preside over judicial proceedings and research and advise on legal matters.

Occupations in this minor group are classified into the following unit groups:

**240  JUDGES AND OFFICERS OF THE COURT**
**241  BARRISTERS AND ADVOCATES**
**242  SOLICITORS**

## 240  JUDGES AND OFFICERS OF THE COURT

Judges and Officers of The Court preside over judicial proceedings, pronounce judgements and perform duties associated with the administration of the court.

### TYPICAL ENTRY ROUTES AND ASSOCIATED QUALIFICATIONS

Entry will require a degree or equivalent qualification and over two years experience in legal practice. Further post-graduate degrees in law may be required.

### TASKS

* conducts trials according to rules of procedure;

* hears, reads and evaluates evidence;

* interprets the law in relation to particular cases;

* in cases tried by jury, summarises the evidence and instructs or advises the jury on points of law or procedure;

* announces the verdict and passes sentence and/or awards costs and damages.

### RELATED JOB TITLES

Judge
Magistrate (*stipendiary*)
Recorder (*legal services*)

## 241  BARRISTERS AND ADVOCATES

Barristers and Advocates prepare and conduct court cases, usually in the higher courts, on behalf of individuals, Government and other organisations.

### TYPICAL ENTRY ROUTES AND ASSOCIATED QUALIFICATIONS

Entry will require a degree or equivalent qualification and to become a Barrister over one years experience in legal practice is required. Further post-graduate degrees in law may be required.

### TASKS

* studies solicitor's brief and discusses the case with solicitor and client;

* investigates circumstances surrounding a case and acquaints him/herself with relevant law and precedent;

* drafts pleadings and questions;

* appears in court to present evidence, cross-examine witnesses and represent client.

### RELATED JOB TITLES

Advocate
Barrister
Queen's Counsel

## 242 SOLICITORS

Solicitors advise clients on and handle the legal aspects of business and personal problems and parliamentary legislation.

### TYPICAL ENTRY ROUTES AND ASSOCIATED QUALIFICATIONS

Entry will usually require a degree or equivalent qualification, although it is possible to enter training as a solicitor with five GCSEs/SCEs (grades A-C/1-3) and two A-levels/H-grades.

### TASKS

- advises client on legal and parliamentary matters;

- undertakes all legal business on behalf of client;

- instructs counsel in higher and lower courts and pleads cases in lower courts as appropriate;

- draws up wills, contracts, Public Bills and Private Members Bills and acts as trustee or executor if required;

- deals with the legal aspects of buying and selling property.

### RELATED JOB TITLES

Articled clerk (*legal services*)
Solicitor
Solicitor's articled clerk

# MINOR GROUP 25
# BUSINESS AND FINANCIAL PROFESSIONALS

Business and financial practice professionals collect and analyse financial and other material, perform accountancy duties and advise industrial, commercial and other establishments on management and business matters.

Occupations in this minor group are classified into the following unit groups:

**250 CHARTERED AND CERTIFIED ACCOUNTANTS**
**251 MANAGEMENT ACCOUNTANTS**
**252 ACTUARIES, ECONOMISTS AND STATISTICIANS**
**253 MANAGEMENT CONSULTANTS, BUSINESS ANALYSTS**

## 250 CHARTERED AND CERTIFIED ACCOUNTANTS

Chartered and Certified Accountants provide accounting and auditing services and advise clients on financial matters.

### TYPICAL ENTRY ROUTES AND ASSOCIATED QUALIFICATIONS

Entry is most common with a degree or equivalent qualification, but is possible with other academic qualifications and professional training.

### TASKS

- plans and oversees implementation of accountancy system and policies;

- prepares financial documents and reports for management, shareholders, statutory or other bodies;

- audits accounts and book-keeping records;

- prepares tax returns, advises on tax problems and contests disputed claim before tax official;

- conducts financial investigations concerning insolvency, fraud, possible mergers, etc.

### RELATED JOB TITLES

Accountant (*qualified*)
Audit examiner
Auditor (*qualified*)
Certified accountant
Chartered accountant
Company accountant (*qualified*)

## 251 MANAGEMENT ACCOUNTANTS

Management accountants collect and analyse financial information and perform other accounting duties required by management for the planning and control of an establishment's income and expenditure.

### TYPICAL ENTRY ROUTES AND ASSOCIATED QUALIFICATIONS

Entry is most common with a degree or equivalent qualification, but is possible with other academic qualifications and professional training.

### TASKS

- evaluates financial information for management purposes;

- liaises with management and other professionals to compile budgets and other costs;

92

- prepares periodic accounts, budgetary reviews and financial forecasts;
- conducts investigations and advises management on financial aspects of productivity, stock holding, sales, new products, etc.

## RELATED JOB TITLES

Cost accountant (*qualified*)
Cost and management accountant (*qualified*)
Cost and works accountant (*qualified*)
Management accountant (*qualified*)

## 252 ACTUARIES, ECONOMISTS AND STATISTICIANS

Actuaries, economists and statisticians apply economic, statistical and actuarial principles and techniques to analyse and interpret data used to assist with the formulation of financial and investment policies, other research and to help solve management and other problems.

## TYPICAL ENTRY ROUTES AND ASSOCIATED QUALIFICATIONS

Entry will usually require a degree, but is possible with a HND, except for actuaries who may be accepted with other academic qualifications.

## TASKS

- establishes the nature and extent of data required for a particular project and determines the appropriate method of data collection;
- analyses and interprets data using statistical and other techniques and advises on economic or other policy in the light of findings;
- prepares reports, charts and tables to summarise main findings and proposals.

## RELATED JOB TITLES

Actuary
Agricultural economist
Consulting actuary
Economist
Statistician

## 253 MANAGEMENT CONSULTANTS, BUSINESS ANALYSTS

Management consultants and business analysts advise industrial, commercial and other establishments on a variety of management, personnel, computing and technical matters.

## TYPICAL ENTRY ROUTES AND ASSOCIATED QUALIFICATIONS

Entry is most common with a degree or equivalent qualification, but is possible with other academic qualifications and professional training.

## TASKS

- assesses the functions, objectives and requirements of the organisation seeking advice;
- identifies and investigates problems concerned with strategy, policy, markets, organisation, computing facilities, procedures and methods;
- analyses information gained with regard to management implications;
- formulates recommendations and discusses and agrees with the client a course of action;
- may assist client in implementing recommendations.

## RELATED JOB TITLES

Business analyst
Management consultant

# MINOR GROUP 26
# ARCHITECTS, TOWN PLANNERS AND SURVEYORS

Architects, town planners and surveyors conduct surveys to determine the exact position of natural and constructed features and design and plan the layout of buildings for commercial, residential, industrial and other uses.

Occupations in this minor group are classified into the following unit groups:

260 ARCHITECTS
261 TOWN PLANNERS
262 BUILDING, LAND, MINING AND 'GENERAL PRACTICE' SURVEYORS

## 260 ARCHITECTS

Architects plan and design the construction and development of buildings and land areas with regard to functional and aesthetic requirements.

### TYPICAL ENTRY ROUTES AND ASSOCIATED QUALIFICATIONS

Entry is most common with a degree or equivalent qualification, but is possible with other academic qualifications and/or professional training as required.

### TASKS

- liaises with client and other professionals to establish building type, style, cost limitations and landscaping requirements;

- studies condition and characteristics of site, taking into account drainage, topsoil, trees, rock formations, etc.;

- analyses site survey and advises client on development and construction details and ensures that proposed design blends in with the surrounding area;

- prepares detailed scale drawings and specifications for design and construction and submits these for planning approval;

- monitors construction work in progress to ensure compliance with specifications.

### RELATED JOB TITLES

Architect
Architectural consultant
Chartered architect
Landscape architect

## 261 TOWN PLANNERS

Town planners direct or undertake the planning of the layout and the co-ordination of plans for the development of urban and rural areas.

### TYPICAL ENTRY ROUTES AND ASSOCIATED QUALIFICATIONS

Entry is most common with a degree or equivalent qualification, but is possible with other academic qualifications and/or professional training.

### TASKS

- analyses information to establish the nature, extent, growth rate and likely development requirements of the area;

- consults statutory bodies and other interested parties to ensure that local interests are catered for and to evaluate competing development proposals;

- drafts and presents graphic and narrative plans, affecting the use of public and private land, housing and transport facilities;

- examines and evaluates development proposals submitted and recommends acceptance, modification or rejection;

- liaises with national and local government and other bodies to advise on urban and regional planning issues.

Land surveyor
Mining surveyor
Surveyor
Surveyor and estimator

## RELATED JOB TITLES

Planning officer (*local government*)
Town planner

## 262 BUILDING, LAND, MINING AND 'GENERAL PRACTICE' SURVEYORS

Building, land, mining and 'general practice' surveyors conduct surveys on buildings, land and mines to provide data for map making, valuations, alterations to buildings and efficient resource exploitation.

## TYPICAL ENTRY ROUTES AND ASSOCIATED QUALIFICATIONS

Entry is most common with GCSE/SCE S-grades plus A-levels/H-grades. Further professional qualifications are required.

## TASKS

- surveys, measures and describes land surfaces to establish property boundaries and to aid with construction or cartographic work;

- surveys mines, prepares drawings of surfaces, hazards and other features, to control the extent and direction of mining;

- surveys buildings to determine necessary alterations and repairs;

- advises clients on repairs and alterations to property and the feasible direction and extent of mining.

## RELATED JOB TITLES

Building surveyor
Chartered surveyor
Contracts surveyor

95

# MINOR GROUP 27
# LIBRARIANS AND RELATED PROFESSIONALS

Librarians and related professionals appraise, obtain, organise, develop and make available collections of written and recorded material, art objects, pictures, artefacts and other items of general and specialised interest.

Occupations in this minor group are classified into the following unit groups:

### 270 LIBRARIANS
### 271 ARCHIVISTS AND CURATORS

## 270 LIBRARIANS

Librarians appraise, obtain, index, collate and make available library acquisitions and organise and control other library services.

### TYPICAL ENTRY ROUTES AND ASSOCIATED QUALIFICATIONS

Entry will require a degree or equivalent qualification. Further professional qualifications are usually required.

### TASKS

- selects and arranges for the acquisition of books, periodicals, audio-visual and other material;

- collects, classifies and catalogues information, books and other material;

- prepares and circulates abstracts, bibliographies, book lists, etc.;

- identifies the information needs of clients, seeks out and evaluates information sources;

- establishes information storage systems to deal with queries and to maintain up to date records;

- manages library borrowing and inter-library loan facilities.

### RELATED JOB TITLES

Assistant librarian

Branch librarian
Chartered librarian
Librarian

## 271 ARCHIVISTS AND CURATORS

Archivists and curators collect, appraise and preserve collections of recorded and other material of historical interest.

### TYPICAL ENTRY ROUTES AND ASSOCIATED QUALIFICATIONS

Entry is most common with a good honours degree or diploma, but is possible with other academic qualifications. Written and spoken fluency in a foreign language is an advantage in some posts.

### TASKS

- examines, appraises and advises on acquisition of exhibits, government papers and other material;

- classifies material and arranges for its safe keeping and preservation;

- maintains indexes, bibliographies and descriptive details of archive material and arranges for reproductions of items where necessary;

- liaises with school and other groups or individuals, publicises exhibits and arranges special displays for general, specialised or educational interest;

- allows access to original material or material not on display for researchers;

- answers verbal or written enquiries and gives advice on exhibits or other material.

**RELATED JOB TITLES**

Archivist
Curator

# MINOR GROUP 29
# PROFESSIONAL OCCUPATIONS NEC

Workers in this minor group perform a variety of professional occupations not elsewhere classified in MAJOR GROUP 2: Professional occupations.

Occupations in this minor group are classified into the following unit groups:

290 PSYCHOLOGISTS
291 OTHER SOCIAL AND BEHAVIOURAL SCIENTISTS
292 CLERGY
293 SOCIAL WORKERS, PROBATION OFFICERS

## 290 PSYCHOLOGISTS

Psychologists study and assess emotional, cognitive and behavioural processes and abnormalities in human beings and animals and how these are affected by genetic, physical and social factors.

### TYPICAL ENTRY ROUTES AND ASSOCIATED QUALIFICATIONS

Entry requires a degree in psychology or a recognised equivalent. For many jobs post-graduate qualifications are also required. Graduate and post-graduate courses usually include study for professional awards.

### TASKS

- develops and administers tests to measure intelligence, abilities, aptitudes, etc. and assesses results;

- develops treatment and guidance methods and gives treatment or guidance using a variety of therapy and counselling techniques;

- observes and experiments on humans and animals to measure mental and physical characteristics;

- analyses the effect of hereditary, social and physical factors on thought and behaviour;

- studies psychological factors in the treatment and prevention of mental illness or emotional and personality disorders.

### RELATED JOB TITLES

Chartered psychologist
Clinical psychologist
Educational psychologist
Occupational psychologist
Psychologist

## 291 OTHER SOCIAL AND BEHAVIOURAL SCIENTISTS

Other social and behavioural scientists study the origin, structure and characteristics of language, the earth's surface and the form, behaviour, social patterns and interrelationships of human beings.

### TYPICAL ENTRY ROUTES AND ASSOCIATED QUALIFICATIONS

Entry is most common with a degree or equivalent qualification but is possible with other academic qualifications or relevant experience.

### TASKS

- organises and controls field excavations to study artifacts, ancient ruins and fossilised remains;

- traces the evolution of word and language forms, compares grammatical structures and analyses the relationships between ancient parent and modern languages;

- compiles and analyses economic, demographic, legal, political, social and other data;

- studies the characteristics and uses of the earth's surface and natural resources;

- arranges findings in a form suitable for publication and advises national/local bodies on policy issues.

## RELATED JOB TITLES

Archaeologist
Anthropologist
Geographer
Historian
Philologist
Sociologist

## 292 CLERGY

Members of the clergy provide spiritual motivation and guidance, conduct worship according to the form of service of a particular faith/denomination and perform related functions associated with religious beliefs and practices.

### TYPICAL ENTRY ROUTES AND ASSOCIATED QUALIFICATIONS

Entry will most commonly require a theology degree or other academic qualifications.

### TASKS

- prepares and delivers sermons and talks and leads congregation in worship;

- interprets doctrines and instructs intending clergy members in religious principles and practices;

- performs marriages, funerals, christenings and other special religious services;

- visits members of the congregation in their homes and in hospitals and counsels those in need of spiritual or moral guidance;

- undertakes administration and social duties as required.

## RELATED JOB TITLES

Clerk in holy orders
Deacon
Minister of Religion
Clergyman/woman
Parish priest
Priest
Vicar

## 293 SOCIAL WORKERS, PROBATION OFFICERS

Social workers and probation officers provide information, advice and support for individuals or groups on emotional, financial, health, housing and other social issues and supervise, counsel and help rehabilitate offenders.

### TYPICAL ENTRY ROUTES AND ASSOCIATED QUALIFICATIONS

Both graduate and non-graduate entry is possible followed by professional training leading to the Certificate of Qualification in Social Work.

### TASKS

- interviews individual, group or offender and assesses the nature and extent of difficulties;

- arranges for further counselling or assistance in the form of financial or material help;

- attempts to resolve family problems and, if necessary, arranges for children to be resettled with foster parents or in a children's home;

- counsels prisoners and supervises those released who are subject to statutory supervision;

- maintains close contact with other social workers and follows progress of case;

- keeps case records and prepares reports.

## RELATED JOB TITLES

Child care officer
Probation officer
Social worker

# MAJOR GROUP 3

## ASSOCIATE PROFESSIONAL AND TECHNICAL OCCUPATIONS

# MAJOR GROUP 3
# ASSOCIATE PROFESSIONAL AND TECHNICAL OCCUPATIONS

This major group covers occupations whose main tasks require experience and knowledge of principles and practices necessary to assume operational responsibility and to give technical support to Professionals in the natural sciences, engineering, life sciences, social sciences, humanities and related fields and to Managers and Administrators.

The main tasks involve the operation and maintenance of complex equipment; legal, financial and design services; software support to Managers and Administrators and Professionals; the provision of skilled nursing care and other support services. Performing artists are also included in this major group. Most occupations in this major group will have an associated high-level vocational qualification, often involving a substantial period of full-time training or further study. Some additional task-related training is usually provided through a formal period of induction.

Occupations in this major group are classified into the following minor groups:

**30 SCIENTIFIC TECHNICIANS**

**31 DRAUGHTSPERSONS, QUANTITY AND OTHER SURVEYORS**

**32 COMPUTER ANALYST/PROGRAMMERS**

**33 SHIP AND AIRCRAFT OFFICERS, AIR TRAFFIC PLANNERS AND CONTROLLERS**

**34 HEALTH ASSOCIATE PROFESSIONALS**

**35 LEGAL ASSOCIATE PROFESSIONALS**

**36 BUSINESS AND FINANCIAL ASSOCIATE PROFESSIONALS**

**37 SOCIAL WELFARE ASSOCIATE PROFESSIONALS**

**38 LITERARY, ARTISTIC AND SPORTS PROFESSIONALS**

**39 ASSOCIATE PROFESSIONAL AND TECHNICAL OCCUPATIONS NEC**

# MINOR GROUP 30
# SCIENTIFIC TECHNICIANS

Workers in this minor group give technical assistance to planners, architects and scientists and perform various technical support functions for engineers.

Occupations in this minor group are classified into the following unit groups:

**300 LABORATORY TECHNICIANS**
**301 ENGINEERING TECHNICIANS**
**302 ELECTRICAL/ELECTRONIC TECHNICIANS**
**303 ARCHITECTURAL AND TOWN PLANNING TECHNICIANS**
**304 BUILDING AND CIVIL ENGINEERING TECHNICIANS**
**309 OTHER SCIENTIFIC TECHNICIANS NEC**

## 300 LABORATORY TECHNICIANS

Laboratory technicians carry out routine laboratory tests and perform a variety of technical support functions requiring the application of established or prescribed procedures and techniques to assist scientists with their research, development, analysis and testing.

### TYPICAL ENTRY ROUTES AND ASSOCIATED QUALIFICATIONS

Entry varies from employer to employer. The usual qualifications are GCSE/SCE S-grades in mathematics and a science subject but some employers require further subjects and/or higher qualifications. Good eyesight and, in some cases, normal colour vision are also required.

### TASKS

- sets up and assists with the construction and the development of scientific apparatus for experimental, demonstration or other purposes;

- prepares and analyses body fluids, secretions and/or tissue to detect infections or to examine the effects of different drugs;

- grows cultures of bacteria and viruses, prepares tissue sections and other organic and inorganic material for examination and stains and fixes slides for microscope work;

- operates and services specialised scientific equipment, undertakes prescribed measurements and analyses and ensures that sterile conditions necessary for some equipment are maintained;

- records and collates data obtained from experimental work and documents all work carried out.

### RELATED JOB TITLES

Geophysical analyst
Laboratory technician
Scientific assistant
Scientific technician

## 301 ENGINEERING TECHNICIANS

Engineering technicians perform a variety of technical support functions to assist engineers with the design, development, operation, installation and maintenance of engineering systems and constructions.

### TYPICAL ENTRY ROUTES AND ASSOCIATED QUALIFICATIONS

Entry to training is possible with GCSE/SCE S-grades but is also possible with BTEC/SCOTVEC or a relevant degree. Some apprenticeships are available. Further professional training is required.

**TASKS**

- plans and prepares work and test schedules based on specifications and drawings;

- sets up equipment, undertakes tests, takes readings, performs calculations and records and interprets data;

- prepares estimates of materials, equipment and labour required for engineering projects;

- diagnoses and detects faults and implements procedures to maintain efficient operation of systems and equipment;

- visits and advises clients on the use and servicing of mechanical and chemical engineering products and services.

**RELATED JOB TITLES**

Commissioning engineer
Contracts engineer
Engineering technician
Engineer's assistant
Technician engineer

## 302 ELECTRICAL/ELECTRONIC TECHNICIANS

Electrical and electronic technicians perform a variety of miscellaneous technical support functions to assist with the design, development, installation, operation and maintenance of electrical and electronic systems.

**TYPICAL ENTRY ROUTES AND ASSOCIATED QUALIFICATIONS**

Entry to training is possible with GCSE/SCE S-grades but is also possible with BTEC/SCOTVEC or a relevant degree. Some apprenticeships are available. Further professional training is required.

**TASKS**

- plans and prepares work and test schedules based on specifications and drawings;

- sets up equipment, undertakes tests, takes readings, performs calculations and records and interprets data;

- plans installation methods, checks completed installation for safety and controls or undertakes the initial running of the new electrical or electronic equipment or system;

- diagnoses and detects faults and implements procedures to maintain efficient operation of systems and equipment;

- visits and advises clients on the use and servicing of electrical and electronic systems and equipment.

**RELATED JOB TITLES**

Electrical technician
Electronic technician

## 303 ARCHITECTURAL AND TOWN PLANNING TECHNICIANS

Architectural and town planning technicians perform a variety of technical support functions to assist architects and planners with the design of buildings and the layout of urban and rural areas.

**TYPICAL ENTRY ROUTES AND ASSOCIATED QUALIFICATIONS**

Entry is most common with GCSE/SCE S-grades followed by the appropriate BTEC/SCOTVEC course, but is possible with other academic qualifications or experience.

**TASKS**

- investigates proposed design with regard to practicality, cost and use;

- prepares building plans, drawings and specifications for use by contractors;

- liaises with engineers and building contractors regarding technical construction problems and attends site meetings on behalf of architect;

- surveys land and property uses and prepares report for planning authority;

- issues development permits as authorised;

- checks that completed work conforms to specifications.

## RELATED JOB TITLES

Architectural assistant
Architectural technician
Planning assistant (*local government*)

## 304 BUILDING AND CIVIL ENGINEERING TECHNICIANS

Building and civil engineering technicians perform a variety of miscellaneous technical support functions to assist civil and building engineers.

### TYPICAL ENTRY ROUTES AND ASSOCIATED QUALIFICATIONS

No academic qualifications are necessary although entry is most common with GCSE/SCE S-grades and A-levels/H-grades followed by a BTEC/SCOTVEC or degree course. Professional examinations passes are required for some posts.

### TASKS

- sets up apparatus and equipment and undertakes field and laboratory tests of soil and work materials;

- performs calculations and collects, records and interprets data;

- prepares estimates of materials, equipment and labour required for civil engineering projects and plans and prepares work schedule;

- inspects construction materials and completed work to ensure compliance with specifications and arranges remedial work as necessary.

### RELATED JOB TITLES

Building technician
Civil engineering technician

## 309 OTHER SCIENTIFIC TECHNICIANS NEC

Workers in this unit group perform a variety of technical support functions not elsewhere classified in MINOR GROUP 30: Scientific Technicians.

### TYPICAL ENTRY ROUTES AND ASSOCIATED QUALIFICATIONS

No academic qualifications are necessary although entry is most common with GCSE/SCE S-grades and A-levels/H-grades followed by a BTEC/SCOTVEC or degree course. Professional qualifications are required for some posts.

### TASKS

- sets up apparatus for experimental, demonstration or other purposes;

- undertakes tests and takes measurements and readings;

- performs calculations and records and interprets data;

- otherwise assists technologists as directed.

### RELATED JOB TITLES

Maintenance technician
Mechanical technician
Process technician
Technical assistant
Technical officer
Technician

# MINOR GROUP 31
# DRAUGHTSPERSONS, QUANTITY AND OTHER SURVEYORS

Workers in this minor group prepare technical drawings, plans and charts, conduct marine, insurance and other surveys, prepare bills of quantities for construction projects and undertake inspections of buildings to ensure compliance with regulations, bye laws and other requirements.

Occupations in this minor group are classified into the following unit groups:

310 DRAUGHTSPERSONS
311 BUILDING INSPECTORS
312 QUANTITY SURVEYORS
313 MARINE, INSURANCE AND OTHER SURVEYORS

## 310 DRAUGHTSPERSONS

Draughtspersons prepare technical drawings, plans, maps, charts and similar items.

### TYPICAL ENTRY ROUTES AND ASSOCIATED QUALIFICATIONS

Entry is possible via an apprenticeship, requiring GCSE/SCE S-grades, a full time college course, requiring GCSE/S-grades (and in some cases A-levels/H-grades), lasting between three and five years or BTEC/SCOTVEC awards in surveying and/or cartography. Some employers have an upper age limit of 25 and some provide on-the-job training.

### TASKS

- examines design specification to determine general requirements;

- considers the suitability of different materials with regard to the dimensions and weight and calculates the likely fatigue, stresses, tolerances, bonds and threads;

- prepares design drawings, plans or sketches and checks feasibility of construction and compliance with safety regulations;

- prepares detailed drawings, plans, charts or maps that include natural features, desired surface finish, elevations, electrical circuitry and other details as required;

- arranges for completed drawings to be reproduced for use as working drawings.

### RELATED JOB TITLES

Cartographer
Designer-detailer
Designer-draughtsman
Draughtsman/woman
Draughtsperson-engineer
Electrical draughtsperson
Engineering-draughtsperson
Mechanical-draughtsperson

## 311 BUILDING INSPECTORS

Building inspectors inspect building plans and structures to ensure compliance with building regulations, bye laws and any other statutory requirements.

### TYPICAL ENTRY ROUTES AND ASSOCIATED QUALIFICATIONS

No academic qualifications are necessary although entry is most common with GCSE/SCE

S-grades and A-levels/H-grades followed by a BTEC/SCOTVEC or degree course. Professional examinations passes are required in some posts.

## TASKS

- examines building plans to ensure compliance with local, statutory and other requirements;

- inspects building structure, sanitation, lighting, ventilation and fire precautions to determine suitability for habitation;

- visits building sites, examines foundations and inspects drains to ensure compliance with regulations;

- inspects structural condition of buildings for insurance and mortgage purposes;

- prepares reports and recommendations on all inspections made.

## RELATED JOB TITLES

Building control officer
Building inspector
District building inspector
NHBRC Inspector

## 312 QUANTITY SURVEYORS

Quantity surveyors advise on financial and contractual matters relating to, and prepare bills of quantities for, construction projects and provide other support functions concerning the financing and materials required for building projects.

## TYPICAL ENTRY ROUTES AND ASSOCIATED QUALIFICATIONS

Qualifications in these occupations is through professional training. Entry to examinations requires GCSE/SCE S-grades and A-levels/H-grades. Degree/Diploma holders may achieve full or partial exemption from professional examinations.

## TASKS

- liaises with client on project costs, formulates detailed cost plan and advises contractors and engineers to ensure that they remain within cost limit;

- examines plans and specifications and prepares details of the material and labour required for the project;

- prepares bills of quantities for use by contractors when tendering for work;

- examines tenders received, advises client on the most acceptable and assists with preparation of a contract document;

- measures and values work in progress and examines any deviations from original contract;

- measures and values completed contract for authorisation of payment.

## RELATED JOB TITLES

Chartered quantity surveyor
Quantity surveyor
Quantity surveyor's assistant

## 313 MARINE, INSURANCE AND OTHER SURVEYORS

Marine, insurance and other surveyors conduct surveys of rivers, harbours and other bodies of water and of industrial, commercial and other buildings for insurance purposes and perform other surveying work not elsewhere classified, including land, water, underground, building and related surveys.

## TYPICAL ENTRY ROUTES AND ASSOCIATED QUALIFICATIONS

Professional qualifications are required. Entry to the professional examinations will require GCSE/SCE S-grades and A-levels/H-grades or BTEC/SCOTVEC national certificate/diploma in building, followed by 2-5 years off- and on-the-job training. Graduate entry is possible and may exempt the holder from some parts of the professional examination. Good binocular vision is required and some posts require a current driving licence.

## TASKS

- measures shore lines, elevations and contours, establishes high and low water marks and plots shore features to be used as navigational aids;

- uses current meters and tide gauges to determine tide patterns and directions of currents;

- directs or undertakes soundings to determine underwater contours, navigable channels and depth of silting;

- examines building construction and location to assess any fire hazard, flood potential and possible cause of injury;

- conducts land, water, underground, building and related surveys not elsewhere classified.

## RELATED JOB TITLES

Hydrographic surveyor
Insurance surveyor
Marine surveyor

# MINOR GROUP 32
# COMPUTER ANALYST/PROGRAMMERS

Workers in this minor group develop procedures for automatic data processing and write and modify computer programs.

Occupations in this minor group are classified into the following unit group:

### 320  COMPUTER ANALYST/PROGRAMMERS

## 320  COMPUTER ANALYST/ PROGRAMMERS

Computer analyst/programmers identify areas in which management and business efficiency can be improved by computerised procedures, design, plan and implement computer systems and design, develop and test software needed to carry out specific tasks such as engineering design, accounts and personnel functions, business processes, etc.

### TYPICAL ENTRY ROUTES AND ASSOCIATED QUALIFICATIONS

Most entrants have a degree or BTEC/SCOTVEC higher national award usually in computer science or business subjects. Some employers recruit programmers on the basis of aptitude tests rather than academic achievement. Many become systems analysts on promotion after experience in programming or business management. Post-recruitment training involves specialised courses and studying for professional qualifications.

### TASKS

- examines user's organisation and procedures and carries out feasibility studies to establish the advantages and disadvantages of computerisation;

- specifies systems requirements, outlines options and makes recommendations;

- designs system matching user requirements to hardware and software available, monitors system testing and modifies system design as necessary;

- specifies structure for software and designs and implements programs;

- creates and applies tests to demonstrate that programs achieve their intended effects and modifies programs as necessary;

- writes reports, program descriptions, interpretations of test results and guides for users of the software produced.

### RELATED JOB TITLES

Analyst programmer
Applications programmer
Computer analyst programmer
Computer programmer
Programmer analyst
Systems analyst

# MINOR GROUP 33
# SHIP AND AIRCRAFT OFFICERS, AIR TRAFFIC PLANNERS AND CONTROLLERS

Workers in this minor group command and navigate aircraft and vessels, perform technical functions to operate and maintain such craft and plan and regulate the ground and air movements of aircraft.

Occupations in this minor group are classified into the following unit groups:

330 AIR TRAFFIC PLANNERS AND CONTROLLERS
331 AIRCRAFT FLIGHT DECK OFFICERS
332 SHIP AND HOVERCRAFT OFFICERS

## 330 AIR TRAFFIC PLANNERS AND CONTROLLERS

Air traffic planners and controllers prepare flight plans, authorise flight departures and arrivals and maintain radio, radar and/or visual contact with aircraft to ensure the safe movement of air traffic.

### TYPICAL ENTRY ROUTES AND ASSOCIATED QUALIFICATIONS

Entry will require GCSE/SCE S-grades and A-levels/H-grades. Candidates with relevant experience or ex-aircrew are also accepted. Training lasts three years and leads to a Civil Aviation Authority licence. Candidates must have normal colour vision and are required to undergo medical examinations on entry and during their careers. Further training is also required.

### TASKS

- maintains radio and/or radar or visual contact with aircraft and liaises with other air traffic controllers and control centres to direct aircraft in and out of controlled airspace and into holding areas ready for landing;

- gives landing instructions to pilot and monitors descent of aircraft;

- directs movement of aircraft and motor vehicles on runways, taxiways and in parking bays;

- obtains information regarding weather conditions, navigational hazards, landing conditions, seating arrangements, loading of cargo, fuel and catering supplies;

- calculates fuel consumption and optimum flying height, plans route and prepares flight plan for aircraft pilot;

- discusses operational requirements with pilot, issues duty schedules for flight deck and cabin crews, maintains records of flight progress and authorises flight departure.

### RELATED JOB TITLES

Air traffic controller
Controller of aircraft
Flight planner
Ground movement controller

## 331 AIRCRAFT FLIGHT DECK OFFICERS

Aircraft flight deck officers check, regulate, adjust and test engines and other equipment prior to take-off, navigate and pilot aircraft and give flying lessons.

### TYPICAL ENTRY ROUTES AND ASSOCIATED QUALIFICATIONS

Common routes of entry are as follows: candidates with GCSE/SCE S-grades and A-levels/H-grades can apply for an airline sponsorship; or private residential training is available to candidates with GCSE/SCE S-grades; or holders of Private Pilots Licences who have 700 hours flying experience; may sit the Civil Aviation Authority examinations. Employers usually require new entrants to be aged 18-24 and between 5'4" and 6'4". Normal colour vision is required and candidates undergo a medical examination. Ex-armed forces pilots may also apply.

## TASKS

- studies flight plan, discusses it with flight deck crew and makes any necessary adjustments;

- directs or undertakes routine checks on engines, instruments, control panels, cargo distribution and fuel supplies;

- directs or undertakes the operation of controls to fly aeroplanes and helicopters, complying with air traffic control and aircraft operating procedures;

- monitors fuel consumption, air pressure, engine performance and other indicators during flight and advises pilot of any factors that affect the navigation or performance of the aircraft;

- maintains radio contact and discusses weather conditions with air traffic controllers;

- performs specified tests to determine aircraft's stability, response to controls and overall performance;

- accompanies pupil on training flights and demonstrates flying techniques.

## RELATED JOB TITLES

Airline captain
Airline pilot
Commercial pilot
Flight engineer
Flying instructor
Pilot
Test pilot

## 332 SHIP AND HOVERCRAFT OFFICERS

Ship and hovercraft officers command and navigate ships and other craft, co-ordinate the activities of officers and deck and engine room ratings, operate and maintain communications equipment on board ship and undertake minor repairs to engines, boilers and other mechanical and electrical equipment.

## TYPICAL ENTRY ROUTES AND ASSOCIATED QUALIFICATIONS

The minimum qualifications for entry into training are GCSE/SCE S-grades including mathematics, English and a science subject. Most candidates also have A-levels/H-grades. Good colour vision without spectacles or contact lenses is required for some posts and candidates must undergo a medical examination. Navigating and engineering officers require a Department of Trade and Industry Certificate of Competence. Ships' captains and chief engineering officers require a Class 1 certificate and hovercraft pilots require a Type Rating certificate.

## TASKS

- allocates duties to ship's officers and co-ordinates and directs the activities of deck and engine room ratings;

- directs or undertakes the operation of controls to inflate air cushions, run engines and propel and steer ships, hovercraft and other vessels;

- locates the position of vessel using electronic and other navigational aids such as charts and compasses and advises on navigation where appropriate;

- monitors the operation of engines, generators and other mechanical and electrical equipment and undertakes any necessary minor repairs;

- maintains radio contact with other vessels and coast stations;

- prepares watch keeping rota and maintains a look-out for other vessels or obstacles;

- maintains log of vessel's progress, weather conditions, conduct of crew, etc.

## RELATED JOB TITLES

Chief engineer (*ship/hovercraft*)
Commander (*ship/hovercraft*)
Navigator (*ship/hovercraft*)
Ship's captain (*merchant navy*)
Ship's officer (*merchant navy*)

# MINOR GROUP 34
# HEALTH ASSOCIATE PROFESSIONALS

Health associate professionals provide nursing care for the sick and injured and pre- and post-natal care for mothers and babies, operate X-ray and other medical equipment, fit hearing aids and artificial limbs, supply and fit spectacles, treat foot, eye, speech, mental and movement disorders, study mental processes and behaviour, advise on diets, technically assist veterinarians, dentists and pharmacists and undertake inspections to ensure compliance with environmental hygiene regulations.

Occupations in this minor group are classified into the following unit groups:

340 NURSES

341 MIDWIVES

342 MEDICAL RADIOGRAPHERS

343 PHYSIOTHERAPISTS

344 CHIROPODISTS

345 DISPENSING OPTICIANS

346 MEDICAL TECHNICIANS, DENTAL AUXILIARIES

347 OCCUPATIONAL AND SPEECH THERAPISTS, PSYCHOTHERAPISTS, THERAPISTS NEC

348 ENVIRONMENTAL HEALTH OFFICERS

349 OTHER HEALTH ASSOCIATE PROFESSIONALS NEC

## 340 NURSES

Nurses provide general and/or specialised nursing care for the sick, injured and others in need of such care, assist medical doctors with their tasks, advise and teach on nursing practice.

### TYPICAL ENTRY ROUTES AND ASSOCIATED QUALIFICATIONS

Both graduate and non-graduate entry is possible. The most common method of entry is with GCSE/SCE S-grades followed by up to four years off- and on-the-job training leading to professional qualifications. There is a lower age limit of 16 and a half years to enter training.

### TASKS

- assists medical doctors, deals with emergencies and prepares patients for examination;

- monitors patients's progress, administers drugs and medicines, applies surgical dressings and gives other forms of treatment;

- participates in the preparation for physical and psychological treatment of mentally ill patients;

- plans duty rotas and organises and directs the work and training of ward and theatre nursing staff;

- advises on nursing care, disease prevention, nutrition, etc. and liaises with hospital board/ management on issues concerning nursing policy.

Health visitor
Nurse
Staff nurse
State enrolled nurse
State registered nurse
Ward sister

## 341 MIDWIVES

Midwives deliver, or assist in the delivery of babies, provide antenatal and postnatal care and advise parents on baby care.

### TYPICAL ENTRY ROUTES AND ASSOCIATED QUALIFICATIONS

Entry is possible with GCSE/SCE S-grades but is most common as a Registered General Nurse (RGN) followed by three years training. There is a lower age limit of 17 to enter training.

### TASKS

- monitors condition and progress of patient during pregnancy;

- delivers babies in normal births and assists doctors with difficult deliveries;

- monitors recovery of mother in postnatal period and supervises the nursing of premature and other babies requiring special attention;

- advises on baby care, exercise, diet and family planning issues.

### RELATED JOB TITLES

Midwife

## 342 MEDICAL RADIOGRAPHERS

Medical radiographers operate X-ray and similar monitoring equipment for diagnostic and therapeutic purposes under the direction of a radiologist or other medical practitioner.

### TYPICAL ENTRY ROUTES AND ASSOCIATED QUALIFICATIONS

Entry is most common with GCSE/SCE A-levels/H-grades followed by three years training. Some medical schools require additional or higher qualifications and some require specific subjects. Graduate entry is possible but no exemption is granted from any part of the training course.

### TASKS

- verifies identity of patient and ensures that necessary preparations have been made for the examination/treatment;

- decides length and intensity of exposure or strength of dosage of isotope;

- positions patient and operates X-ray, scanning or fluoroscopic equipment;

- maintains records of all radiographic/therapeutic work undertaken.

### RELATED JOB TITLES

Diagnostic radiographer (*medical services*)
Medical radiographer

## 343 PHYSIOTHERAPISTS

Physiotherapists plan and apply massage, exercise, hydro- and electrotherapy in the treatment of injuries, diseases or disabilities.

### TYPICAL ENTRY ROUTES AND ASSOCIATED QUALIFICATIONS

Entry is most common with GCSE/SCE A-levels/H-grades followed by up to four years training, but is possible with other academic qualifications. There is a lower age limit of 17.

### TASKS

- examines medical reports and assesses patient to determine the condition of muscles, nerves or joints in need of treatment;

- plans and undertakes therapy to improve circulation, restore joint mobility, strengthen muscles and reduce pain;

- explains treatment to and instructs patient in posture and other exercises and adapts treatment as necessary;

- monitors patient's progress and liaises with others concerned with the treatment and rehabilitation of patient.

## RELATED JOB TITLES

Chartered physiotherapist
Physiotherapist
Superintendant physiotherapist

## 344 CHIROPODISTS

Chiropodists diagnose and treat ailments and abnormalities of the human foot.

### TYPICAL ENTRY ROUTES AND ASSOCIATED QUALIFICATIONS

Entry is most common with GCSE/SCE A-levels/H-grades followed by three years training. Some medical schools require higher or specific qualifications. There is a lower age limit of 18.

### TASKS

- examines patient's feet to determine the nature and extent of disorder;

- treats conditions of the skin, nails and soft tissues of feet by minor surgery, massage and heat treatment, padding and strapping or drugs;

- prescribes, makes and fits pads and other appliances to correct and/or protect foot disorders;

- advises patient on aspects of foot care;

- where necessary, refers patient to specialist.

### RELATED JOB TITLES

Chiropodist
Chiropodist/podiatrist

## 345 DISPENSING OPTICIANS

Dispensing opticians supply and fit spectacles according to prescription.

### TYPICAL ENTRY ROUTES AND ASSOCIATED QUALIFICATIONS

Entry is most common with GCSE/SCE S-grades followed by up to three years training. There is a lower age limit of 17.

### TASKS

- examines prescription and measures patient's face to determine distance between pupil centres, height of bridge of nose, etc.;

- advises patient on choice of spectacle frames;

- prepares detailed instructions for workshop;

- ensures that completed spectacles conform to specification;

- fits spectacles and advises patient on lens care and any other difficulties likely to be experienced.

### RELATED JOB TITLES

Dispensing optician

## 346 MEDICAL TECHNICIANS, DENTAL AUXILIARIES

Medical technicians and dental auxiliaries operate cardiographic and encephalographic testing equipment, give simple dental treatment, fit artificial limbs and hearing aids, assist pharmacists and undertake related medical, dental and pharmaceutical tasks.

### TYPICAL ENTRY ROUTES AND ASSOCIATED QUALIFICATIONS

Entry is most common with GCSE/SCE S-grades or A-levels/H-grades but is possible with other academic qualifications. Between one and four years training is also required.

### TASKS

- operates equipment to diagnose and record or treat hearing, heart, brain, lung and kidney ailments;

- undertakes scaling and polishing of teeth, applies medicaments, carries out post-operative hygiene work and advises on preventative dentistry;

- measures patient's for, and fits them with, surgical appliances, hearing aids and artificial limbs;

- prepares, under supervision, drugs and medicaments according to prescription, advises patient on use of drug or medicament and may undertake research;

- performs related medical tasks including treating hair and scalp disorders and conducting tests on glaucoma patients.

**RELATED JOB TITLES**

Audiologist
Cardiographer
Dental hygienist
Dispensary assistant
Pharmacy technician

## 347 OCCUPATIONAL AND SPEECH THERAPISTS, PSYCHOTHERAPISTS, THERAPISTS NEC

Workers in this unit group study mental processes and behaviour and plan and apply physical and therapeutic treatments and activities to assist recovery from illness and to minimise the effects of disabilities.

**TYPICAL ENTRY ROUTES AND ASSOCIATED QUALIFICATIONS**

Entry is possible with GCSE/SCE A-levels/H-grades but some medical schools require specific or higher qualifications. Some posts have lower age limits for entry into training which lasts between two and four years.

**TASKS**

- examines patient and medical records to assess condition;

- plans exercises to treat eye muscle disorders and improve speech and mobility;

- studies psychological factors involved in diagnosis and treatment and helps patient regain emotional stability and independence;

- manipulates and massages patient to relieve pain and correct irregularities in body structure;

- prescribes diet therapy as part of a patient's treatment and gives advice on dietetic and nutritional matters.

**RELATED JOB TITLES**

Dietician
Masseur
Occupational therapist
Orthoptist
Osteopath
Psychotherapist
Speech therapist

## 348 ENVIRONMENTAL HEALTH OFFICERS

Environmental health officers undertake inspections and investigations to verify and ensure compliance with government acts, orders and regulations relating to environmental hygiene and the general health of the public.

**TYPICAL ENTRY ROUTES AND ASSOCIATED QUALIFICATIONS**

Entry will require GCSE/SCE A-levels/H-grades followed by three to four years training and work experience leading to a diploma. Graduate entry is also possible.

**TASKS**

- inspects and investigates housing and working conditions, conditions under which food, drink and drugs are manufactured and stored, atmospheric pollution, drainage, sewage and refuse disposal, noise levels, etc. to ensure compliance with government regulations;

- makes visits and inspections in accordance with a planned programme or in response to complaints;

- advises on ways of rectifying conditions that contravene regulations;

- prepares reports and recommendations on all inspections made;

- recommends legal action in cases of persistent contravention of regulations.


## RELATED JOB TITLES

Authorised meat inspector
Divisional environmental health officer
Environmental health officer
Environmental health inspector
Public health officer


# 349 OTHER HEALTH ASSOCIATE PROFESSIONALS NEC

Workers in this unit group provide technical assistance to veterinarians and perform a variety of health associate professional occupations not elsewhere classified in MINOR GROUP 34: Health Associate Professionals.


## TYPICAL ENTRY ROUTES AND ASSOCIATED QUALIFICATIONS

Entry is most common with GCSE/SCE S-grades or A-levels/H-grades but is possible with other academic qualifications.


## TASKS

- carries out tests, operates X-ray equipment to aid the diagnosis and treatment of animal injuries and disorders and prepares animals for autopsies;

- prepares operating theatre, sterilises equipment and assists in theatre as required;

- dispenses medicines and applies dressings to animals;

- feeds, waters and exercises animals and keeps their quarters clean and tidy.


## RELATED JOB TITLES

Animal technician
Veterinary assistant

# MINOR GROUP 35
# LEGAL ASSOCIATE PROFESSIONALS

Legal associate professionals consider and decide disputed housing, planning and other tribunal cases, organise the administrative work of legal practices and perform specialised legal duties.

Occupations in this minor group are classified into the following unit group:

## 350   LEGAL SERVICE AND RELATED OCCUPATIONS

## 350  LEGAL SERVICE AND RELATED OCCUPATIONS

Legal service and related workers provide administrative support for legal professionals and investigate and make recommendations on legal matters which do not fall within the province of a normal court of law.

### TYPICAL ENTRY ROUTES AND ASSOCIATED QUALIFICATIONS

Entry is most common with GCSE/SCE S-grades but is possible without any specific educational qualifications.  Some employees may expect entrants to be qualified to A-level standard.  Further professional qualifications will be required.

### TASKS

- decides, on behalf of principals, which cases to accept and arranges appropriate fees;

- collates information, drafts briefs and other documents;

- assists with property conveyancing and probate and common law practice;

- presides over local public enquiries and hearings;

- considers oral and written evidence, appropriate regulations and precedent and reaches verdict;

- keeps financial records on behalf of chambers and clients.

### RELATED JOB TITLES

Barrister's clerk
Conveyancer
Legal assistant
Legal executive
Housing and planning inspector

# MINOR GROUP 36
# BUSINESS AND FINANCIAL ASSOCIATE PROFESSIONALS

Business and financial associate professionals calculate probable costs of projects, assess values of real and other property, assess liability regarding insurance claims, deal in stocks, shares and bills of exchange and advise clients on industrial relations, personnel, resource utilisation, work methods, taxation and other financial matters.

Occupations in this minor group are classified into the following unit groups:

**360 ESTIMATORS, VALUERS**

**361 UNDERWRITERS, CLAIMS ASSESSORS, BROKERS, INVESTMENT ANALYSTS**

**362 TAXATION EXPERTS**

**363 PERSONNEL AND INDUSTRIAL RELATIONS OFFICERS**

**364 ORGANISATION AND METHODS AND WORK STUDY OFFICERS**

## 360 ESTIMATORS, VALUERS

Estimators and valuers plan and undertake the calculation of probable costs of civil, mechanical, electrical, electronic and other projects and estimate the value of property and chattels.

### TYPICAL ENTRY ROUTES AND ASSOCIATED QUALIFICATIONS

Entry is possible with no academic qualifications, but GCSE/SCE S-grades and A-levels/H-grades are usually required. Professional qualifications are required.

### TASKS

- examines plans, drawings, specifications, parts lists, etc.;

- assesses condition, location, desirability and amenities of property to be valued;

- computes and specifies materials and components required;

- assesses costs of materials, labour time and other factors such as required profit margins, transport costs, tariffs and fare structures, possible hazards, etc.;

- prepares comprehensive estimates of time and costs and presents these in report or tender form.

### RELATED JOB TITLES

Building estimator
Chief estimator
Estimator
Estimator-engineer
Planner estimator
Rates and charges officer
Surveyor and valuer
Valuation surveyor
Valuer

## 361 UNDERWRITERS, CLAIMS ASSESSORS, BROKERS, INVESTMENT ANALYSTS

Workers in this unit group evaluate risks and underwrite insurance, investigate insurance claims to assess their validity and to assign liability, deal in stocks and shares and advise clients and employers on investment and insurance matters.

117

Entry is possible with GCSE/SCE S-grades. Holders of higher academic qualifications are also recruited. Professional qualifications are required for senior positions.

## TASKS

- considers risk involved with insurance application and, if acceptable, computes and/or quotes premium;

- examines insurance documents to assess extent of liability and gathers information about incident from police, medical records, ship's log, etc. and investigates potential fraudulent claims;

- analyses information concerning market trends for securities, bonds and stocks, government regulations and financial status of customer;

- records and transmits buy and sell orders for stocks, shares and bonds and calculates transaction costs;

- advises client/employer on the suitability of particular investment and insurance schemes;

- negotiates with stockbrokers and insurance companies on client's/employer's behalf and arranges appropriate investment and insurance.

## RELATED JOB TITLES

Claims adjuster
Claims inspector
Finance broker
Financial analyst
Foreign exchange dealer
Insurance assessor
Insurance broker
Insurance underwriter
Investment analyst
Loss adjuster
Money broker
Stockbroker

## 362 TAXATION EXPERTS

Taxation experts advise clients on tax matters and assess tax liabilities.

Entry is possible with GCSE/SCE S-grades. Holders of higher academic qualifications are also recruited. Further professional qualifications may be required.

## TASKS

- examines accounts of industrial, commercial and other establishments to determine their tax liability and makes adjustments to claims where necessary;

- considers particular problems concerning all forms of personal and company taxation;

- stays abreast of all changes in tax law and precedent;

- discusses disputed cases with accountants and other specialists;

- represents Government/client in contested claims before tax officials or an independent tribunal.

## RELATED JOB TITLES

Inspector of taxes
Tax consultant
Taxation adviser

## 363 PERSONNEL AND INDUSTRIAL RELATIONS OFFICERS

Personnel and industrial relations officers conduct research and advise on recruitment, training, staff appraisal and industrial relations policies and assist specialist managers with negotiations on behalf of a commercial enterprise, trades union or other organisation.

## TYPICAL ENTRY ROUTES AND ASSOCIATED QUALIFICATIONS

Entry does not depend on academic qualifications but some employers require candidates to have GCSE/SCE, A-levels/H-grades or higher qualifications or relevant experience.

## TASKS

- undertakes research into pay differentials, productivity and efficiency bonuses and other payments;

- develops and recommends personnel and industrial relations policies and assists with their implementation;

- arranges meetings between management and employees or trades unions and assists with negotiations concerning pay and conditions of employment;

- advises on training and recruitment, negotiating procedures, salary agreements and other personnel and industrial relations issues.

## RELATED JOB TITLES

Industrial relations officer
Personnel officer

## 364 ORGANISATION AND METHODS AND WORK STUDY OFFICERS

Workers in this unit group advise on the effectiveness of an organisation's procedures, systems and methods and recommend ways of improving utilisation of labour, equipment and materials.

## TYPICAL ENTRY ROUTES AND ASSOCIATED QUALIFICATIONS

Entry will require GCSE/SCE S-grades, A-levels/H-grades, BTEC/SCOTVEC or equivalent. Professional qualifications are available and are required by most employers.

## TASKS

- studies particular department or problem area and assesses its interrelationships with other activities;

- studies work methods and procedures by measuring work involved and computing standard times for specified activities;

- analyses project components, organises them into a logical sequence and establishes the minimum time required for the project;

- produces report detailing suggestions for increasing efficiency and lowering costs.

## RELATED JOB TITLES

Organisation and methods officer
Time management officer
Time study engineer
Work study engineer
Work study officer

# MINOR GROUP 37
# SOCIAL WELFARE ASSOCIATE PROFESSIONALS

Social welfare associate professionals direct, organise and provide social welfare and related services for individuals and direct and co-ordinate the running of residential homes for the young and the elderly.

Occupations in this minor group are classified into the following unit groups:

> 370 MATRONS, HOUSEPARENTS
> 371 WELFARE, COMMUNITY AND YOUTH WORKERS

## 370 MATRONS, HOUSEPARENTS

Matrons and houseparents organise and control the work of day or residential nurseries and residential homes for children or the elderly and supervise the care and control of young people in homes, schools or institutions for young offenders.

### TYPICAL ENTRY ROUTES AND ASSOCIATED QUALIFICATIONS

Entry to training does not depend on academic qualifications. Training lasts for up to two years and leads to the Certificate of Qualification in Social Work. Further on-the-job training is provided and other professional qualifications are available.

### TASKS

- organises staffing resources and arranges duty rotas;

- creates friendly, secure atmosphere and tries to gain the trust and confidence of those in the home or under supervision;

- plans and participates in games and leisure activities to encourage emotional, social, physical and intellectual development;

- ensures that all material needs of residents are provided and endeavours to resolve any problems that they may have;

- establishes and maintains contact with members of the neighbouring community and/or the resident's family and friends;

- maintains contact and discusses problems/ progress with other staff and social workers.

### RELATED JOB TITLES

Deputy matron
Houseparent
Matron
Warden (*home for elderly*)

## 371 WELFARE, COMMUNITY AND YOUTH WORKERS

Welfare, community and youth workers organise and co-ordinate group social activities for youth and community groups, assist the blind, deaf, sick, elderly, physically handicapped and mentally ill with problems relating to their condition, investigate cases of child neglect or ill treatment and perform other welfare tasks not elsewhere classified.

### TYPICAL ENTRY ROUTES AND ASSOCIATED QUALIFICATIONS

Entry is most common with a degree or equivalent qualification but is possible with other academic qualifications and/or relevant experience.

### TASKS

- organises social, recreational and educational activities in youth groups and local community centres;

- investigates allegations of child neglect or abuse, liaises with other social workers, probation officers and the police and, where necessary, recommends legal action;

- helps the handicapped and sick to adjust to the limitations imposed by their condition and arranges for any necessary alterations in the home;

- performs other welfare tasks not elsewhere classified including working in a Citizens Advice Bureau, developing community participation in planning issues, dealing with free milk and clothing grants in schools and organising local authority home help services.


## RELATED JOB TITLES

Community officer
Community worker
Education welfare officer
Welfare officer
Youth leader
Youth worker

# MINOR GROUP 38
# LITERARY, ARTISTIC AND SPORTS PROFESSIONALS

Literary, artistic and sports professionals compose, edit and arrange written material for publication, translate written and spoken statements into different languages, conceive, create or perform various works of art and direct or assist with the interpretation, filming, sound recording and production of entertainment or information for transmission through a variety of media, introduce and host radio and television programmes, create designs for industrial and commercial products, negotiate engagements for entertainers, manage and coach sports teams or individual sportsmen/women and participate in and control sporting events.

Occupations in this minor group are classified into the following unit groups:

**380 AUTHORS, WRITERS, JOURNALISTS**

**381 ARTISTS, COMMERCIAL ARTISTS, GRAPHIC DESIGNERS**

**382 INDUSTRIAL DESIGNERS**

**383 CLOTHING DESIGNERS**

**384 ACTORS, ENTERTAINERS, STAGE MANAGERS, PRODUCERS AND DIRECTORS**

**385 MUSICIANS**

**386 PHOTOGRAPHERS, CAMERA, SOUND AND VIDEO EQUIPMENT OPERATORS**

**387 PROFESSIONAL ATHLETES, SPORTS OFFICIALS**

## 380 AUTHORS, WRITERS, JOURNALISTS

Authors, writers and journalists write, edit and evaluate literary material for publication and translate spoken and written statements into different languages.

### TYPICAL ENTRY ROUTES AND ASSOCIATED QUALIFICATIONS

Entry is possible with GCSE/SCE S-grades. Holders of higher academic qualifications are also recruited. Some occupations require post-graduate qualifications.

### TASKS

- determines subject matter and researches as necessary by interviewing, attending public events, seeking out records, etc.;

- reads written work, attends film or stage performances or art exhibition and drafts report, critique or manuscript and submits to editor, theatrical or film producer;

- selects material for publication, checks style, grammar and accuracy of content and arranges for any necessary revisions;

- negotiates contracts with freelance agents and with buyer on behalf of writer

- converts written or spoken statements from one language into another.

### RELATED JOB TITLES

Author
Copywriter (*advertising*)
Editor

Interpreter
Journalist
News editor
Press officer
Script writer
Technical author
Translator

# 381 ARTISTS, COMMERCIAL ARTISTS, GRAPHIC DESIGNERS

Artists, commercial artists and graphic designers create artistic works by painting, drawing, printing, sculpting and engraving, design artwork and illustrations and plan and arrange displays of artistic work.

## TYPICAL ENTRY ROUTES AND ASSOCIATED QUALIFICATIONS

Entry is most common with a degree or equivalent qualification but is possible without specific academic qualifications.

## TASKS

- conceives and develops ideas for artistic composition or studies design specifications from client;

- selects appropriate materials, medium and method;

- prepares sketches, scale drawings or colour schemes and submits them for approval if necessary;

- builds up composition into finished work by carving, sculpting, etching, painting, engraving and drawing.

## RELATED JOB TITLES

Animator (*cartoon films*)
Art director
Artist
Commercial artist
Display assistant
Graphic artist
Graphic designer
Illustrator
Interior designer
Sculptor

# 382 INDUSTRIAL DESIGNERS

Industrial designers plan, direct and undertake the creation of designs for new industrial and commercial products, combining aesthetic and utilitarian features.

## TYPICAL ENTRY ROUTES AND ASSOCIATED QUALIFICATIONS

Entry is most common with a degree/BTEC/SCOTVEC or equivalent qualification. Postgraduate and professional qualifications are required for some posts. Entry is possible without specific academic qualifications but a portfolio for prospective clients will be required.

## TASKS

- liaises with client to determine the purpose, cost, technical specification and potential uses/users of product;

- prepares sketches, designs, patterns or prototypes for textiles, plastics, footwear, jewellery, ceramics, motor vehicles, domestic appliances and engineering products;

- submits design to management, sales department and client for approval;

- makes any necessary alterations;

- oversees production of sample product.

## RELATED JOB TITLES

Commercial designer
Industrial designer
Textile designer

# 383 CLOTHING DESIGNERS

Clothing designers plan, direct and undertake the creation of designs for new clothing and fashion accessories, combining aesthetic and utilitarian features.

Entry is most common with a degree/BTEC/
SCOTVEC or equivalent qualification. Post-
graduate and professional qualifications are required for some posts. Entry is possible without
specific academic qualifications but a portfolio for
prospective clients will be required.

## TASKS

- undertakes research to determine market trends
  or liaises with client to discuss the prospective
  design and its cost;

- prepares patterns and sketches of clothing, fashion accessories, handbags, gloves, shoes and
  hats;

- discusses patterns/sketches with client and
  makes any necessary alterations;

- oversees production of sample product.

## RELATED JOB TITLES

Bridal consultant
Clothing designer
Costume designer
Dress designer
Fashion designer

# 384 ACTORS, ENTERTAINERS, STAGE MANAGERS, PRODUCERS AND DIRECTORS

Actors, entertainers, stage managers, producers and
directors sing, portray roles in dramatic productions, perform comedy routines, gymnastic feats
and tricks of illusion, introduce radio and television programmes and read news bulletins, adapt
stories, themes and ideas into dance routines, direct
the production of motion pictures and radio and
television programmes, train animals to perform
and perform with them and manage the business
affairs of entertainers.

## TYPICAL ENTRY ROUTES AND ASSOCIATED QUALIFICATIONS

Entry does not depend on academic qualifications
although some drama schools require candidates to
have GCSE/SCE S-grades. Entry to drama/dance
schools may require a medical examination and
an audition to determine the candidates' potential.
Some colleges prefer students to be under 25 and
most dance schools have minimum and maximum
height levels. Mature entry is possible but difficult.
Membership of the appropriate Trades Union is
usually required.

## TASKS

- studies, rehearses and performs songs, roles in
  dramatic productions, comedy and conjuring
  routines and creates, rehearses and performs
  dances;

- reads script, play or book and prepares and
  rehearses interpretation;

- plans set and lighting designs, camera work,
  costume and sound effects for stage, television,
  radio and motion picture presentations;

- introduces radio and television programmes,
  reads news bulletins and makes announcements;

- edits film and videotape and co-ordinates the
  activities of performers and radio, television,
  stage and motion picture workers;

- trains animals to perform entertaining routines
  and may perform with them;

- organises and controls the financial and/or business aspects of individuals, theatrical companies
  and film studios.

## RELATED JOB TITLES

Actor
Ballet dancer
Dancer
Disc Jockey
Entertainer
Film editor
Film producer
Producer (*entertainment*)
Singer
Stage Manager

# 385 MUSICIANS

Musicians write, arrange, orchestrate, conduct and
perform musical compositions.

## TYPICAL ENTRY ROUTES AND ASSOCIATED QUALIFICATIONS

Entry to a degree/diploma course requires A-levels/H-grades. Entry to the performers course requires GCSE/SCE S-grades. Some colleges do not require academic qualifications. Candidates also require Associated Board examination passes in their chosen instrument(s) and will be required to audition for places. Classical musicians usually enter formal full-time training by 16. In popular music, formal training is not essential as most are self-taught.

## TASKS

- conceives and writes original music;

- tunes instrument and studies and rehearses score;

- plays instrument as a soloist or as a member of a group or orchestra;

- scores music for different combinations of voices and instruments to produce desired effect;

- auditions and selects performers and rehearses and conducts them in the performance of the composition.

## RELATED JOB TITLES

Cellist
Music composer
Musician
Organist
Pianist
Violinist

# 386 PHOTOGRAPHERS, CAMERA, SOUND AND VIDEO EQUIPMENT OPERATORS

Workers in this unit group operate and assist with still, cine and television cameras and operate equipment other than cameras to record and project sound and vision for entertainment, commercial and industrial purposes.

## TYPICAL ENTRY ROUTES AND ASSOCIATED QUALIFICATIONS

There is no common/usual entry route to these occupations. City and Guilds, BTEC and SCOTVEC courses are available and these usually require GCSE/ SCE S-grades or A-levels/H-grades but mature students may be admitted without academic qualifications. In some posts, off- and on-the-job training is provided.

## TASKS

- selects subject and conceives composition of picture or discusses composition with colleagues;

- arranges subject, lighting, camera equipment and any microphones;

- checks that camera is loaded, inserts lenses and adjusts aperture and speed settings as necessary;

- photographs subject or follows action by moving camera

- checks operation and positioning of projectors, videotape machines, mobile microphones and mixing and dubbing equipment;

- operates telecine, projection and video equipment to record and play back films and television programmes;

- operates sound mixing and dubbing equipment to obtain desired mix, level and balance of sound.

## RELATED JOB TITLES

Camera operator
Film technician
Photographer
Photographic technician
Press photographer
Projectionist
Sound recordist

# 387 PROFESSIONAL ATHLETES, SPORTS OFFICIALS

Professional athletes and sports officials officiate at, train competitors for and participate in, sporting events for financial gain.

## TYPICAL ENTRY ROUTES AND
## ASSOCIATED QUALIFICATIONS

No academic qualifications are required. Entry is based on ability and professional qualifications.

## TASKS

- arranges matches, contests or appearances for athlete or team, controls team selection and discipline and recruits ancillary staff such as coaches or physiotherapists;

- coaches teams or individuals by demonstrating techniques and directing training and exercise sessions;

- starts race or competition and controls its progress according to established rules;

- trains regularly to develop ability in a particular sport;

- decides tactics or receives instructions from manager and performs in a competitive event.

## RELATED JOB TITLES

Golfer
Horse jockey
Professional footballer
Referee
Riding instructor
Sports coach
Sports umpire
Swimming teacher
Umpire

# MINOR GROUP 39
# ASSOCIATE PROFESSIONAL AND TECHNICAL OCCUPATIONS NEC

Workers in this unit group perform a variety of associate professional occupations not elsewhere classified in MAJOR GROUP 3: Associate Professional and Technical Occupations.

Occupations in this minor group are classified into the following unit groups:

| | |
|---|---|
| 390 | INFORMATION OFFICERS |
| 391 | VOCATIONAL AND INDUSTRIAL TRAINERS |
| 392 | CAREERS ADVISERS AND VOCATIONAL GUIDANCE SPECIALISTS |
| 393 | DRIVING INSTRUCTORS (EXCLUDING HGV) |
| 394 | INSPECTORS OF FACTORIES, UTILITIES AND TRADING STANDARDS |
| 395 | OTHER STATUTORY AND SIMILAR INSPECTORS NEC |
| 396 | OCCUPATIONAL HYGIENISTS AND SAFETY OFFICERS (HEALTH AND SAFETY) |
| 399 | OTHER ASSOCIATE PROFESSIONAL AND TECHNICAL OCCUPATIONS NEC |

## 390 INFORMATION OFFICERS

Information officers organise, maintain and make available collections of written or recorded material and collect, appraise and disseminate information.

### TYPICAL ENTRY ROUTES AND ASSOCIATED QUALIFICATIONS

Entry is most common with GCSE/SCE S-grades and A-levels/H-grades, but is possible with other academic qualifications. Further professional qualifications/training is required.

### TASKS

- ensures that all material is catalogued, classified and indexed;
- arranges material on shelves for convenience of users;
- seeks out and evaluates information sources and organises the collection of information;
- answers inquiries regarding information or sources of information;
- prepares abstracts, bibliographies, reports and memorandums as appropriate.

### RELATED JOB TITLES

Computer tape librarian
Information officer
Intelligence officer (*government*)
Political research officer

## 391 VOCATIONAL AND INDUSTRIAL TRAINERS

Vocational and industrial trainers provide instruction in manual, manipulative and other vocational

127

skills and advise on, plan and organise vocational instruction within industrial, commercial and other establishments.

## TYPICAL ENTRY ROUTES AND ASSOCIATED QUALIFICATIONS

Entry is most common with a degree or equivalent qualification but is possible with other academic qualifications and/or relevant experience.

## TASKS

- assesses training requirements and prepares lectures, demonstrations and study aids;

- supervises trainee development, assists trainees with difficulties and prepares regular progress reports on each trainee for management;

- arranges work experience and instructional visits for trainees;

- plans curriculum and rota of staff duties and updates or amends them in light of developments;

- advises on training programmes and discusses progress or problems with staff and trainees;

- devises general and specialised training courses in response to particular needs.

## RELATED JOB TITLES

Technical instructor
Training instructor
Training officer
Training supervisor

## 392 CAREERS ADVISERS AND VOCATIONAL GUIDANCE SPECIALISTS

Workers in this unit group give advice on careers or occupations, training courses and related matters, direct school leavers and other job seekers into employment and assess their progress.

## TYPICAL ENTRY ROUTES AND ASSOCIATED QUALIFICATIONS

Entry into training will require a degree, CNAA, a Diploma in Higher Education or equivalent, all leading to a professional qualification (Diploma in Careers Guidance) which is awarded by the Local Government Training Board.

## TASKS

- uses an interview, questionnaire and/or psychological or other test to determine the aptitude, preferences and temperament of the client;

- advises on appropriate courses of study or avenues into employment;

- visits educational and other establishments to give talks and distribute information regarding careers;

- liaises with employers to determine employment opportunities and advises schools, colleges or individuals accordingly;

- organises careers forums and exhibitions and establishes and maintains contact with local employers and/or training boards;

- monitors progress and welfare of young people in employment and advises them on any difficulties.

## RELATED JOB TITLES

Careers adviser
Careers officer
Placement co-ordinator
Placement officer

## 393 DRIVING INSTRUCTORS (EXCLUDING HGV)

Driving instructors (excluding HGV) co-ordinate and undertake the instruction of people learning to drive cars and light commercial vehicles.

## TYPICAL ENTRY ROUTES AND ASSOCIATED QUALIFICATIONS

No academic qualifications are required. Candidates must have held a current driving licence for four out of the last six years and had no disqualifications from driving for the last four years. A one to three week training course is available leading to a three-part examination to become an Approved Driving Instructor. Further training leading to higher qualifications is available.

## TASKS

- checks instruction and learning standards and discusses teaching plans with other instructors;

- plans lessons in accordance with the needs and abilities of individual pupils;

- explains driving techniques and assists pupil with difficulties;

- familiarises pupil with the Highway Code and different road and traffic conditions;

- advises pupil when to apply for a driving test and familiarises them with test procedures and standards.

## RELATED JOB TITLES

Advanced driving instructor (*not HGV*)
Driving instructor (*not HGV*)

## 394 INSPECTORS OF FACTORIES, UTILITIES AND TRADING STANDARDS

Inspectors of factories, utilities and trading standards undertake investigations and inspections to verify and ensure compliance with acts, regulations and other requirements regarding weights, measures and trade descriptions, the installation and safety of electrical, gas and water supplies and equipment and the welfare, health and safety in factories and all work sites subject to the provisions in the Factory Acts.

## TYPICAL ENTRY ROUTES AND ASSOCIATED QUALIFICATIONS

Entry is most common with an honours degree or equivalent but is possible with other academic qualifications and/or relevant experience. Up to three years off- and on-the-job training is provided.

## TASKS

- inspects measuring and similar equipment in factories and visits street traders, shops, garages and other premises to check scales, weights and measuring equipment;

- inspects factories and other work sites to ensure adequate cleanliness, temperature, lighting and ventilation, checks for fire hazards and inspects storage and handling arrangements of dangerous materials;

- visits sites during construction and inspects completed installations of electricity, gas or water supply;

- draws attention to any irregularities or infringements of regulations and advises on ways of rectifying them;

- investigates industrial accidents or any complaints made by the public, prepares reports and recommendations on all inspections made and recommends legal action where necessary.

## RELATED JOB TITLES

Gas inspector
Inspector of factories
Inspector of weights and measures
Installation inspector (*electricity, gas*)
Plumbing inspector
Trading standards officer

## 395 OTHER STATUTORY AND SIMILAR INSPECTORS NEC

Workers in this unit group conduct driving tests and undertake investigations and inspections to ensure compliance with bye-laws, acts and other regulations concerning river pollution and use of fishing grounds, the condition and standard of ships' structures, equipment and accommodation, the treatment of animals, the operation of commercial, passenger and road goods vehicles and other miscellaneous concerns/issues not elsewhere classified.

## TYPICAL ENTRY ROUTES AND ASSOCIATED QUALIFICATIONS

Entry is most common with experience gained in employment, but is possible with GCSE/SCE S-grades or A-levels/H-grades. On-the-job training is provided and professional qualifications are available and are mandatory for some posts.

**TASKS**

- verifies the weight of vehicles, checks drivers licence and the number of hours worked;

- takes regular samples of river water for laboratory analysis and removes any diseased fish from the river;

- visits premises discharging effluent into river and advises on ways of preventing pollution;

- prevents illegal fishing and inspects and verifies fishing licences;

- visits kennels, race courses, slaughterhouses and other areas where animals are kept, investigates any complaints and advises on animal care;

- provides first aid treatment for animals and undertakes humane killing where necessary;

- conducts driving tests to assess the competence of learners applying for road vehicle licences;

- undertakes other inspections not elsewhere classified, including alkali, drugs, explosives, flight operations, horticulture, wages and mining inspections.

**RELATED JOB TITLES**

Alkali inspector
Driving examiner
Fishery officer
Flight examiner
Inspector of mines
RSPCA inspector
Ship surveyor
Water bailiff

## 396 OCCUPATIONAL HYGIENISTS AND SAFETY OFFICERS (HEALTH AND SAFETY)

Workers in this unit group counsel employees on personal, domestic and other problems and grievances, advise on industrial health and safety and co-ordinate accident prevention and safety measures within an establishment or organisation.

**TYPICAL ENTRY ROUTES AND ASSOCIATED QUALIFICATIONS**

Entry is possible with either a degree or equivalent qualification or with other academic qualifications and/or relevant experience.

**TASKS**

- assists employees in need of accommodation and maintains contact with those off work due to illness;

- counsels individuals on any personal or domestic problems affecting their work;

- inspects factory and other work areas to ensure compliance with health and safety legislation;

- instructs workers in the proper use of protective clothing and safety devices;

- compiles statistics on accidents and injuries, analyses their causes and makes recommendations to management accordingly;

- gives talks and distributes information on accident prevention;

- carries out routine tests on safety devices and protective clothing.

**RELATED JOB TITLES**

Occupational hygienist
Safety adviser
Safety officer

## 399 OTHER ASSOCIATE PROFESSIONAL AND TECHNICAL OCCUPATIONS NEC

Workers in this unit group perform a variety of associate professional occupations not elsewhere classified in MINOR GROUP 39: Associate Professional and Technical Occupations n.e.c.

**TYPICAL ENTRY ROUTES AND ASSOCIATED QUALIFICATIONS**

Entry is possible with either a degree or equivalent qualification or with other academic qualifications and/or relevant experience.

**TASKS**

- performs scientific and technical tasks related to a variety of associate professional and technical occupations not elsewhere classified.

## RELATED JOB TITLES

Appraiser
Bank inspector
Committee secretary
Materials planner
Research officer (*government*)

# MAJOR GROUP 4

## CLERICAL AND SECRETARIAL OCCUPATIONS

# MAJOR GROUP 4
# CLERICAL AND SECRETARIAL OCCUPATIONS

This major group covers occupations whose main tasks require the knowledge and experience necessary to record, organise, store and retrieve information, compute data and perform client-orientated clerical duties. The main tasks involve typing, work processing and other secretarial skills; business machines; sorting, classifying, filing and despatching administrative and business records; providing information to clients; collecting debts; assisting librarians and draughtspersons and routing information through organisations.

Most occupations in this major group will require a good standard of general education. Certain occupations will require further additional vocational training to a well defined standard (e.g. typing or shorthand).

Occupations in this major group are classified into the following minor groups:

40    ADMINISTRATIVE/CLERICAL OFFICERS AND
      ASSISTANTS IN CIVIL SERVICE
      AND LOCAL GOVERNMENT

41    NUMERICAL CLERKS AND CASHIERS

42    FILING AND RECORDS CLERKS

43    CLERKS (NOT OTHERWISE SPECIFIED)

44    STORES AND DESPATCH CLERKS, STOREKEEPERS

45    SECRETARIES, PERSONAL ASSISTANTS, TYPISTS,
      WORD PROCESSOR OPERATORS

46    RECEPTIONISTS, TELEPHONISTS AND RELATED
      OCCUPATIONS

49    CLERICAL AND SECRETARIAL OCCUPATIONS NEC

# MINOR GROUP 40
# ADMINISTRATIVE/CLERICAL OFFICERS AND ASSISTANTS IN CIVIL SERVICE AND LOCAL GOVERNMENT

Workers in this minor group undertake a variety of clerical work in national and local government departments.

Occupations in this minor group are classified into the following unit groups:

**400 CIVIL SERVICE ADMINISTRATIVE OFFICERS AND ASSISTANTS**
**401 LOCAL GOVERNMENT CLERICAL OFFICERS AND ASSISTANTS**

## 400 CIVIL SERVICE ADMINISTRATIVE OFFICERS AND ASSISTANTS

Civil Service administrative officers and assistants undertake a variety of clerical duties in national government offices and departments.

### TYPICAL ENTRY ROUTES AND ASSOCIATED QUALIFICATIONS

Entry is most common with GCSE/SCE S-grades but is possible with other academic qualifications.

### TASKS

- maintains and updates correspondence, documents, data and other records for storage in files or on computer tape;

- classifies, sorts and files publications, correspondence, etc. in offices and libraries;

- provides analyses, reports, statistics and other information for senior officers;

- performs miscellaneous clerical tasks not elsewhere classified including preparing statistical information, proof reading printed material and drafting letters in reply to correspondence or telephone enquiries.

### RELATED JOB TITLES

Administrative assistant (*central government*)
Administrative officer (*central government*)

## 401 LOCAL GOVERNMENT CLERICAL OFFICERS AND ASSISTANTS

Local government clerical officers and assistants undertake a variety of clerical duties in local government offices and departments.

### TYPICAL ENTRY ROUTES AND ASSOCIATED QUALIFICATIONS

Entry is most common with GCSE/SCE S-grades but is possible without specific academic qualifications.

### TASKS

- computes cost of product/services and maintains and balances records of financial transactions;

- prepares and checks invoices and verifies accuracy of records;

- receives and pays out cash and cheques and performs closely related clerical duties;

- operates data processing equipment to update and maintain data, correspondence and other records for storage or despatch;

- arranges, classifies and indexes publications, correspondence and other material in libraries and offices;

- performs other clerical duties not elsewhere classified including preparing financial information for management, proof reading printed material and drafting letters in reply to correspondence or telephone enquiries.

## RELATED JOB TITLES

Clerical assistant (*local government*)
Clerical officer (*local government*)

# MINOR GROUP 41
# NUMERICAL CLERKS AND CASHIERS

Numerical clerks and cashiers record and produce financial information and receive and pay out cash.

Occupations in this minor group are classified into the following unit groups:

    **410   ACCOUNTS AND WAGES CLERKS, BOOK-KEEPERS, OTHER FINANCIAL CLERKS**

    **411   COUNTER CLERKS AND CASHIERS**

    **412   DEBT, RENT AND OTHER CASH COLLECTORS**

## 410  ACCOUNTS AND WAGES CLERKS, BOOK-KEEPERS, OTHER FINANCIAL CLERKS

Accounts and wages clerks, book-keepers, and other financial clerks, maintain and balance records of financial transactions, calculate hours worked, wages due and other relevant contributions/deductions and perform other financial and related clerical duties.

### TYPICAL ENTRY ROUTES AND ASSOCIATED QUALIFICATIONS

Entry does not depend on academic qualifications but is most common with GCSE/SCE/S-grades. On-the-job training is provided.

### TASKS

- checks and records accuracy of daily records of financial transactions;

- prepares provisional balances and reconciles these with appropriate accounts;

- calculates and records hours worked, wages due, deductions and voluntary contributions;

- compiles schedules and distributes or arranges distribution of wages and salaries;

- calculates costs and overheads and prepares analyses for management.

### RELATED JOB TITLES

Accountant's clerk
Accounts assistant
Audit assistant
Book-keeper
Claims assistant
Cost clerk
Invoice clerk
Wages clerk

## 411  COUNTER CLERKS AND CASHIERS

Counter clerks and cashiers receive and pay out cash and record and balance such transactions. Other financial clerks compile data.

### TYPICAL ENTRY ROUTES AND ASSOCIATED QUALIFICATIONS

Entry does not depend on academic qualifications but is most common with GCSE/SCE/S-grades. On-the-job training is provided.

### TASKS

- deals with enquiries from customers, other banks and other authorised enquirers;

- maintains records of transactions and compiles statistical information;

- receives and pays out cash, cheques, money orders, credit notes, foreign currency or travellers cheques.

**RELATED JOB TITLES**

Bank cashier
Bank clerk
Building Society clerk
Cash clerk
Cashier
Counter clerk

## 412 DEBT, RENT AND OTHER CASH COLLECTORS

Debt, rent and other cash collectors collect payments due or overdue from households and businesses and empty cash from prepayment meters or machines.

**TYPICAL ENTRY ROUTES AND ASSOCIATED QUALIFICATIONS**

Academic qualifications may not be required. On-the-job training is provided.

**TASKS**

- receives payment at centralised office or calls on household/business premises;

- records details of transaction, issues receipt or annotates rent book;

- remits cash, cheques or credit notes to cashier, supervisor or bank, Building Society or Post Office.

**RELATED JOB TITLES**

Collector agent
Debt collector
Meter collector
Meter reader
Rent collector
Toll collector

# MINOR GROUP 42
# FILING AND RECORDS CLERKS

Filing and records clerks compile, sort and file correspondence, data and other documents for storage and despatch.

Occupations in this minor group are classified into the following unit groups:

> **420 FILING, COMPUTER AND OTHER RECORDS CLERKS (INCLUDING LEGAL CONVEYANCING)**
>
> **421 LIBRARY ASSISTANTS/CLERKS**

## 420 FILING, COMPUTER AND OTHER RECORDS CLERKS (INCLUDING LEGAL CONVEYANCING)

Filing, computer and other records clerks maintain and update documents, correspondence and other records and arrange and store them in files or on computer cards or tapes.

### TYPICAL ENTRY ROUTES AND ASSOCIATED QUALIFICATIONS

Academic qualifications may not be required. On-the-job training is provided.

### TASKS

- examines and sorts incoming material;

- classifies and files documents and other records;

- copies or duplicates documents or other records;

- enters numerical and other data from source material into computer-compatible storage and processing devices;

- performs specialised clerical tasks in connection with the conveying of property.

### RELATED JOB TITLES

Census enumerator
Computer clerk

Export clerk
Filing clerk
Goods checker
Progress chaser
Records clerk
School secretary
Shipping clerk
Technical clerk

## 421 LIBRARY ASSISTANTS/CLERKS

Library assistants and clerks classify, sort and file publications, documents, audio-visual material and correspondence in libraries and offices.

### TYPICAL ENTRY ROUTES AND ASSOCIATED QUALIFICATIONS

Academic qualifications may not be required. On-the-job training is provided.

### TASKS

- sorts, catalogues and maintains library records;

- locates and retrieves material on request for borrowers;

- issues library material and records date of issue/due date for return;

- classifies, labels and indexes new books;

- performs simple repairs on old books.

**RELATED JOB TITLES**

Library assistant
Library clerk

# MINOR GROUP 43
# CLERKS (NOT OTHERWISE SPECIFIED)

Clerks (n.o.s.) perform a variety of clerical tasks and comprise people described as 'clerk', 'clerical assistant' or with other job titles lacking specific details.

Occupations in this minor group are classified into the following unit group:

## 430   CLERKS (NOT OTHERWISE SPECIFIED)

## 430  CLERKS (NOT OTHERWISE SPECIFIED)

Clerks (n.o.s.) are responsible for recording, filing and disseminating information for a business or private individual.

### TYPICAL ENTRY ROUTES AND ASSOCIATED QUALIFICATIONS

Entry is most common with GCSE/SCE S-grades or equivalent but is possible with no specific academic qualifications. Off- and on-the-job training is provided.

### TASKS

- records and retrieves information;

- compiles, sorts and files correspondence;

- receives and pays out cash.

### RELATED JOB TITLES

Clerical assistant
Clerical officer
Clerk
Clerk/telephonist
Clerk/typist
Commercial assistant
General assistant
Office supervisor
Office worker

# MINOR GROUP 44
# STORES AND DESPATCH CLERKS, STOREKEEPERS

Stores and despatch clerks and storekeepers receive orders for merchandise, prepare requisitions or despatch documents for ordered goods, maintain records of stock movements and store, select and issue freight, baggage, furniture, goods and other items.

Occupations in this minor group are classified into the following unit groups:

**440 STORES, DESPATCH AND PRODUCTION CONTROL CLERKS**
**441 STOREKEEPERS AND WAREHOUSEMEN/WOMEN**

## 440 STORES, DESPATCH AND PRODUCTION CONTROL CLERKS

Stores, despatch and production control clerks receive orders from customers, prepare requisitions or despatch documents for ordered goods and check and maintain records of stocks held and stock movements.

### TYPICAL ENTRY ROUTES AND ASSOCIATED QUALIFICATIONS

Academic qualifications may not be required. On-the-job training is provided.

### TASKS

- receives enquiries and orders by mail, telephone or personally from a customer;

- quotes prices, discounts, delivery dates and other relevant information to customers;

- prepares requisitions, consignments and other despatch documents;

- checks requisitions against stock records and forwards to issuing department;

- adjusts stock records as orders are received, reports on damaged stock and prepares requisitions to replenish stock.

### RELATED JOB TITLES

Despatch clerk
Stock clerk
Stock control clerk
Stores clerk

## 441 STOREKEEPERS AND WAREHOUSEMEN/WOMEN

Storekeepers and warehousemen/women store, maintain stock records and store, select and issue freight, furniture, equipment and other items.

### TYPICAL ENTRY ROUTES AND ASSOCIATED QUALIFICATIONS

Academic qualifications may not be required. On-the-job training is provided.

### TASKS

- directs or undertakes unloading of goods from vans and supervises the sorting of passengers' baggage for hold or baggage room;

- checks items against invoices and inventories, records issue and despatch of goods and maintains records of goods in stock;

- stores or directs the storage of goods in appropriate section of warehouse, cellar, hold or cupboard;

- makes up orders against requisitions from customers and arranges for despatch.

141

## RELATED JOB TITLES

Despatcher
Partsman/woman
Stockroom assistant
Storekeeper
Storeman/woman
Stores assistant
Warehouse assistant

# MINOR GROUP 45
# SECRETARIES, PERSONAL ASSISTANTS, TYPISTS, WORD PROCESSOR OPERATORS

Secretaries and personal assistants perform filing, typing, shorthand or audio dictation services and clerical and organisational duties in support of management or other workers. Typists and word processor operators record oral or written matter in shorthand and type, edit and print documents using either typewriters or word processors.

Occupations in this minor group are classified into the following unit groups:

450 MEDICAL SECRETARIES
451 LEGAL SECRETARIES
452 TYPISTS AND WORD PROCESSOR OPERATORS
459 OTHER SECRETARIES, PERSONAL ASSISTANTS, TYPISTS, WORD PROCESSOR OPERATORS NEC

## 450 MEDICAL SECRETARIES

Medical secretaries file and maintain medical and other records, transcribe notes and dictation into typewritten form and perform other routine clerical tasks in hospitals/surgeries and other medical establishments.

### TYPICAL ENTRY ROUTES AND ASSOCIATED QUALIFICATIONS

Entry is most common with GCSE/SCE S-grades. Further proficiency certificates are required.

### TASKS

- sorts and files correspondence;

- writes down dictated matter in shorthand and transcribes it into typewritten form;

- transcribes audio dictation into typewritten form;

- maintains patients' records and arranges appointments;

- answers enquiries and refers patient to appropriate experts;

- organises and attends meetings and keeps records of proceedings.

### RELATED JOB TITLES

Medical secretary

## 451 LEGAL SECRETARIES

Legal secretaries file and maintain legal and other records, transcribe notes and dictation into typewritten form and perform other routine clerical tasks in legal practices.

### TYPICAL ENTRY ROUTES AND ASSOCIATED QUALIFICATIONS

Entry is most common with SCE/SCE S-grades. Further proficiency certificates are required.

### TASKS

- sorts and files correspondence;

- writes down dictated matter into shorthand and transcribes it into typewritten form;

- transcribes audio dictation into typewritten form;

- maintains court and clients' records and arranges appointments;

- answers enquiries and directs clients to appropriate experts;
- attends meetings and keeps records of proceedings.

## RELATED JOB TITLES

Legal secretary

## 452  TYPISTS AND WORD PROCESSOR OPERATORS

Typists and word process operators type letters, minutes, memos, reports and other documents from written or dictated matter, using typewriters or word processing machines.

## TYPICAL ENTRY ROUTES AND ASSOCIATED QUALIFICATIONS

Entry is most common with GCSE/SCE S-grades and professional certificates but is possible with other academic qualifications.

## TASKS

- types letters, minutes, memos, reports and other documents;
- proof reads, edits and corrects errors to produce clean copy to specified layout;
- operates printing machine attached to word processor.

## RELATED JOB TITLES

Audio typist
Shorthand typist
Typist
Word processor operator

## 459  OTHER SECRETARIES, PERSONAL ASSISTANTS, TYPISTS, WORD PROCESSOR OPERATORS NEC

Other secretaries, personal assistants, typists and word processor operators perform filing, clerical and organisational duties, transcribe notes into typewritten form and a variety of secretarial tasks not elsewhere classified in MINOR GROUP 45: Secretaries, Personal Assistants, Typists, Word Processor Operators.

## TYPICAL ENTRY ROUTES AND ASSOCIATED QUALIFICATIONS

Entry is most common with GCSE/SCE S-grades. Further proficiency certificates are required. Written and spoken fluency in one or more foreign language is required for some posts.

## TASKS

- sorts and files correspondence;
- writes down dictated matter in shorthand and transcribes it into typewritten form;
- arranges appointments and receives telephone calls on behalf of superior(s);
- attends meetings and keeps records of proceedings;
- organises travel arrangements and makes reservations.

## RELATED JOB TITLES

Bi-lingual secretary
Farm secretary
Manager's personal assistant
Personal managerial assistant
Secretary

# MINOR GROUP 46
# RECEPTIONISTS, TELEPHONISTS AND RELATED OCCUPATIONS

Receptionists, telephonists and related workers operate public and private switchboards, radios, telegraph and teleprinter equipment to transmit and receive signals and messages. They also receive callers, deal with enquiries and provide information concerning the goods and services offered by an establishment.

Occupations in this minor group are classified into the following unit groups:

460 **RECEPTIONISTS**

461 **RECEPTIONISTS/TELEPHONISTS**

462 **TELEPHONE OPERATORS**

463 **RADIO AND TELEGRAPH OPERATORS, OTHER OFFICE COMMUNICATION SYSTEM OPERATORS**

## 460 RECEPTIONISTS

Receptionists receive and direct clients and callers, make appointments, and deal with enquiries in commercial, industrial and other establishments.

### TYPICAL ENTRY ROUTES AND ASSOCIATED QUALIFICATIONS

Academic qualifications may not be required, but some employers ask for GCSE/SCE S-grades. On-the-job training is provided.

### TASKS

- receives callers and clients and directs them to the appropriate person or department;

- records details of enquiries and makes appointments and reservations;

- deals with telephone enquiries;

- supplies brochures, pamphlets and other information for clients.

### RELATED JOB TITLES

Dental receptionist

Doctor's receptionist
Medical receptionist
Receptionist

## 461 RECEPTIONIST/ TELEPHONISTS

Receptionists and telephonists receive and direct callers, deal with enquiries and operate telephone switchboards in commercial, industrial and other establishments.

### TYPICAL ENTRY ROUTES AND ASSOCIATED QUALIFICATIONS

Academic qualifications may not be required, but some employers ask for GCSE/SCE S-grades. On-the-job training is provided.

### TASKS

- receives callers and directs them to appropriate person or department;

- records details of enquiries and makes appointments and reservations;

- operates switchboard to connect outgoing calls or to relay incoming or internal calls;

- reports any faults on telephone operating system.

145

## RELATED JOB TITLES

Receptionist/telephonist
Telephonist/receptionist

## 462 TELEPHONE OPERATORS

Telephone operators operate telephone (public) and office (private) switchboards to advise on, and assist with, dialling and to relay incoming, outgoing and internal calls.

### TYPICAL ENTRY ROUTES AND ASSOCIATED QUALIFICATIONS

Academic qualifications may not be required. On-the-job training is provided.

### TASKS

- operates switchboard to connect outgoing calls and to relay incoming or internal calls;

- gives advice on dialling and other special features available;

- provides directory information, dialling codes and details of charges;

- alerts emergency services in cases of fire, crime or accident;

- may monitor calls and record call details for charging purposes.

### RELATED JOB TITLES

Night telephonist
Telephone operator
Telephonist
Switchboard operator

## 463 RADIO AND TELEGRAPH OPERATORS, OTHER OFFICE COMMUNICATION SYSTEM OPERATORS

Workers in this unit group operate radio, telegraphic, telex and other teleprinter equipment to transmit and receive signals and messages.

### TYPICAL ENTRY ROUTES AND ASSOCIATED QUALIFICATIONS

Academic qualifications may not be required. On-the-job training is provided.

### TASKS

- receives messages, weather reports and other material to transmit;

- tunes transmitter to required channel or wavelength and relays or receives message to/from person or vehicle;

- uses a teleprinter or telex keyboard to transmit messages to other teleprinters or telexes;

- keeps record of messages sent and received;

- performs routine tests and maintenance on equipment and reports faults.

### RELATED JOB TITLES

Communications operator
Control room operator (*fire service*)
Radio operator
Telecommunications officer
Telegraphist
Telex operator

# MINOR GROUP 49
# CLERICAL AND SECRETARIAL OCCUPATIONS NEC

Workers in this minor group perform a variety of clerical and secretarial occupations not elsewhere classified in MAJOR GROUP 4: Clerical and Secretarial Occupations.

Occupations in this minor group are classified into the following unit groups:

**490   COMPUTER OPERATORS, DATA PROCESSING OPERATORS, OTHER OFFICE MACHINE OPERATORS**

**491   TRACERS, DRAWING OFFICE ASSISTANTS**

## 490   COMPUTER OPERATORS, DATA PROCESSING OPERATORS, OTHER OFFICE MACHINE OPERATORS

Workers in this unit group operate accounting, calculating, key punch, duplicating and addressing machines and data processing and computing equipment.

### TYPICAL ENTRY ROUTES AND ASSOCIATED QUALIFICATIONS

Academic qualifications may not be required. On-the-job training is provided.

### TASKS

- sets machine or computer for required operation or process;

- loads machine with data tapes, discs, punched cards or stationery;

- transcribes data onto computer-compatible storage devices using key punch machine;

- operates keyboard to enter, edit and retrieve data or to perform calculations;

- starts machine and monitors operation for error messages, paper misfeeds, etc.;

- removes blockages and replaces damaged cards or paper.

### RELATED JOB TITLES

Accounts machine operator
Computer operator
Data preparation operator
Data processor
Key punch operator
Key-to-disc operator

## 491   TRACERS, DRAWING OFFICE ASSISTANTS

Tracers and drawing office assistants make tracings of the whole or parts of original drawings.

### TYPICAL ENTRY ROUTES AND ASSOCIATED QUALIFICATIONS

Academic qualifications may be required. On-the-job training is provided.

### TASKS

- places appropriate tracing material over the original drawing;

- traces required details in pencil or ink using T-square, dividers, compasses and other draughting instruments;

- inserts additional detail on tracing if required;

- colours tracing as directed.

**RELATED JOB TITLES**

Drawing office assistant
Leading tracer
Tracer

# MAJOR GROUP 5

## CRAFT AND
## RELATED OCCUPATIONS

# MAJOR GROUP 5
# CRAFT AND RELATED OCCUPATIONS

This major group covers occupations whose tasks involve the performance of complex physical duties which normally require a degree of initiative, manual dexterity and other practical skills. The main tasks of these occupations require experience with, and understanding of, the work situation, the materials worked with and the requirements of the structures, machinery and other items produced.

Most occupations in this major group have a level of skill commensurate with a substantial period of training, often provided by means of work-based training programme.

Occupations in this major group are classified into the following minor groups:

      **50   CONSTRUCTION TRADES**

      **51   METAL MACHINING, FITTING AND INSTRUMENT
            MAKING TRADES**

      **52   ELECTRICAL/ELECTRONIC TRADES**

      **53   METAL FORMING, WELDING AND RELATED TRADES**

      **54   VEHICLE TRADES**

      **55   TEXTILES, GARMENTS AND RELATED TRADES**

      **56   PRINTING AND RELATED TRADES**

      **57   WOODWORKING TRADES**

      **58   FOOD PREPARATION TRADES**

      **59   OTHER CRAFT AND RELATED OCCUPATIONS NEC**

# MINOR GROUP 50
# CONSTRUCTION TRADES

Construction trades workers construct, install, finish, maintain and repair internal and external structures of domestic, commercial and industrial buildings and civil constructions, erect and dismantle scaffolding and working platforms, set up lifting equipment and splice, maintain and repair ropes and wires.

Occupations in this minor group are classified into the following unit groups:

> **500 BRICKLAYERS, MASONS**
>
> **501 ROOFERS, SLATERS, TILERS, SHEETERS, CLADDERS**
>
> **502 PLASTERERS**
>
> **503 GLAZIERS**
>
> **504 BUILDERS, BUILDING CONTRACTORS**
>
> **505 SCAFFOLDERS, STAGERS, STEEPLEJACKS, RIGGERS**
>
> **506 FLOORERS, FLOOR COVERERS, CARPET FITTERS AND PLANNERS, FLOOR AND WALL TILERS**
>
> **507 PAINTERS AND DECORATORS**
>
> **509 OTHER CONSTRUCTION TRADES NEC**

## 500 BRICKLAYERS, MASONS

Bricklayers and masons erect and repair structures of stone, brick and similar materials and cut, shape and polish granite, marble, slate and other stone for building, ornamental and other purposes.

### TYPICAL ENTRY ROUTES AND ASSOCIATED QUALIFICATIONS

Entry may not depend on academic qualifications. Training is by apprenticeship.

### TASKS

- examines drawings, photographs and specifications to determine job requirements;

- marks and cuts stone using hammers, mallet and hand or pneumatic chisels;

- spreads mortar on foundations and bricks and places, levels and aligns brick in mortar bed;

- uses hand and power tools to shape, trim, carve, cut letters in and polish stone;

- levels, aligns and embeds stone in mortar and faces brick, concrete or steel frame with stone to make and repair structures.

### RELATED JOB TITLES

Bricklayer
Mason
Monumental mason
Stone mason

## 501 ROOFERS, SLATERS, TILERS, SHEETERS, CLADDERS

Workers in this unit group cover roofs and exterior walls with felting, sheeting, slates, tiles and thatch to provide a waterproof surface.

Entry may not depend on academic qualifications.
Training is by apprenticeship.

## TASKS

- measures roof or exterior wall and calculates
required amounts of underfelt, tiles, slates or
thatching material;

- cuts wooden battens, felt and underfelt to required size;

- lays and secures underfelt and covers with hot
bitumen or other adhesive compound;

- lays, aligns and secures successive overlapping
layers of roofing material;

- seals edges of roof with mortar and ensures that
joints are watertight.

## RELATED JOB TITLES

Felter (*building and contracting*)
Roof sheeter
Roof tiler
Roofer
Roofing felt fixer
Sheeter (*building and contracting*)
Slater
Slater and tiler
Thatcher

# 502 PLASTERERS

Plasterers apply plaster and cement mixtures to
walls and ceilings, fix fibrous sheets and cast and fix
ornamental plaster work to the interior or exterior
of buildings.

## TYPICAL ENTRY ROUTES AND
ASSOCIATED QUALIFICATIONS

Entry may not depend on academic qualifications.
Training is by apprenticeship.

## TASKS

- mixes, or directs the mixing of, plaster to desired
consistency;

- applies and smoothes one or more coats of plaster
and produces a finished surface, using hand tools
or mechanical spray;

- pours liquid plaster into mould to cast ornamental plaster work;

- measures, cuts, installs and secures plaster board
and/or ornamental plasterwork to walls and ceilings;

- covers and seals joints between boards and finishes surface;

- checks surface level using line, spirit level and
straight edge.

## RELATED JOB TITLES

Plasterer
Plastering contractor

# 503 GLAZIERS

Glaziers cut, fit and set glass in windows, doors,
shop fronts, and other structural frames.

## TYPICAL ENTRY ROUTES AND
ASSOCIATED QUALIFICATIONS

Entry may not depend on academic qualifications.
Training is by apprenticeship.

## TASKS

- examines drawings or specifications to determine job requirements;

- scores plain, coloured, safety and ornamental
glass with hand cutter and breaks off glass by
hand or with pliers;

- smoothes edges of glass and positions and secures in frame or grooved lead strips;

- applies mastic, putty or adhesive between glass
and frame and trims off excess with knife;

- fixes mirror panels to interior and exterior walls
and repairs and replaces broken glass.

Glass fitter
Glazier
Leaded light maker

# 504 BUILDERS, BUILDING CONTRACTORS

Builders and building contractors undertake a variety of tasks in the construction, alteration, maintenance and repair of buildings.

## TYPICAL ENTRY ROUTES AND ASSOCIATED QUALIFICATIONS

Entry may not depend on academic qualifications. Training is by apprenticeship.

## TASKS

- makes, alters and repairs woodwork structures and fittings;

- lays bricks, tiles and building blocks to construct, repair and decorate buildings;

- prepares interior and exterior surfaces for painting and plastering;

- pours and levels concrete and mixes and applies plaster and paint;

- installs, maintains and repairs electrical wiring and plumbing fixtures and appliances in building;

- covers and weatherproofs roofs and cuts, fits and sets glass in frames.

## RELATED JOB TITLES

Builder (*building and contracting*)
Builder and contractor
Builder and decorator
Building contractor
General builder
Master builder
Housebuilder

# 505 SCAFFOLDERS, STAGERS, STEEPLEJACKS, RIGGERS

Workers in this unit group erect and dismantle scaffolding and working platforms, set up lifting equipment and ships' rigging, maintain and repair steeples, industrial chimneys and other tall structures and install, maintain and repair ropes, wires and cables.

## TYPICAL ENTRY ROUTES AND ASSOCIATED QUALIFICATIONS

Academic qualifications may not be required. Scaffolding is a strictly regulated occupation and skilled workers must obtain CITB recognised scaffolders record scheme cards.

## TASKS

- examines drawings and specifications to determine job requirements;

- examines scaffold tubing and couplings for defects and selects, fits and bolts scaffold tubes until scaffolding reaches required height;

- lays and secures wooden planking to form working platforms and fixes guard rails, ladders, cradles and awnings as required;

- erects jib, derrick and similar hoisting equipment and installs ropes, pulleys and other lifting tackle;

- forms rope slings, ladders, netting and other rigging and measures, cuts and repairs wire or fibre rope;

- maintains and repairs steeples and other high structures and installs and repairs lightning conductors.

## RELATED JOB TITLES

Rigger
Scaffolder
Stager (*shipbuilding*)
Steeplejack

## 506 FLOORERS, FLOOR COVERERS, CARPET FITTERS AND PLANNERS, FLOOR AND WALL TILERS

Workers in this unit group lay composition mixtures (other than mastic asphalt) to form flooring, plan, fit and secure carpet, underlay and linoleum and cover and decorate walls and floors with terrazzo and granolithic mixtures, tiles and mosaic panels.

### TYPICAL ENTRY ROUTES AND ASSOCIATED QUALIFICATIONS

Entry may not depend on academic qualifications and training is mainly on-the-job for floorers and carpet fitters. Training is by apprenticeship for tile setters.

### TASKS

- examines drawings and specifications to determine job requirements;

- cleans floor surface, fixes wooden laying guides and mixes, pours and levels granite and terrazzo mixtures, bitumen, synthetic resin or other composition mixtures to form flooring;

- examines premises to plan suitable layout and cuts, lays and secures underlay, carpet and linoleum;

- finishes covering by rolling, smoothing, grouting or polishing;

- mixes cement screed or other adhesive, cuts and positions floor and wall tiles and checks alignment of tiling with spirit level.

### RELATED JOB TITLES

Carpet fitter
Carpet layer
Carpet planner
Floor layer
Floor tiler
Tile setter (*building and contracting*)
Wall tiler

## 507 PAINTERS AND DECORATORS

Workers in this unit group apply paint, varnish, wallpaper and other protective and decorative materials to walls and ceilings, make signs and show-cards, paint designs and lettering on wood, glass, metal, plastics and other materials and stain, wax and french polish wood surfaces by hand.

### TYPICAL ENTRY ROUTES AND ASSOCIATED QUALIFICATIONS

Academic qualifications may not be required (but normal colour vision is necessary). Training is by apprenticeship.

### TASKS

- erects working platform or scaffolding up to five metres in height;

- prepares surfaces by cleaning, sanding and filling cracks and holes with appropriate filler;

- applies primer, undercoat and finishing coat(s) using brush, roller, or spray equipment;

- mixes adhesive or removes self-adhesive backing and positions covering material on wall, matching up patterns where appropriate and removing wrinkles and air bubbles by hand or brush;

- sketches outline of lettering or design onto surface and paints, or presses gold or similar leaf onto adhesive, as required to reproduce design;

- stains, waxes and french polishes wood surfaces by hand.

### RELATED JOB TITLES

Decorator
French polisher
House painter
Painter
Painter and decorator
Sign writer

## 509 OTHER CONSTRUCTION TRADES NEC

Workers in this unit group perform a variety of construction trades not elsewhere classified in MINOR GROUP 50: Construction Trades.

### TYPICAL ENTRY ROUTES AND ASSOCIATED QUALIFICATIONS

Entry may not depend on academic qualifications. Training is by apprenticeship.

### TASKS

- cuts, shapes and fits wood to form structures and fittings;

- lays bricks, tiles and building blocks to construct, repair and decorate buildings;

- installs, maintains and repairs electrical wiring and plumbing fixtures and appliances in buildings;

- pours and levels concrete and mixes and applies plaster and paint;

- covers and waterproofs roofs and cuts, fits and sets glass in frames;

- excavates and enlarges underground roadways and tunnels and sinks wells, other than in a coalmine, using hand and powered excavating equipment.

### RELATED JOB TITLES

Building worker
Jobbing builder
Maintenance hand (*building and contracting*)
Property repairer
Shaft sinker
Tunnel miner

# MINOR GROUP 51
# METAL MACHINING, FITTING AND INSTRUMENT MAKING TRADES

Metal machining, fitting and instrument making trades workers mark out metal for machine tool working, set up and operate lathes, boring, drilling, grinding, milling machines and presses, assemble and repair machine tools, install and repair plant and industrial machinery, fit and assemble parts and sub-assemblies in the manufacture of metal products, make, assemble and repair jewellery, precious metalware, precision instruments, watches and clocks and set, cut and polish gems.

Occupations in this minor group are classified into the following unit groups:

**510 CENTRE, CAPSTAN, TURRET AND OTHER LATHE SETTERS AND SETTER-OPERATORS**

**511 BORING AND DRILLING MACHINE SETTERS AND SETTER-OPERATORS**

**512 GRINDING MACHINE SETTERS AND SETTER-OPERATORS**

**513 MILLING MACHINE SETTERS AND SETTER-OPERATORS**

**514 PRESS SETTERS AND SETTER-OPERATORS**

**515 TOOL MAKERS, TOOL FITTERS AND MARKERS-OUT**

**516 METAL WORKING PRODUCTION AND MAINTENANCE FITTERS**

**517 PRECISION INSTRUMENT MAKERS AND REPAIRERS**

**518 GOLDSMITHS, SILVERSMITHS, PRECIOUS STONE WORKERS**

**519 OTHER MACHINE TOOL SETTERS AND SETTER-OPERATORS NEC (INCLUDING CNC SETTER-OPERATORS)**

## 510 CENTRE, CAPSTAN, TURRET AND OTHER LATHE SETTERS AND SETTER-OPERATORS

Centre, capstan, turret and other lathe setters and setter-operators set up and may operate centre, capstan, turret and other lathes to shape metal workpieces.

### TYPICAL ENTRY ROUTES AND ASSOCIATED QUALIFICATIONS

Some GCSE/SCE qualifications may be required. Training is usually via an apprenticeship including work experience and practical and technical training leading to recognised awards.

### TASKS

- examines drawings and specifications to determine appropriate method, sequence of operations and machine setting;

- selects and fixes appropriate cutting, shaping and/or forming tools;

- sets machine controls for rotation speeds, depth of cut and stroke, duration, etc.;

- operates machine to check accuracy of settings and makes any necessary adjustments;

- instructs operators on the safe and correct method of operation of the machine;

155

- changes tools and resets machine as necessary during production run.

## RELATED JOB TITLES

Capstan setter
Capstan setter-operator
Centre lathe turner
Lathe turner
Roll turner
Turner (*metal trades*)
Turret lathe turner

# 511 BORING AND DRILLING MACHINE SETTERS AND SETTER-OPERATORS

Boring and drilling machine setters and setter-operators set up and may operate boring and drilling machines to bore and drill metal workpieces.

## TYPICAL ENTRY ROUTES AND ASSOCIATED QUALIFICATIONS

Some GCSE/SCE qualifications may be required. Training is usually via an apprenticeship including work experience and practical and technical training leading to recognised awards.

## TASKS

- examines drawings and specifications to determine appropriate method and sequence of operations;

- selects and fixes appropriate work-holding devices and cutting tools;

- sets drill or boring machine controls for rotation speed, depth of stroke and adjusts machine table, stops and guides;

- operates drill or boring machine automatically or manually and checks accuracy of machining;

- repositions workpiece and changes bits and controls as necessary.

## RELATED JOB TITLES

Borer (*metal trades*)
Driller (*metal trades*)
Horizontal borer
Jig borer
Radial arm driller
Universal borer
Vertical borer

# 512 GRINDING MACHINE SETTERS AND SETTER-OPERATORS

Grinding machine setters and setter-operators set up and may operate grinding machines to shape or otherwise machine the surfaces of metal workpieces by means of a rotating grinding wheel.

## TYPICAL ENTRY ROUTES AND ASSOCIATED QUALIFICATIONS

Some GCSE/SCE qualifications may be required. Training is usually via an apprenticeship including work experience and practical and technical training leading to recognised awards.

## TASKS

- examines drawings and specifications to determine appropriate method and sequence of operations;

- selects and fixes appropriate work-holding devices and grinding tools;

- sets controls and trues cutting surface of grinding wheel;

- operates automatic or manual controls to feed tool to workpiece, or workpiece to tool and checks accuracy of machining;

- repositions workpiece and changes tools and machine controls as necessary.

## RELATED JOB TITLES

Grinder (*metal trades*)
Precision grinder
Surface grinder
Tool grinder
Universal grinder

## 513 MILLING MACHINE SETTERS AND SETTER-OPERATORS

Milling machine setters and setter-operators set up and may operate milling machines to cut or otherwise machine the surfaces of metal workpieces by means of one or more multi-toothed rotary cutting tools.

### TYPICAL ENTRY ROUTES AND ASSOCIATED QUALIFICATIONS

Some GCSE/SCE qualifications may be required. Training is usually via an apprenticeship including work experience and practical and technical training leading to recognised awards.

### TASKS

- examines drawings and specifications to determine appropriate method and sequence of operations;

- selects and fixes appropriate work-holding devices and cutting tools;

- sets controls and may copy a machined workpiece or model using tracer attachment;

- operates automatic or manual controls of milling machine and checks accuracy of machining;

- repositions workpiece and changes tools and machine controls as necessary.

### RELATED JOB TITLES

Gear cutter
Miller (*metal trades*)
Miller setter-operator
NC miller
Universal miller

## 514 PRESS SETTERS AND SETTER-OPERATORS

Press setters and setter-operators set up and may operate hand or power presses to shape and form metal workpieces.

### TYPICAL ENTRY ROUTES AND ASSOCIATED QUALIFICATIONS

Some GCSE/SCE qualifications may be required. Training is usually via an apprenticeship including work experience and practical and technical training leading to recognised awards.

### TASKS

- examines drawings and specifications to determine appropriate method and sequence of operations;

- calculates length of ram stroke and pressures involved;

- positions and secures workpieces on press;

- sets machine controls, adjusts stops and guides and may operate machine as appropriate;

- instructs operators on the safe and correct method of operation of the machine;

- changes press tools and dies and resets machine as necessary during production runs.

### RELATED JOB TITLES

Power press setter
Press setter-operator
Press tool setter

## 515 TOOL MAKERS, TOOL FITTERS AND MARKERS-OUT

Tool makers, tool fitters and markers-out mark out metal for machining and fit, assemble and repair machine and press tools, dies, jigs, fixtures and other tools.

### TYPICAL ENTRY ROUTES AND ASSOCIATED QUALIFICATIONS

Some GCSE/SCE qualifications may be required. Training is usually via an apprenticeship including work experience and practical and technical training leading to recognised awards.

## TASKS

- examines drawings and specifications to determine appropriate method and sequence of operations;

- marks out reference points using measuring instruments and tools such as punches, rules and squares;

- operates hand and machine tools to shape work-pieces to specifications and checks accuracy of machining;

- assembles prepared parts, checks their alignment with micrometers, optical projectors and other measuring equipment and adjusts as necessary;

- repairs damaged or worn tools.

## RELATED JOB TITLES

Die sinker (*metal trades*)
Jig and tool fitter
Marker off (*engineering*)
Tool maker (*metal trades*)
Toolroom fitter

# 516 METAL WORKING PRODUCTION AND MAINTENANCE FITTERS

Metal working production and maintenance fitters erect, install and repair electrical and mechanical plant and industrial machinery, fit and assemble parts and sub-assemblies in the manufacture of metal products and test and adjust new motor vehicles and engines.

## TYPICAL ENTRY ROUTES AND ASSOCIATED QUALIFICATIONS

Some GCSE/SCE qualifications may be required. Training is usually via an apprenticeship including work experience and practical and technical training leading to recognised awards. Further professional examinations are required to become a licensed aircraft engineer.

## TASKS

- examines drawings and specifications to determine appropriate methods and sequence of operations;

- fits and assembles parts and/or metal sub-assemblies to fine tolerances to make aircraft and marine engines, prototype metal products, agricultural machinery and machine tools;

- fits and assembles, other than to fine tolerances, prepared parts and sub-assemblies to make motor vehicles, printing and agricultural machinery, orthopaedic appliances and other metal goods;

- examines operation of, and makes adjustments to, internal combustion and jet engines and motor vehicles;

- erects, installs, repairs and services plant and industrial machinery, including railway stock, textile machines, aircraft frames and engines, coin operated machines, locks, sewing machines, bicycles and gas and oil appliances.

## RELATED JOB TITLES

Aircraft engineer
Aircraft fitter
Aircraft ground engineer
Bench fitter
Engineering fitter
Fitter and turner
Machine fitter
Maintenance fitter
Mechanic-fitter
Millwright
Plant fitter

# 517 PRECISION INSTRUMENT MAKERS AND REPAIRERS

Precision instrument makers and repairers make, calibrate, test and repair precision and optical instruments such as barometers, compasses, cameras, calibrators, watches, clocks and chronometers.

## TYPICAL ENTRY ROUTES AND ASSOCIATED QUALIFICATIONS

Some GCSE/SCE qualifications may be required. Training is usually via an apprenticeship including work experience and practical and technical training leading to recognised awards.

## TASKS

- examines drawings or specifications to determine appropriate methods, materials and sequence of operation;

- marks out and machines aluminium, brass, steel and plastics using machine tools such as grinders, lathes and shapers;

- tests watches and clocks for repair to diagnose faults and removes, repairs or replaces damaged and worn parts;

- tests completed timepiece for accuracy using electronic or other test equipment;

- carries out service tasks such as cleaning, oiling and regulating;

- checks prepared parts for accuracy using measuring equipment;

- assembles parts and adjusts as necessary using hand and machine tools;

- positions, aligns and secures optical lenses in mounts;

- tests, adjusts and repairs precision and optical instruments.

## RELATED JOB TITLES

Clockmaker
Horologist
Instrument maker
Instrument mechanic
Optical fitter
Precision instrument fitter
Precision instrument maker
Watch and clock repairer
Watchmaker

## 518 GOLDSMITHS, SILVERSMITHS, PRECIOUS STONE WORKERS

Goldsmiths, silversmiths and precious stone workers make and repair jewellery and precious metalware, set, cut and polish gems and other stones, decorate metalware and make master patterns for articles of jewellery.

## TYPICAL ENTRY ROUTES AND ASSOCIATED QUALIFICATIONS

GCSE/SCE qualifications are not usually required, though some may be required for full-time courses. Training is either by apprenticeship or study for a pre-vocational qualification. These range from craft to degree level awards.

## TASKS

- marks out and cleans stone and operates lathe, grinding wheel, or rotating disc to cut, shape and smooth stone;

- uses hand and machine tools to make mounts and then to set gems in prepared mounts;

- cuts blank metal pieces and uses hand and machine tools to beat, spin or form metal to required shape;

- assembles metal pieces by soldering, bolting, brazing and riveting to form tea services, tankards, jewellery and other precious metal articles;

- anneals, butts, decorates, etches out monographs, crests and designs using hand and machine tools;

- makes master pattern of articles using wood, wax, metal, or other materials.

## RELATED JOB TITLES

Diamond mounter
Diamond polisher
Gem setter
Goldsmith
Silversmith

## 519 OTHER MACHINE TOOL SETTERS AND SETTER-OPERATORS NEC (INCLUDING CNC SETTER-OPERATORS)

Other machine tool setters and setter-operators n.e.c. set up and may operate machine tools not otherwise specified to cut, grind, mill, turn, bore, drill or otherwise shape metal workpieces.

## TYPICAL ENTRY ROUTES AND ASSOCIATED QUALIFICATIONS

Some GCSE/SCE qualifications may be required. Training is usually via an apprenticeship including work experience and practical and technical training leading to recognised awards.

## TASKS

- examines drawings and specifications to determine appropriate method and sequence of operations;

- selects and fixes appropriate work-holding devices and tools;

- sets controls and adjusts machine table, stops and guides;

- operates automatic or manual controls to feed tool to workpiece, or workpiece to tool and checks accuracy of machining;

- repositions workpiece and changes tools and machine controls as necessary.

## RELATED JOB TITLES

Machine setter (*metal trades*)
Machine tool setter
Setter (*metal trades*)
Setter-operator (*metal trades*)
Tool setter-operator

# MINOR GROUP 52
# ELECTRICAL/ELECTRONIC TRADES

Electrical and electronic trade workers install wiring in road and rail vehicles and aircraft and assemble, install, maintain, test and repair electrical and electronic equipment, components and systems concerned with lighting, signalling, telecommunications, radio and television, computing and other commercial industrial and domestic functions.

Occupations in this minor group are classified into the following unit groups:

520 PRODUCTION FITTERS (ELECTRICAL/ELECTRONIC)
521 ELECTRICIANS, ELECTRICAL MAINTENANCE FITTERS
522 ELECTRICAL ENGINEERS (NOT PROFESSIONAL)
523 TELEPHONE FITTERS
524 CABLE JOINTERS, LINES REPAIRERS
525 RADIO, TV AND VIDEO ENGINEERS
526 COMPUTER ENGINEERS, INSTALLATION AND MAINTENANCE
529 OTHER ELECTRICAL/ELECTRONIC TRADES NEC

## 520 PRODUCTION FITTERS (ELECTRICAL/ELECTRONIC)

Production fitters fit, assemble, test and repair parts and/or sub-assemblies in the manufacture of electrical and electronic equipment.

### TYPICAL ENTRY ROUTES AND ASSOCIATED QUALIFICATIONS

Academic qualifications may not be required, though some GCSE/SCE qualifications are an advantage. Training is by apprenticeship including work experience and practical and technical training leading to recognised awards.

### TASKS

- examines drawings, specifications and wiring diagrams to determine method and sequence of operations;

- makes and modifies metal parts using hand and machine tools;

- assembles parts and sub-assemblies using hand tools and by brazing, riveting or welding;

- checks alignments during assembly using measuring instruments;

- selects, cuts and connects wire or cable to appropriate terminals/connectors by crimping, brazing, soldering or bolting;

- tests completed circuit and undertakes repair work as required.

### RELATED JOB TITLES

Electrical fitter
Electronic fitter
Production fitter (*electrical/electronic*)

## 521 ELECTRICIANS, ELECTRICAL MAINTENANCE FITTERS

Electricians and electrical maintenance fitters install, maintain and repair electrical wiring, fittings, plant, machinery and other equipment in rail vehicles, aircraft, theatres and other commercial, industrial or domestic premises.

161

Academic qualifications may not be required, though some GCSE/SCE qualifications are an advantage. Training is by apprenticeship including work experience and practical and technical training leading to recognised awards.

## TASKS

- examines drawings, wiring diagrams and specifications to determine appropriate method and sequence of operations;

- selects, cuts and lays wire and connects to socket, plug, or terminal by crimping, soldering, brazing, or bolting;

- cuts, bends, assembles and installs electrical conduit and plans cable runs in ships;

- installs fuse boxes, switches, generators, transformers, light sockets, power points, water heaters, illuminated signs, floodlights, spotlights, domestic and other electrical appliances;

- examines electrical plant or machinery, domestic appliances, aircraft equipment and office electrical machinery for faults using test equipment and dismantles and replaces worn parts and faulty wiring;

- rebuilds electrical equipment, tests for correct functioning and makes any necessary adjustments;

- operates lighting and sound systems in theatres, film and television studios.

## RELATED JOB TITLES

Electrical contractor
Electrician

## 522 ELECTRICAL ENGINEERS (NOT PROFESSIONAL)

Electrical engineers install, maintain and repair electrical plant and machinery and electrical wiring, fixtures and appliances in buildings and on site.

Academic qualifications may not be required, though some GCSE/SCE qualifications are an advantage. Training is by apprenticeship including work experience and practical and technical training leading to recognised awards.

## TASKS

- examines drawings, wiring diagrams and specifications to determine appropriate method and sequence of operations;

- selects, cuts and lays wire and connects to socket, plug, or terminal by crimping, soldering, brazing or bolting;

- cuts, bends, assembles and installs electrical conduit;

- installs plant and machinery and other electrical fixtures and appliances such as fuse boxes, switches, light sockets, etc.;

- examines electrical plant and machinery, aircraft and rail vehicle equipment for faults and dismantles and replaces worn parts or faulty wiring;

- rebuilds electrical equipment, tests for correct functioning and makes any necessary adjustments;

- operates lighting and sound systems in theatres, film and television studios.

## RELATED JOB TITLES

Electrical engineer (*not professional*)

## 523 TELEPHONE FITTERS

Telephone fitters install, maintain and repair public and private telephone systems.

## TYPICAL ENTRY ROUTES AND ASSOCIATED QUALIFICATIONS

Academic qualifications may not be required, though some GCSE/SCE qualifications are an advantage. Trainees are given both practical and technical training, attend courses and receive on-the-job training.

## TASKS

- installs internal cabling and wiring for telephone systems and fits and wires junction and distribution boxes;

- fixes connecting wires from underground and aerial lines to premises and connects cable terminals to inside wiring;

- installs telephones, switchboards and coin operated phone boxes;

- uses testing equipment to locate defective components of circuitry and makes any necessary repairs;

- tests installation and makes any further necessary adjustments.

## RELATED JOB TITLES

Telecommunications engineer (*telephones*)
Telephone installation engineer
Telephone technician

## 524 CABLE JOINTERS, LINES REPAIRERS

Cable jointers and lines repairers install, maintain, test and repair overhead, underground, surface and submarine electricity and telecommunications cables.

## TYPICAL ENTRY ROUTES AND ASSOCIATED QUALIFICATIONS

Academic qualifications may not be required, though some GCSE/SCE qualifications are an advantage. Trainees are given technical and practical training at special training centres.

## TASKS

- assists with the erection of wood poles or steel towers to carry overhead lines;

- removes protective sheath from cables, joins conductor wires by brazing, soldering or crimping and applies conductor insulation and protective coverings;

- connects and installs transformers, fuse gear, lightning arrestors, aircraft warning lights, cable boxes and other equipment;

- connects cables to test equipment and tests for balance, resistance, insulation and any defects;

- locates and repairs faults to lines and ancillary equipment.

## RELATED JOB TITLES

Cable jointer
Cable repairer (*electric*)
Overhead linesman
Overhead wireman

## 525 RADIO, TV AND VIDEO ENGINEERS

Radio, TV and video engineers service and repair domestic radios and television receivers.

## TYPICAL ENTRY ROUTES AND ASSOCIATED QUALIFICATIONS

Academic qualifications may not be required, though some GCSE/SCE qualifications are an advantage. Training is usually by apprenticeship including work experience and practical and technical training leading to recognised awards. Full-time courses are also available.

## TASKS

- examines equipment and observes reception to determine nature of defect;

- uses electronic testing equipment to diagnose faults and check voltages and resistance;

- dismantles equipment and repairs or replaces faulty components or wiring;

- re-assembles equipment, tests for correct functioning and makes any necessary further adjustments;

- carries out service tasks such as cleaning and insulation testing according to schedule.

## RELATED JOB TITLES

Radio and television engineer
Radio mechanic
Service engineer (*radio and television*)
Television engineer
Television service engineer
Video engineer (*service and repair*)

## 526 COMPUTER ENGINEERS, INSTALLATION AND MAINTENANCE

Computer engineers, installation and maintenance workers install, maintain and repair computer hardware.

### TYPICAL ENTRY ROUTES AND ASSOCIATED QUALIFICATIONS

Entry is most common with a BTEC/SCOTVEC national or higher national award or a degree. Trainees are sometimes recruited with GCSE/SCE qualifications and study for recognised technical awards part-time.

### TASKS

- examines drawings, specifications and wiring diagrams to determine appropriate method and sequence of operations;

- advises on heating, ventilation and electricity supply and installs computer equipment;

- locates and diagnoses faults by running test programmes and using measuring instruments;

- places prepared parts and sub-assemblies in position, checks alignment and secures with hand tools;

- adjusts replaces or repairs worn or defective components;

- carries out preventative servicing tasks such as cleaning equipment and monitoring equipment operation.

### RELATED JOB TITLES

Computer engineer
Computer maintenance engineer
Computer service engineer
Computer service technician

## 529 OTHER ELECTRICAL/ELECTRONIC TRADES NEC

Workers in this group perform a variety of electrical and electronic occupations not elsewhere classified in MINOR GROUP 52: Electrical/Electronic Trades.

### TYPICAL ENTRY ROUTES AND ASSOCIATED QUALIFICATIONS

Academic qualifications may not be required, though some GCSE/SCE qualifications are an advantage. Training is usually by apprenticeship including work experience and practical and technical training leading to recognised awards. Full-time courses are also available in some trades.

### TASKS

- examines drawings, wiring diagrams and specifications to determine appropriate methods and sequence of operations;

- places prepared parts and sub-assemblies in position, checks their alignment and secures with hand tools to install x-ray and medical equipment, aircraft instruments and other electronic equipment not elsewhere classified;

- connects wire or cable to specified terminals or connectors by crimping, brazing, bolting or soldering;

- examines for defect and repairs, x-ray equipment, aircraft and ground control electronic equipment, teleprinters, accounting machines, dictating machines, electronic test equipment, railway electrical signalling equipment, sound and television transmission equipment, radar equipment, microwave ovens, metal detectors, medical equipment and other electronic and related equipment not elsewhere classified;

- tests for correct functioning and makes any further necessary adjustments;

- performs routine service tasks, such as cleaning and insulation testing.

### RELATED JOB TITLES

Alarm engineer
Electronic engineer (*maintenance*)
Service engineer (*office machines*)
Signal technician (*railways*)

# MINOR GROUP 53
# METAL FORMING, WELDING AND RELATED TRADES

Metal forming, welding and related trades workers shape, cast, finish and join metal and erect, install, maintain and repair metal structures and fixtures.

Occupations in this minor group are classified into the following unit groups:

530 SMITHS AND FORGE WORKERS

531 MOULDERS, CORE MAKERS, DIE CASTERS

532 PLUMBERS, HEATING AND VENTILATING ENGINEERS AND RELATED TRADES

533 SHEET METAL WORKERS

534 METAL PLATE WORKERS, SHIPWRIGHTS, RIVETERS

535 STEEL ERECTORS

536 BARBENDERS, STEEL FIXERS

537 WELDING TRADES

## 530 SMITHS AND FORGE WORKERS

Smith and forge workers operate or direct the operation of power hammers and presses to shape heated metal to requirements and to make and repair a variety of metal articles by heating, hammering and bending.

### TYPICAL ENTRY ROUTES AND ASSOCIATED QUALIFICATIONS

Some GCSE/SCE qualifications are usually required. Training is by apprenticeship including work experience and practical and technical training leading to recognised awards.

### TASKS

- heats or supervises the heating of metal to be forged in furnace;

- positions or directs the positioning of heated metal on anvil or other work surface;

- operates or directs operation of press or hammer and repositions workpiece between strokes;

- holds special forging tools against workpiece to shape and cut metal as required;

- bends or shapes metal by hand forging methods using hammers, punches, drifts and other hand tools;

- tempers and hardens forged pieces, as required, by quenching in oil or water;

- fits and secures horses shoes.

### RELATED JOB TITLES

Blacksmith
Farrier
Forger
Smith

## 531 MOULDERS, CORE MAKERS, DIE CASTERS

Moulders, core makers and die casters make sand, loam and plaster moulds and cores for casting metal and pour or inject molten metal into dies by hand or machine.

TYPICAL ENTRY ROUTES AND
ASSOCIATED QUALIFICATIONS

Some GCSE/SCE qualifications are usually required. Training is by apprenticeship including work experience and practical and technical training leading to recognised awards.

## TASKS

- positions moulding frame over pattern, fills it with sand, loam, or plaster and compacts by hand or machine;

- transfers mould unit to oven for baking or hardens by injecting carbon dioxide;

- separates mould from pattern and repairs damaged mould surfaces;

- applies refractory bonding solution to moulds and dies to prevent molten metal fusing with sand;

- fits cores in mould to form hollow parts in casting;

- prepares casting pit with vents to allow the escape of gases.

- scoops molten metal from furnace using ladle and pours it into die or die casting machine.

## RELATED JOB TITLES

Core moulder
Coremaker (*metal trades*)
Die caster
Floor moulder
Moulder and coremaker (*foundry*)

## 532 PLUMBERS, HEATING AND VENTILATING ENGINEERS AND RELATED TRADES

Workers in this unit group assemble, install, maintain and repair plumbing fixtures, heating and ventilating systems and pipes and pipeline systems in commercial, residential and industrial establishments.

TYPICAL ENTRY ROUTES AND
ASSOCIATED QUALIFICATIONS

Some GCSE/SCE qualifications are usually required. Training is by apprenticeship including work experience and practical and technical training leading to recognised awards.

## TASKS

- examines drawings and specifications to determine layout of system;

- measures and cuts required lengths of copper, lead, steel, iron, aluminium or plastic using hand or machine tools;

- installs fittings such as storage tanks, cookers, baths, toilets, taps and valves, refrigerators, boilers, radiators, fires and drainage pipes;

- tests completed installation for leaks and makes any necessary adjustments;

- attaches fittings and joins piping by welding, soldering, cementing, fusing, screwing or other methods;

- repairs burst pipes and mechanical and combustion faults, clears blocked drains and replaces faulty taps, washers, valves, etc.

## RELATED JOB TITLES

Central heating engineer
Gas fitter
Heating engineer
Pipe fitter
Pipe fitter welder
Plumber
Plumbing and heating engineer

## 533 SHEET METAL WORKERS

Sheet metal workers mark out, cut, shape and join sheet metal using hand or machine tools, to make and repair sheet metal products and components (excluding vehicle bodywork).

TYPICAL ENTRY ROUTES AND
ASSOCIATED QUALIFICATIONS

Some GCSE/SCE qualifications are usually required. Training is by apprenticeship including work experience and practical and technical training leading to recognised awards.

## TASKS

- examines drawings and specifications to assess job requirements;

- uses template, measuring instruments and tools to mark out layout lines and reference points;

- cuts sheet metal to markings using hand tools, power shears or guillotine;

- uses hand or machine tools to bend, roll, fold, press or beat cut sheet metal;

- assembles prepared parts and joins them by bolting, welding, or soldering;

- finishes product by grinding, filing, cleaning and polishing;

- repairs damaged metal parts such as copper sheets and tubes by beating, riveting, soldering, welding and fitting replacement parts.

## RELATED JOB TITLES

Coppersmith
Metal finisher
Panel beater (*metal trades*)
Sheet metal worker

## 534  METAL PLATE WORKERS, SHIPWRIGHTS, RIVETERS

Metal plate workers, shipwrights and riveters mark off, drill, shape, position, rivet and seal metal plates and girders to form structures and frameworks.

## TYPICAL ENTRY ROUTES AND ASSOCIATED QUALIFICATIONS

Some GCSE/SCE qualifications are usually required.  Training is by apprenticeship including work experience and practical and technical training leading to recognised awards.

## TASKS

- examines drawings and specifications and uses rules, scribes and punches to mark out metal plate with guidelines and reference points;

- cuts metal plate to markings using hand or machine tools;

- uses machine tools to bend, curve, punch, drill and straighten metal plate as required;

- uses hydraulic jacks to position and align metal platework or frame for welding and bolting;

- selects suitable rivets and rivets together metal plates and girders;

- seals seams with caulking compound, smoothes welds, fixes metal doors, metal collars, portholes, tank and hatch covers and performs other metal plate finishing tasks using a variety of hand and power tools.

## RELATED JOB TITLES

Boilermaker
Caulker-burner
Plater-welder
Shipwright

## 535  STEEL ERECTORS

Steel erectors fit and erect structural metal framework for buildings and other structures such as chimneys.

## TYPICAL ENTRY ROUTES AND ASSOCIATED QUALIFICATIONS

Some GCSE/SCE qualifications may be required. In-company training schemes are usual.

## TASKS

- examines drawings and specifications to assess job requirements;

- erects ladders, scaffolding or working cage;

- directs hoisting and positioning of girders and other metal parts and checks alignment;

- arranges for or undertakes bolting and welding of metal parts;

- checks alignment of metal parts using spirit level and plumb-rule.

## 536  BARBENDERS, STEEL FIXERS

Barbenders and steel fixers make up metal framework by hand to form reinforcing core for concrete structures of products.

### TYPICAL ENTRY ROUTES AND ASSOCIATED QUALIFICATIONS

Some GCSE/SCE qualifications may be required together with an aptitude assessment. Training is by apprenticeship including work experience and practical and technical training leading to recognised awards.

### TASKS

- examines drawings and specifications to determine job requirements;

- selects, measures and cuts steel bars, rods, wire or wire mesh to required lengths;

- positions and fixes reinforcing bars, rods, etc. on site, in mould or through channel in concrete and links with metal clips, wire or tension rods;

- tensions reinforcing wire as required using hydraulic jacks.

### RELATED JOB TITLES

Barbender
Steel fixer (*building and contracting*)

## 537  WELDING TRADES

Welding trades workers join metal parts by welding, brazing and soldering and cut and remove defects from metal using a variety of equipment and techniques.

### TYPICAL ENTRY ROUTES AND ASSOCIATED QUALIFICATIONS

Some GCSE/SCE qualifications may be required. Training is by an apprenticeship including work experience and practical and technical training leading to recognised awards.

### TASKS

- selects appropriate welding equipment such as electric arc, gas torch, etc.;

- connects wires to power supply, or hoses to oxygen, acetylene, argon, carbon dioxide, electric arc, or other source and adjusts controls to regulate gas pressure and rate of flow;

- guides electrode or torch along line of weld, burns away damaged areas, and melts brazing alloy or solder into joints;

- cleans and smoothes weld.

### RELATED JOB TITLES

Arc welder
Electric welder
Fitter-welder
Solderer
Spot welder
Welder

# MINOR GROUP 54
# VEHICLE TRADES

Vehicle trades workers repair, service and maintain the bodies, engines, parts, sub-assemblies, internal trimmings, upholstery and exterior surfaces of vehicles.

Occupations in this minor group are classified into the following unit groups;

**540  MOTOR MECHANICS, AUTO ENGINEERS
(INCLUDING ROAD PATROL ENGINEERS)**

**541  COACH AND VEHICLE BODY BUILDERS**

**542  VEHICLE BODY REPAIRERS, PANEL BEATERS**

**543  AUTO ELECTRICIANS**

**544  TYRE AND EXHAUST FITTERS**

## 540  MOTOR MECHANICS, AUTO ENGINEERS (INC. ROAD PATROL ENGINEERS)

Motor mechanics and auto engineers accept calls for help and repair and service the mechanical parts of cars, lorries, buses, motorcycles and other motor vehicles.

### TYPICAL ENTRY ROUTES AND ASSOCIATED QUALIFICATIONS

Academic qualifications are not essential, though some GCSE/SCE S-grades are an advantage. Trainees are given work experience and practical and technical training leading to recognised awards. Full-time BTEC/SCOTVEC courses are also available. Separate training is given for light or heavy vehicles or motor cycles.

### TASKS

- may drive to site of breakdown and visually checks, test drives or uses test equipment to diagnose engine and mechanical faults;

- removes, dismantles and checks the appropriate parts, systems or entire engine;

- repairs and replaces defective parts;

- prepares new parts using hand and machine tools;

- reassembles, tests, adjusts and tunes the appropriate parts, systems or entire engine;

- carries out routine maintenance checks on oil and air filters, brakes and other vehicle parts/systems.

### RELATED JOB TITLES

Car mechanic
Diesel vehicle fitter
Garage mechanic
Motor fitter
Motor mechanic
Motor vehicle technician
Motorcycle mechanic
Vehicle mechanic
Vehicle patrolman/woman
Vehicles fitter

## 541  COACH AND VEHICLE BODY BUILDERS

Coach and vehicle body builders construct bodies for road vehicles or railway coaches and fix interior and exterior fittings to aircraft and vehicle bodies.

### TYPICAL ENTRY ROUTES AND ASSOCIATED QUALIFICATIONS

Academic qualifications may not be required. Trainees are given work experience and practical and technical training leading to recognised awards.

## TASKS

- diagnoses job requirements or ascertains work specifications from drawings or instructions;

- selects, cuts, bends and shapes materials to form parts of vehicle underframe, framework and body;

- machines, bolts, welds, rivets and otherwise assembles sheet metal, wood, glass fibre and plastic laminate parts;

- positions, secures and repairs external fittings including windows, doors, door handles, catches and roof attachments;

- installs and repairs interior fittings including seats, seatbelts and panelling in cars, sinks and special features in caravans and mobile shops and bulkheads in aircraft.

## RELATED JOB TITLES

Body builder (*vehicles*)
Body maker (*vehicles*)
Coach builder
Coach finisher
Commercial vehicle body builder
Vehicle builder
Vehicle body builder

## 542  VEHICLE BODY REPAIRERS, PANEL BEATERS

Vehicle body repairers and panel beaters repair the bodies and chassis of damaged motor vehicles.

### TYPICAL ENTRY ROUTES AND ASSOCIATED QUALIFICATIONS

Academic qualifications may not be required. Trainees are given work experience and practical and technical training leading to recognised awards.

## TASKS

- beats out dents in bodywork using hammer and blocks;

- fills small depressions with solder, plastic, or other filler compound;

- repairs damage to chassis and engine mountings using hydraulic rams, jacks and jigs;

- rivets and welds replacement panels into position using hand and power tools;

- prepares and smoothes surfaces for painting and mixes paint to correct colour specification;

- applies paint by spray or brush.

## RELATED JOB TITLES

Panel beater (*vehicle repair*)
Vehicle body repairer

## 543  AUTO ELECTRICIANS

Auto electricians repair and service the electrical/electronic circuitry and components of cars, lorries, buses, motorcycles and other motor vehicles.

### TYPICAL ENTRY ROUTES AND ASSOCIATED QUALIFICATIONS

Some GCSE/SCE qualifications may be required. Trainees are given work experience and practical and technical training leading to recognised awards. Full-time BTEC/SCOTVEC courses are also available.

## TASKS

- uses portable and bench test equipment to diagnose faults in electrical/electronic circuitry;

- removes faulty components and fits replacements using hand tools and by simple brazing/soldering;

- makes new parts using hand and machine tools;

- checks condition of electrical/electronic systems and carries out servicing tasks;

- installs additional electrical amenities such as radio/cassette players, aerials and radio suppressors.

## RELATED JOB TITLES

Auto electrician
Automobile electrician

## 544 TYRE AND EXHAUST FITTERS

Tyre and exhaust fitters fit, repair and adjust tyres and exhausts on cars, buses, motorcycles and other motor vehicles.

## TYPICAL ENTRY ROUTES AND ASSOCIATED QUALIFICATIONS

Academic qualifications may not be required. Training is mostly on-the-job learning from experienced fitters. Training varies according to the equipment used and the range of vehicles worked on.

## TASKS

- carries out inspection and assesses the nature and extent of repair necessary;

- raises vehicle on ramp or hydraulic jack and removes wheel or exhaust using semi-automatic machinery or hand and power tools;

- replaces faulty parts and/or refits exhaust;

- separates tyre from wheel and fits replacement tyre using automatic machine or by using a wheel stand and hand tools;

- inflates tyre to correct pressure, refits wheel to axle and balances wheel using balancing machine.

## RELATED JOB TITLES

Tyre and exhaust fitter
Tyre fitter
Vehicle exhaust fitter

# MINOR GROUP 55
# TEXTILES, GARMENTS AND RELATED TRADES

Textiles, garments and related trades workers prepare textile fibres, make textile products by spinning, weaving, knitting and other techniques, repair shoes and garments, prepare, cut out and sew patterns and upholster furniture .

Occupations in this minor group are classified into the following unit groups:

550 WEAVERS

551 KNITTERS

552 WARP PREPARERS, BLEACHERS, DYERS AND FINISHERS

553 SEWING MACHINISTS, MENDERS, DARNERS
    AND EMBROIDERERS

554 COACH TRIMMERS, UPHOLSTERERS AND MATTRESS MAKERS

555 SHOE REPAIRERS, LEATHER CUTTERS AND SEWERS,
    FOOTWEAR LASTERS, MAKERS AND FINISHERS,
    OTHER LEATHER MAKING AND REPAIRING

556 TAILORS AND DRESSMAKERS

557 CLOTHING CUTTERS, MILLINERS, FURRIERS

559 OTHER TEXTILES, GARMENTS AND RELATED TRADES NEC

## 550 WEAVERS

Weavers set up and operate or attend hand and power looms to weave natural and synthetic fibres into fabric and carpet.

### TYPICAL ENTRY ROUTES AND ASSOCIATED QUALIFICATIONS

Entry may not depend on academic qualifications. Training is mainly on-the-job.

### TASKS

- prepares loom by installing required attachments and mounting spools;

- ties new pile and warp ends to corresponding old ends and draws them through appropriate guides and tensioners;

- positions pile and warp yarn beams and packages of feedstock;

- sets metre counter, starts loom or operates foot treadle and monitors its operation;

- examines fabric/carpet being woven to check pattern, evenness of warp tension and to detect broken threads;

- pulls out and replaces broken weft threads (picks) and repairs breaks in yarn;

- cleans and oils machine and reports any mechanical faults.

### RELATED JOB TITLES

Carpet weaver
Pattern weaver
Textile weaver
Weaver

## 551 KNITTERS

Knitters set up and operate or attend hand and power operated machines to knit fabric, garments and other articles from yarn.

Entry may not depend on academic qualifications.
Training is mainly on-the-job.

## TASKS

- places yarn packages on spindles/machine and thread ends through guides and tensioners;

- sets machine controls to produce article of specified size and pattern;

- starts and stops machine as required, or moves carriage across needle bed by hand;

- monitors operation to detect yarn breaks or faulty knitting;

- completes or reinforces garment by hand if necessary.

- cleans and oils machine and reports any mechanical faults;

## RELATED JOB TITLES

Hosiery worker
Knitter

# 552 WARP PREPARERS, BLEACHERS, DYERS AND FINISHERS

Warp preparers, bleachers, dyers and finishers operate machines to wind warp yarn onto packages and beams, prepare yarn for dyeing, knitting or weaving and then bleach, dye, finish or otherwise treat textile fibres, yarn, hosiery, etc.

## TYPICAL ENTRY ROUTES AND ASSOCIATED QUALIFICATIONS

Entry may not depend on academic qualifications.
Training is mainly on-the-job.

## TASKS

- prepares hand or power operated warp winding machine to draw warp threads through eyelets, guides and reeds ready for knitting, weaving and dyeing;

- joins new warp to old warp by hand twisting and/or mechanical knotting;

- prepares dye, bleaching, starching, water repellent, fixing salt and other chemical solutions;

- operates controls to regulate temperature, flow and treatment times;

- monitors operation to detect broken or tangled threads and to assess the evenness of dyeing/bleaching/finishing;

- stretches, shrinks, brushes, dampens and presses fabric and shears or burns off protruding fabric fibres as required;

- cleans machine and reports any mechanical faults.

## RELATED JOB TITLES

Beamer (*textile mfr*)
Cloth finisher
Crimper (*textile mfr*)
Dyer (*textile mfr*)
Reeder
Stenterer
Warper

# 553 SEWING MACHINISTS, MENDERS, DARNERS AND EMBROIDERERS

Workers in this unit group rectify faults in manufactured textile goods, repair worn garments and sew and embroider garments by hand or machine.

## TYPICAL ENTRY ROUTES AND ASSOCIATED QUALIFICATIONS

Entry may not depend on academic qualifications.
Training is mainly on-the-job.

## TASKS

- examines natural and synthetic fabrics of all types to identify imperfections and determine best method of repair;

- operates standard and specialised machines to sew and repair garments and other textile, fabric, fur and skin products;

- performs hand sewing tasks in the making and finishing of fur, sheepskin, leather, upholstery, mats, carpets, umbrellas and other textile products;

- embroiders decorative designs on, or secures trimmings to, textile fabric with hand or machine stitching;

- cleans and oils machine and reports or remedies any mechanical faults.

## RELATED JOB TITLES

Burler
Darner (*textile mfr*)
Embroiderer
Hand sewer
Lockstitch machinist
Mender (*textile mfr*)
Sample machinist
Seamstress
Sewing machinist (*clothing mfr*)

## 554 COACH TRIMMERS, UPHOLSTERERS AND MATTRESS MAKERS

Coach trimmers, upholsterers and mattress makers upholster vehicle, aircraft and other seating, fix trimmings to the interiors of vehicles and aircraft and make mattresses, curtains and other soft furniture.

## TYPICAL ENTRY ROUTES AND ASSOCIATED QUALIFICATIONS

Entry may not depend on academic qualifications. Training is mainly on-the-job.

## TASKS

- measures frame to be covered or examines drawings or other specifications and cuts material with shears, knife or scissors;

- tacks and staples or otherwise secures webbing to furniture frame;

- pads springs and secures padding by stitching, stapling, tacking, etc.;

- pins sections of coverings together, joins by sewing and inserts trims, braids and buttons as required;

- operates machine to compress padded spring assemblies and inserts them into mattress covers;

- encases bed springs and padding with selected covering material by hand or machine stitching and fits castors where required;

- fits upholstery unit to frame or replaces covering, padding, webbing or springs to repair upholstered furniture.

## RELATED JOB TITLES

Coach trimmer
Interior sprung mattress maker
Upholsterer

## 555 SHOE REPAIRERS, LEATHER CUTTERS AND SEWERS, FOOTWEAR LASTERS, MAKERS AND FINISHERS, OTHER LEATHER MAKING AND REPAIRING

Workers in this unit group repair shoes, cut out, make up, sew, decorate and finish leather and leather substitute goods other than garments.

## TYPICAL ENTRY ROUTES AND ASSOCIATED QUALIFICATIONS

Entry may not depend on academic qualifications. Training is mainly on-the-job.

## TASKS

- cuts off worn heels and soles, cuts replacements and sews, nails or glues them onto shoe, replaces insoles, rubber and steel tips and smoothes and finishes repair;

- uses hand tools or machine to cut out, trim, punch holes in or stitch guide lines on leather or leather substitute component parts;

- positions leather and rubber footwear component parts on lasts and shapes and joins uppers to insoles and soles;

- uses hand tools or machine to make up and repair saddles, harnesses, belts, straps and other leather products;

- uses hand and machine tools to sew and stitch leather in the making and decoration of footwear and leather goods other than garments;

- prepares paper or paperboard master patterns of component parts of footwear;

- waxes, cleans and finishes footwear and other leather goods.

## RELATED JOB TITLES

Clicker (*footwear mfr*)
Cobbler
Laster
Saddler
Shoe repairer
Shoemaker

## 556 TAILORS AND DRESSMAKERS

Tailors and dressmakers prepare patterns and make, fit and alter tailored garments, dresses and other articles of light clothing.

## TYPICAL ENTRY ROUTES AND ASSOCIATED QUALIFICATIONS

Entry may not depend on academic qualifications. Training is mainly on-the-job. Apprenticeships may be available.

## TASKS

- takes customer's measurements and discusses required style and material;

- prepares individual or adapts stock pattern;

- arranges pattern on correct grain of fabric, in most economical layout, marks position and cuts out garment parts with shears;

- pins garment on customer or dummy model and makes any necessary alterations;

- sews garment parts together by hand or machine, makes buttonholes and sews on fasteners and trimmings;

- shapes garment by pressing seams, pleats, etc.;

- determines any necessary alterations and removes or inserts stitching, lengthens or shortens garment parts and adjusts seams, darts, etc. as required.

## RELATED JOB TITLES

Alteration hand
Dressmaker
Tailor/ess

## 557 CLOTHING CUTTERS, MILLINERS, FURRIERS

Clothing cutters cut out material for garment making. Milliners and furriers make fur garments and womens or childrens hats.

## TYPICAL ENTRY ROUTES AND ASSOCIATED QUALIFICATIONS

Entry does not depend on academic qualifications. Training is mainly on-the-job.

## TASKS

- examines and estimates fabrics or skins for flaws, grain and stretch;

- cuts out blemishes, brushes, combs and moistens skins;

- discusses customer's requirements or examines photographs or sketches of hat or garment;

- marks out or cuts garment parts and linings;

- shapes, moulds and glues hat foundation;

- arranges covering material over foundation and stretches, moulds, steams, sews or glues to required shape;

- sews in stiffeners, lining and headband.

## RELATED JOB TITLES

Bandknife cutter
Clothing cutter
Furrier (*not retail trades*)
Garment cutter
Marker (*clothing mfr*)
Milliner (*not retail trades*)
Nailer (*fur goods*)
Tailor's cutter

## 559  OTHER TEXTILES, GARMENTS AND RELATED TRADES NEC

Workers in this unit group perform a variety of textiles and related craft occupations not elsewhere classified in MINOR GROUP 55: Textiles, Garments and Related Trades.

## TYPICAL ENTRY ROUTES AND ASSOCIATED QUALIFICATIONS

Entry may not depend on academic qualifications. Training is mainly on-the-job.

## TASKS

- marks out, cuts and sews corsets, light clothing and hoods and aprons and makes and repairs sails, boat covers and other canvas goods;

- fills and stuffs cushions, quilts, soft toys and furniture;

- examines sketches and draws out patterns for the manufacture of garments and upholstery;

- shapes and steams fabric into hats or hoods and gives final shape to fibre helmets and felt hats;

- performs other tasks not elsewhere classified, for example, forms mounts for wigs, makes powder puffs and buttons, shapes hat brims, and staples seams of industrial gloves.

## RELATED JOB TITLES

Corsetiere
Cushion filler
Felt hat finisher
Sailmaker

# MINOR GROUP 56
# PRINTING AND RELATED TRADES

Printing and related trades workers compose and set type and printing blocks, produce printing plates, cylinders and film, operate printing machines and bind the finished printed product.

Occupations in this minor group are classified into the following unit groups:

**560 ORIGINATORS, COMPOSITORS AND PRINT PREPARERS**

**561 PRINTERS**

**562 BOOKBINDERS AND PRINT FINISHERS**

**563 SCREEN PRINTERS**

**569 OTHER PRINTING AND RELATED TRADES NEC**

## 560 ORIGINATORS, COMPOSITORS AND PRINT PREPARERS

Originators, compositors and print preparers prepare printing layouts, compose and assemble metal type and other materials, make printing plates from moulds, set out photographed material, transfer film images to plates or cylinders and lay out printing copy to be photographed.

### TYPICAL ENTRY ROUTES AND ASSOCIATED QUALIFICATIONS

Academic qualifications may not be required. Training is by apprenticeship.

### TASKS

- lays sheet of plastic, rubber, wax or pulp board on former and passes under hydraulic press to form mould;

- determines from specification the kind and size of type to be used and prepares page layout;

- arranges lines of type in composing stick and operates keyboard of perforating, composing, computer or filmsetting machine;

- examines proof copies and makes any necessary alterations to type;

- processes output from filmsetting machine to produce image on film or sensitised paper;

- chemically treats plates and cylinders to produce film positives;

- arranges and pastes printing material onto paper ready for photographing.

### RELATED JOB TITLES

Compositor
Lino type operator
Lithographic planner
Lithographic plate maker
Paste-up artist
Photoengraver
Stereotyper
Type setter

## 561 PRINTERS

Printers operate printing presses, prepare printing plates and compose and assemble type and printing blocks.

### TYPICAL ENTRY ROUTES AND ASSOCIATED QUALIFICATIONS

Academic qualifications may not be required. Training is by apprenticeship.

## TASKS

- examines customer's requirements to determine appropriate format and kind and size of type;

- prepares composed type or printing plate according to type of press used;

- positions forme or plate on machine, sets press and prints proof copies;

- examines proof copies and adjusts press as necessary;

- starts or directs start of printing run and ensures that printing proceeds smoothly.

## RELATED JOB TITLES

General printer
Master printer
Printer

## 562  BOOKBINDERS AND PRINT FINISHERS

Bookbinders and print finishers bind and/or finish printed products by hand or machine.

## TYPICAL ENTRY ROUTES AND ASSOCIATED QUALIFICATIONS

Academic qualifications may not be required. Training may be by apprenticeship.

## TASKS

- folds, collates and sews printed sheets by hand or machine;

- compresses sewn book in nipping machine to expel air and reduce swelling caused by sewing;

- trims head, tail and fore-edge of book and gilds and marbles page edges as necessary;

- cuts board and cloth for book cover and spine;

- embosses lettering or decoration on cover by hand or machine;

- repairs worn book bindings.

## RELATED JOB TITLES

Binder's assistant
Book finisher (*printing*)
Bookbinder
Collator (*printing*)

## 563  SCREEN PRINTERS

Screen printers set and operate screen printing machines and print lettering and designs on metal, glass, plastics, paper and other materials by hand or machine.

## TYPICAL ENTRY ROUTES AND ASSOCIATED QUALIFICATIONS

No formal academic qualifications are required. Training is by apprenticeship.

## TASKS

- positions item for printing against guide marks on work bench;

- pours colour into machine or directly onto screen and positions screen over item;

- operates squeegee by hand or machine to press colour through screen;

- dips wooden pattern block into colour tray and lays different colours on top of, and adjacent to, others to form the required pattern;

- examines screen print during run and makes any necessary adjustments.

## RELATED JOB TITLES

Block printer
Screen printer
Silk screen printer

## 569  OTHER PRINTING AND RELATED TRADES NEC

Workers in this unit group perform a variety of printing and related occupations not elsewhere classified in MINOR GROUP 56: Printing and Related Trades.

## TYPICAL ENTRY ROUTES AND ASSOCIATED QUALIFICATIONS

Academic qualifications may not be required. Training is by apprenticeship or is on-the-job according to occupation.

## TASKS

- sets and/or operates presses printing proof copies and die stamping, paper and textiles printing, embossing, roll mounting, spooling, paper pattern cutting, duplicating and footwear marking machines;

- transfers outline of lettering or design onto roller, cylinder, plate or die using varnish, gelatine sheets or a copper roller machine;

- cuts out design using hand graving tools or a pantographic machine;

- arranges, cuts, develops, prints and mounts negative film and cleans, reconditions and retouches negatives and finished prints;

- assists with the preparation of printing screens, wallpaper, textile printing and paper, paper board and carton making machines;

- performs other tasks not elsewhere classified, including stamping pottery, cutting stencils for use in screen printing, making up hand samples of paper or paper board products and reproducing master patterns for footwear and garments.

## RELATED JOB TITLES

Grader (*photographic processing*)
Prover
Retoucher

179

# MINOR GROUP 57
# WOODWORKING TRADES

Woodworking trades workers construct, erect, install, repair and renovate wooden furniture, structures and fittings on site or on ships and cut, shape, carve, bend and assemble wood to make templates, jigs, models, patterns and block floors.

Occupations in this minor group are classified into the following unit groups:

> 570 CARPENTERS AND JOINERS
> 571 CABINET MAKERS
> 572 CASE AND BOX MAKERS
> 573 PATTERN MAKERS (MOULDS)
> 579 OTHER WOODWORKING TRADES NEC

## 570 CARPENTERS AND JOINERS

Carpenters and joiners construct, erect, install and repair wooden structures and fittings used in internal and external frameworks and cut, shape, fit and assemble wood to make templates, jigs, scale models and scenic equipment for theatres.

### TYPICAL ENTRY ROUTES AND ASSOCIATED QUALIFICATIONS

Academic qualifications may not be required. Training is by apprenticeship.

### TASKS

- examines drawings and specifications to determine job requirements;

- selects and measures appropriate wood and cuts, shapes and drills to specification using saws, planes, chisels and other power or hand tools;

- aligns and fixes prepared wood pieces by screwing, nailing, glueing and dowelling to form frames, shop fronts, counter units, decking, theatrical sets, furniture, small wooden craft, scale models and wooden templates;

- checks accuracy of work with square, rule and spirit level;

- maintains and repairs woodwork and fittings.

### RELATED JOB TITLES

Boat builder
Builder's joiner
Carpenter
Carpenter and joiner
Shop fitter

## 571 CABINET MAKERS

Cabinet makers make and repair wooden furniture and piano and cabinet cases.

### TYPICAL ENTRY ROUTES AND ASSOCIATED QUALIFICATIONS

Academic qualifications may not be required. Training is by apprenticeship.

### TASKS

- examines drawings and specifications to determine job requirements;

- selects, measures, cuts and shapes wood using saws, chisels, planes, powered hand tools and woodworking machines;

- fits parts together to form cabinets, tables, drawers, chairs and piano cases;

- reinforces joints with nails, screws or dowels and fits locks, catches, hinges, castors, drawers or shelves;

- removes and replaces or repairs damaged parts of wooden furniture.

## RELATED JOB TITLES

Antiques restorer
Cabinet maker
Coffin maker
Furniture fitter

## 572  CASE AND BOX MAKERS

Case and box makers make, assemble and repair wood to make packing cases, crates, barrels or casks.

## TYPICAL ENTRY ROUTES AND ASSOCIATED QUALIFICATIONS

Academic qualifications may not be required. Training is by apprenticeship.

## TASKS

- examines written instructions and specifications to determine job requirements;

- selects measures, cuts and shapes wood using planes, chisels and powered hand tools;

- assembles parts of container by bolting, nailing, clipping and stapling or uses temporary hoop to draw staves together to make barrels;

- makes up bases and lids as required and fits metal strips, corner pieces, wire or wooden hoops to strengthen the container;

- repairs barrels and casks by removing and replacing damaged staves.

## RELATED JOB TITLES

Box maker (*wood*)
Case maker
Cooper
Crate maker
Pallet maker

## 573  PATTERN MAKERS (MOULDS)

Pattern makers (moulds) make patterns from wood, metal, plaster and plastics for use in making moulds for metal castings.

## TYPICAL ENTRY ROUTES AND ASSOCIATED QUALIFICATIONS

Academic qualifications may not be required. Training is by apprenticeship.

## TASKS

- examines drawings and specifications to determine job requirements and appropriate materials;

- selects, measures, cuts and shapes wood using hand and machine tools to form wooden patterns;

- machines and fits metal castings and/or metal parts to form metal

- pours plaster around wooden pattern and fills plaster mould with resin to form pattern;

- compares pattern dimensions with original drawings using calipers, micrometers, protractors, etc.;

- smoothes surface of pattern with grinding machine or emery cloth.

## RELATED JOB TITLES

Engineer's pattern maker
Metal pattern maker
Pattern maker (*metal trades*)
Wood pattern maker

## 579  OTHER WOODWORKING TRADES NEC

Workers in this unit group perform a variety of woodworking occupations not elsewhere classified in MINOR GROUP 57: Woodworking Trades.

## TYPICAL ENTRY ROUTES AND ASSOCIATED QUALIFICATIONS

Academic qualifications may not be required. Training is by apprenticeship.

## TASKS

- examines drawings and specifications to determine job requirements and appropriate materials;

- uses hand tools and machines to cut, shape, bend and carve wooden parts as required;

- assembles parts with nails, screws, pins or adhesive to make ladders, picture frames, wheels, textile shuttles, sports equipment, orthopaedic appliances and wooden stocks and foreparts for bespoke guns;

- measures floor areas to be covered and lays wood blocks, parquet panels or hardwood strips;

- matches and marks out veneers ready for cutting and examines and repairs defects in veneer or plywood sheets.

## RELATED JOB TITLES

Ladder maker
Picture frame maker
Veneer splicer
Wood carver

# MINOR GROUP 58
# FOOD PREPARATION TRADES

Workers in food preparation trades slaughter livestock, cut, trim and prepare meat, poultry and fish and prepare, bake and finish bread and flour confectionery products.

Occupations in this minor group are classified into the following unit groups:

**580    BAKERS, FLOUR CONFECTIONERS**
**581    BUTCHERS, MEAT CUTTERS**
**582    FISHMONGERS, POULTRY DRESSERS**

## 580 BAKERS, FLOUR CONFECTIONERS

Bakers, flour confectioners and related operatives prepare and bake dough, pastry and cake mixtures and make and finish flour confectioners products by hand.

### TYPICAL ENTRY ROUTES AND ASSOCIATED QUALIFICATIONS

Entry may not depend on academic qualifications. Training is either by apprenticeship or on-the-job.

### TASKS

● weighs flour and other ingredients according to recipe;

● mixes ingredients using hand or machine and adds water or other liquids to obtain the required consistency;

● rolls, cuts, stretches, kneads and moulds mixture to form bread, rolls, buns, cakes and pastry shapes;

● allows dough to rise and fills and glazes pastry;

● makes cake decorations, spreads icing, fillings and toppings and sprinkles sugar and other confections on products.

### RELATED JOB TITLES

Baker
Baker and confectioner
Confectioner (*not retail trade*)

## 581 BUTCHERS, MEAT CUTTERS

Butchers and meat cutters direct and undertake the slaughter of animals and prepare carcasses for storage, processing and sale.

### TYPICAL ENTRY ROUTES AND ASSOCIATED QUALIFICATIONS

Entry may not depend on academic qualifications. Training is mainly on-the-job and professional qualifications can be obtained.

### TASKS

● slaughters animal and removes skin, hide, hairs, internal organs, etc.;

● cuts or saws carcasses into manageable proportions;

● removes bones, gristle, surplus fat, rind and other waste material;

● cuts carcass parts into chops, joints, steaks, etc. for sale;

● prepares meat for curing or other processing;

● cleans tools and work surfaces.

## RELATED JOB TITLES

Butcher
Butcher's cutter
Meat Cutter
Slaughterer

## 582 FISHMONGERS, POULTRY DRESSERS

Fishmongers and poultry dressers clean, cut and prepare poultry carcasses and fish for processing or sale.

### TYPICAL ENTRY ROUTES AND ASSOCIATED QUALIFICATIONS

Academic qualifications may not be required. Training is on-the-job.

### TASKS

- removes feathers and internal organs, extracts edible offal and cuts off feet and head from poultry carcass as required;

- scrubs, heads, guts, washes and bones fish;

- cuts and slits fish for curing by hand or machine;

- cleans tools and work surfaces.

### RELATED JOB TITLES

Filleter (*fish*)
Fishmonger
Poultry dresser

# MINOR GROUP 59
# OTHER CRAFT AND RELATED OCCUPATIONS NEC

Workers in this unit group perform a variety of craft and related trades not elsewhere classified in MAJOR GROUP 5: Craft and Related Occupations.

Occupations in this minor group are classified into the following unit groups:

**590  GLASS PRODUCT AND CERAMICS MAKERS**

**591  GLASS PRODUCT AND CERAMICS FINISHERS AND DECORATORS**

**592  DENTAL TECHNICIANS**

**593  MUSICAL INSTRUMENT MAKERS, PIANO TUNERS**

**594  GARDENERS, GROUNDSMEN/GROUNDSWOMEN**

**595  HORTICULTURAL TRADES**

**596  COACH PAINTERS, OTHER SPRAY PAINTERS**

**597  FACE TRAINED COALMINING WORKERS, SHOTFIRERS AND DEPUTIES**

**598  OFFICE MACHINERY MECHANICS**

**599  OTHER CRAFT AND RELATED OCCUPATIONS NEC**

## 590  GLASS PRODUCT AND CERAMICS MAKERS

Glass product and ceramics makers form and shape glassware and glass products by blowing, moulding and pressing and form and repair pottery, earthenware, refractory goods, clay bricks, tiles and other ceramic goods by casting, moulding, extruding, cutting and shaping.

### TYPICAL ENTRY ROUTES AND ASSOCIATED QUALIFICATIONS

Entry may not depend on academic qualifications. On-the-job training is provided. Professional qualifications can be obtained.

### TASKS

- blows through pipe to inflate and shape molten glass;

- uses hand tools and operates machinery to heat, bend, shape, press, drill and cut glass;

- makes artificial eyes, laminated glass sheets or blocks, glass fibre tissue, wool, filament and matting, marks optical lenses and assembles rimless spectacles;

- makes models and moulds from moulding clay and plaster for use in the making and casting of pottery and other ceramic goods;

- throws, casts and presses clay by hand or machine to form pottery, stoneware or refractory goods such as bricks, crucibles, ornaments, sanitary furnishings, saggars, cups, saucers, plates and roofing tiles;

- cuts and joins unfired stoneware pipes to form junctions and gullies, moulds sealing bands on clay pipes, prepares and joins porcelain or earthenware components and assists crucible makers and stone workers with their tasks.

### RELATED JOB TITLES

Brick maker
Caster (*ceramic mfr*)
Clay potter
Figure maker

185

Glass blower
Glass cutter
Glass maker
Potter
Presser (*glass/ceramic mfr*)
Sponger (*ceramic mfr*)

## 591 GLASS PRODUCT AND CERAMICS FINISHERS AND DECORATORS

Glass product and ceramics finishers and decorators smooth, polish, etch, paint, varnish and otherwise finish glass and ceramic goods and transfer decorative patterns onto ceramic goods.

### TYPICAL ENTRY ROUTES AND ASSOCIATED QUALIFICATIONS

Entry may not depend on academic qualifications but some employers ask for GCSE/SCE S-grades. Training is mainly on-the-job.

### TASKS

- uses hand tools and operates machinery to grind, sandblast, smooth and polish glass, optical glass and ceramic products;

- marks out, cuts and etches decorative patterns on glass and pottery goods;

- paints decorative designs on glass and ceramic goods using hand brushes or paint spraying equipment;

- applies glaze, colour, varnish, slip or oil onto ceramic goods with brushes or by dipping or spraying;

- transfers patterns, pattern outlines or painted labels to ceramic goods by hand.

### RELATED JOB TITLES

Aerographer (*ceramic mfr*)
Bander (*ceramic mfr*)
Ceramic artist
Dipper (*ceramic mfr*)
Etcher (*ceramic mfr*)
Glass decorator
Glass painter
Lithographer (*ceramic mfr*)
Polisher (*lenses*)
Scourer (*ceramic mfr*)

## 592 DENTAL TECHNICIANS

Dental technicians make and repair dentures according to individual requirements.

### TYPICAL ENTRY ROUTES AND ASSOCIATED QUALIFICATIONS

Entry is only available via an apprenticeship, sandwich course or full-time college course plus two years consolidation in an approved laboratory and requires GCSE/SCE S-grades or equivalent.

### TASKS

- examines prescription and specification to determine job requirements;

- prepares plaster mould using wax, hydrocolloid or other impression taken by dentist;

- casts plastic or metal plate and sets selected artificial teeth during casting, or cements teeth onto cast plate;

- ensures that teeth are correctly adjusted for biting and chewing;

- finishes dentures with hand or machine tools;

- repairs broken dentures or dental plate.

### RELATED JOB TITLES

Dental technician

## 593 MUSICAL INSTRUMENT MAKERS, PIANO TUNERS

Musical instrument makers and piano tuners make, adjust, string, tune and repair musical instruments, make bows and assemble, install and regulate piano action parts.

### TYPICAL ENTRY ROUTES AND ASSOCIATED QUALIFICATIONS

Entry is most common with GCSE/SCE S-grades. Training is by apprenticeship or on-the-job. Or by specialised college courses.

## TASKS

- examines drawings and specifications to determine appropriate materials and job requirements;

- selects, cuts, drills, carves and planes wood to make up parts for the assembly of pianos, organs, violins, cellos and other instruments;

- assembles and joins prepared parts such as body sections, springs, pads, keys, pipes, dampers, bellows, stretched vellum, etc. to make wind and string instruments, drums, organs and bows;

- uses tuning fork and hand tools to tune pianos and organs and adjusts organ pipes to improve tone quality, volume and pitch;

- fits prepared action assemblies and pedal movements into piano cases and repairs or replaces worn or broken strings, dampers, hammers and felt.

## RELATED JOB TITLES

Musical instrument maker
Organ builder
Piano tuner
Violin maker
Violin repairer

## 594 GARDENERS, GROUNDS-MEN/GROUNDSWOMEN

Gardeners and groundsmen/groundswomen cultivate flowers, trees, shrubs and other plants in public and private gardens, construct artificial features to improve the appearance of existing terrain, cut and lay turf and maintain areas for sports and recreation.

## TYPICAL ENTRY ROUTES AND ASSOCIATED QUALIFICATIONS

Academic qualifications may not be required, though some GCSE/SCE qualifications are an advantage. Training is usually by apprenticeship including work experience and practical and technical training leading to recognised awards.

## TASKS

- levels ground and installs drainage system as required;

- prepares soil and plants and transplants, prunes, weeds and otherwise tends plant life;

- protects plants from pests and diseases;

- cuts and lays turf using hand and machine tools and repairs damaged turf;

- moves soil to alter surface contour of land using mechanical equipment and constructs paths, rockeries, ponds and other features;

- rolls, mows and waters grass.

## RELATED JOB TITLES

Gardener
Greenkeeper
Groundsman/groundswoman
Landscape gardener
Turf cutter

## 595 HORTICULTURAL TRADES

Horticultural trades workers intensively cultivate vegetables, plants, fruit, shrubs, trees and flowers in greenhouses, market gardens, nurseries and orchards.

## TYPICAL ENTRY ROUTES AND ASSOCIATED QUALIFICATIONS

Academic qualifications may not be required for entry, though some GCSE/SCE qualifications are an advantage. Training is usually by apprenticeship including work experience and practical and technical training leading to recognised awards.

## TASKS

- prepares soil in field, bed or pot by hand or machine;

- mixes soil, composts, fertilizers and/or organic matter and spreads fertilizer and manure;

- sows seeds and bulbs and transplants seedlings;

- propagates plants by taking cuttings and by grafting and budding;

- applies weedkiller, fungicide and insecticide to control pests and diseases;

- prunes and thins trees and shrubs;

- supports trees by staking and wiring.

## RELATED JOB TITLES

Greenhouse worker
Horticultural worker
Nursery hand
Nursery worker

## 596 COACH PAINTERS, OTHER SPRAY PAINTERS

Coach painters and other spray painters use brushes and spray equipment to apply paint, cellulose and other protective or decorative materials to the body-work of motor vehicles or railway coaches and wagons and spray paint, cellulose and other materials onto furniture, musical instruments, leather pieces and other items/materials excluding ceramics, ships, buildings and other structures.

### TYPICAL ENTRY ROUTES AND ASSOCIATED QUALIFICATIONS

Academic qualifications may not be required. On-the-job training is provided.

### TASKS

- removes old paint and cleans, files or smoothes surface to be coated;

- mixes paint, polish, dye or other protective and decorative materials to desired consistency or colour and fills hand or electrostatic spray gun;

- protects areas not to be covered with masking material;

- uses brushes, hand or electrostatic spray to coat surfaces and adjusts nozzle and pressure valves of gun if necessary;

- rubs down coated surfaces between applications using abrasive paper or sanding machine;

- removes masking material and cleans equipment.

## RELATED JOB TITLES

Cellulose sprayer
Coach painter
Paint sprayer
Spray painter
Sprayer

## 597 FACE TRAINED COALMINING WORKERS, SHOTFIRERS AND DEPUTIES

Workers in this unit group drill holes, set and detonate charges to loosen coal and rock, stow waste, remove rock to enlarge road and air ways, extract coal and build and dismantle roof and wall supports in underground coal workings;

### TYPICAL ENTRY ROUTES AND ASSOCIATED QUALIFICATIONS

Academic qualifications may not be required to commence training which is both off- and on-the-job. Certificates of competence are required at each stage of training. There is a minimum age limit of 18 for underground work.

### TASKS

- uses machine or portable drill to drill holes to required depth for blasting, bursting, release of gas or water infusion;

- inserts and compacts appropriate explosive, primer and detonator in drilling hole and detonates charge to break and loosen coal and rock from solid formations;

- operates heading and ripping machines to remove material from working face, monitors conveyor carrying away loose material and makes and maintains refuge holes and road and airways;

- directs and undertakes the moving, positioning and operation of a coal cutting-loading machine;

- erects permanent and temporary wall and roof supports from dry stone material, timber and metal and withdraws supports and serviceable material/equipment from worked out or abandoned faces;

- stows waste in area from which coal has been removed using feed hopper or stowing machine.

## RELATED JOB TITLES

Coal face worker
Collier
Face worker (*coal mine*)
Face working coal miner
Power loader (*coal mine*)
Ripper (*coal mine*)
Shotfirer (*coal mine*)

## 598 OFFICE MACHINERY MECHANICS

Office machinery mechanics service and repair office machinery and cash registers and tills.

### TYPICAL ENTRY ROUTES AND ASSOCIATED QUALIFICATIONS

Entry may not depend on academic qualifications. Off- and on-the-job training is provided. Some employers require candidates to hold a current driving licence.

### TASKS

- examines cash registers and tills, typewriters, accounting and other office machinery to detect nature and location of defects;

- dismantles machine and replaces worn or defective parts using hand tools and soldering equipment;

- repairs or replaces defective wiring and lubricates any moving parts;

- tests machine for correct functioning and makes any further necessary adjustments;

- carries out routine service tasks such as cleaning and lubricating.

### RELATED JOB TITLES

Customer engineer (*office machinery mfr*)
Office machinery mechanic
Office machines engineer
Typewriter mechanic
Typewriter repairer

## 599 OTHER CRAFT AND RELATED OCCUPATIONS NEC

Workers in this unit group cover a variety of other trades not elsewhere classified in MINOR GROUP 59: Other Craft and Related Occupations n.e.c.

### TYPICAL ENTRY ROUTES AND ASSOCIATED QUALIFICATIONS

Some academic qualifications may be required. Training is either on-the-job or by apprenticeship.

### RELATED JOB TITLES

Basket maker (*not wire*)
Billiard table fitter
Blind maker
Brush maker
Diver
Jewellery engraver
Lampshade maker
Lens fixer
Orthodontic technician
Orthopaedic appliance maker
Toy maker
Wig maker

# MAJOR GROUP 6

# PERSONAL AND PROTECTIVE SERVICE OCCUPATIONS

# MAJOR GROUP 6
## PERSONAL AND PROTECTIVE SERVICE OCCUPATIONS

This major group covers occupations whose tasks involve the provision of a service to customers, whether in a public protective or personal care capacity. The main tasks associated with these occupations involve a knowledge of defensive techniques, law enforcement and security provision; the preparation of food and drink for consumption; travel services; personal care and hygiene.

Most occupations in this major group require a good standard of general education, a high degree of integrity and skills in interpersonal communication.

Occupations in this major group are classified into the following minor groups:

**60  NCOs AND OTHER RANKS, ARMED FORCES**

**61  SECURITY AND PROTECTIVE SERVICE OCCUPATIONS**

**62  CATERING OCCUPATIONS**

**63  TRAVEL ATTENDANTS AND RELATED OCCUPATIONS**

**64  HEALTH AND RELATED OCCUPATIONS**

**65  CHILDCARE AND RELATED OCCUPATIONS**

**66  HAIRDESSERS, BEAUTICIANS AND RELATED OCCUPATIONS**

**67  DOMESTIC STAFF AND RELATED OCCUPATIONS**

**69  PERSONAL AND PROTECTIVE SERVICE OCCUPATIONS NEC**

# MINOR GROUP 60
# NCOs AND OTHER RANKS, ARMED FORCES

Workers in this minor group serve in Her Majesty's, foreign and Commonwealth armed forces.

Occupations in this minor group are classified into the following unit groups:

**600** NCOs AND OTHER RANKS, UK ARMED FORCES
**601** NCOs AND OTHER RANKS, FOREIGN AND COMMONWEALTH ARMED FORCES

## 600 NCOs AND OTHER RANKS, UK ARMED FORCES

Workers in this unit group are full-time members of the armed forces of the UK and perform duties for which there is no civilian equivalent.

### TYPICAL ENTRY ROUTES AND ASSOCIATED QUALIFICATIONS

Entry may not depend on academic qualifications although candidates will require GCSE/SCE S-grades to enter certain trades. Basic training lasts between 6 and 20 weeks; specialist training lasts up to 2 years.

### TASKS

- monitors, operates, services and repairs military equipment;

- stands watch and guards military establishments and other buildings;

- trains and exercises using various military equipment and tactics;

- patrols areas of possible military activity;

- leads and trains new recruits and lower ranks.

### RELATED JOB TITLES

Airman/woman
Corporal
Petty officer
Private
Sapper
Sergeant
Sergeant-major

## 601 NCOs AND OTHER RANKS, FOREIGN AND COMMONWEALTH ARMED FORCES

Workers in this unit group are full-time members of the armed forces of foreign and Commonwealth countries and perform duties for which there is no civilian equivalent.

### TYPICAL ENTRY ROUTES AND ASSOCIATED QUALIFICATIONS

Entry requirements depend on which force the person serves in. Some academic qualifications are required.

### TASKS

- monitors, operates, services and repairs military equipment;

- stands watch and guards military establishments and other buildings;

- trains and exercises using various military equipment and tactics;

- patrols areas of possible military activity;

- leads and trains new recruits and lower ranks.

## RELATED JOB TITLES

Airman/woman
Corporal
Petty officer
Private
Sapper
Sergeant
Sergeant-major

# MINOR GROUP 61
# SECURITY AND PROTECTIVE SERVICE OCCUPATIONS

Workers in this minor group investigate crimes and maintain law and order, fight fires and advise on fire prevention, guard prisoners, serve summonses, protect individuals or property from injury, theft or damage, inspect goods and persons entering the UK to ensure compliance with Customs and Excise and immigration regulations and perform other miscellaneous fire fighting and protective service occupations.

Occupations in this minor group are classified into the following unit groups:

**610 POLICE OFFICERS (SERGEANT AND BELOW)**

**611 FIRE SERVICE OFFICERS (LEADING FIRE OFFICER AND BELOW)**

**612 PRISON SERVICE OFFICERS (BELOW PRINCIPAL OFFICER)**

**613 CUSTOMS AND EXCISE OFFICERS, IMMIGRATION OFFICERS (CUSTOMS: BELOW CHIEF PREVENTIVE OFFICER; EXCISE: BELOW SURVEYOR)**

**614 TRAFFIC WARDENS**

**615 SECURITY GUARDS AND RELATED OCCUPATIONS**

**619 OTHER SECURITY AND PROTECTIVE SERVICE OCCUPATIONS NEC**

## 610 POLICE OFFICERS (SERGEANT AND BELOW)

Police officers (Sergeant and below) co-ordinate and undertake the investigation of crimes, patrol public areas, arrest offenders and suspects and enforce law and order.

### TYPICAL ENTRY ROUTES AND ASSOCIATED QUALIFICATIONS

Entry to the civilian (Home Office) police will require a minimum of GCSE/SCE S-grades and is also possible with a degree or equivalent. There are lower height limits of 5'4" for women and 5'8" for men. Other statutory police forces have varying academic, age, height and eyesight requirements. Candidates must pass a medical examination and undergo a two-year period of probation and training.

### TASKS

- receives instructions from senior officer and patrols an assigned area on foot, horseback, motorcycle, motor car or boat to check security and enforce regulations;

- directs and controls traffic or crowds and demonstrations;

- investigates complaints, crimes, accidents, any suspicious activities or other incidents;

- interviews suspects, takes statements from witnesses and stops, searches and/or arrests suspects;

- prepares briefs or reports for senior officers;

- gives evidence in court cases.

### RELATED JOB TITLES

Constable
Police cadet

Police constable
Police officer
Policeman/woman

## 611 FIRE SERVICE OFFICERS (LEADING FIRE OFFICER AND BELOW)

Workers in this unit group direct, co-ordinate and participate in fire fighting, advise on fire prevention and salvage goods during and after fires.

### TYPICAL ENTRY ROUTES AND ASSOCIATED QUALIFICATIONS

Entry will require GCSE/SCE S-grades. Candidates should be between 18 and 30 years of age, over 5'6" tall and have a chest measurement of at least 38" (expanded). Good colour vision without spectacles or contact lenses is required. Candidates must also pass a medical examination and a strength test. Initial training lasts between 12 and 16 weeks and is followed by further off- and on-the-job training.

### TASKS

- inspects premises to identify potential fire hazards and to check that statutory fire fighting equipment is available and in working order;

- arranges fire drills and tests alarm systems and equipment;

- travels to fire or other emergency by vehicle and locates water mains if necessary;

- operates hosepipes, ladders, chemical, foam, gas or powder fire extinguishing appliances;

- rescues people or animals trapped by fire and administers first aid;

- removes goods from fire damaged premises, clears excess water, makes safe any structural hazards and takes any other necessary steps to reduce damage to property;

- may fill or empty large water holders.

### RELATED JOB TITLES

Fire officer (*coal mine*)
Fireman (*fire service*)

## 612 PRISON SERVICE OFFICERS (BELOW PRINCIPAL OFFICER)

Prison service officers (below Principal Officer) direct, co-ordinate and participate in guarding inmates and maintaining discipline in prisons and other detention centres.

### TYPICAL ENTRY ROUTES AND ASSOCIATED QUALIFICATIONS

Academic qualifications may not be required but candidates must pass a pre-entry test. Candidates must be between 21 and 49 and a half years of age, have good eyesight with or without spectacles or contact lenses and be at least 5'3" (women) and 5'6" (men) tall. Between 10 and 12 weeks off- and on-the-job training is provided.

### TASKS

- escorts prisoners to and from cells and supervises them during meals, recreation and visiting periods;

- watches for any infringements of regulations and searches prisoners and cells for weapons, drugs and other contraband items;

- guards entrances and perimeter walls;

- investigates disturbances or any other unusual occurrences;

- escorts prisoners transferred from one institution to another;

- reports on prisoners' conduct as necessary.

### RELATED JOB TITLES

Prison officer
Warder (*prison service*)

## 613 CUSTOMS AND EXCISE OFFICERS, IMMIGRATION OFFICERS (CUSTOMS: BELOW CHIEF PREVENTIVE OFFICER; EXCISE: BELOW SURVEYOR)

Workers in this unit group undertake inspections and investigations of goods and persons to ensure compliance with acts, orders and regulations concerning payment of Customs and Excise duties and the entry of aliens and Commonwealth citizens into the UK.

### TYPICAL ENTRY ROUTES AND ASSOCIATED QUALIFICATIONS

Entry is most common with GCSE/SCE S-grades and A-levels/H-grades or a degree/BTEC/SCOTVEC, but is possible with other academic qualifications.

### TASKS

- examines, weighs, gauges and counts goods imported by ship or aircraft;

- ensures that declared value of goods is satisfactory and that duties and taxes have been paid;

- maintains revenue control at breweries, tobacco factories and other premises where dutiable goods are manufactured, processed or stored;

- prevents unlicensed trading and controls movement of goods in and out of bond;

- visits racecourses, greyhound stadiums and betting shops to ensure compliance with legal requirements;

- examines passports, visas, work permits and other immigration documents and allows or refuses entry into the UK.

### RELATED JOB TITLES

Customs and excise officer
Immigration officer

## 614 TRAFFIC WARDENS

Traffic wardens direct, co-ordinate and participate in patrolling assigned areas to detect and prevent infringements of local parking regulations.

### TYPICAL ENTRY ROUTES AND ASSOCIATED QUALIFICATIONS

Academic qualifications may not be required but relevant experience may be advantageous. Candidates should be at least 18 years of age (in some areas 20–25+) and may be required to pass a medical examination. On-the-job training is provided.

### TASKS

- patrols assigned area to detect vehicles parked in no-parking zones and vehicles parked in excess of permitted time in restricted parking zones;

- warns offenders or issues tickets;

- advises motorists on local parking facilities and directs them as required;

- notes any cases of obstruction, evasion of tax or other infringement and reports them to the police;

- gives evidence in court as required.

### RELATED JOB TITLES

Parking meter attendant
Traffic warden

## 615 SECURITY GUARDS AND RELATED OCCUPATIONS

Workers in this unit group direct, co-ordinate and undertake investigations on behalf of individuals or commercial organisations and protect merchandise, individuals, hotels, offices, factories, public grounds and private estates.

### TYPICAL ENTRY ROUTES AND ASSOCIATED QUALIFICATIONS

Academic qualifications may not be required but relevant experience is advantageous. Candidates are usually between 21 and 45 years of age, at least 5'6" tall and must pass a medical examination. For some vacancies a current and clean driving licence is required.

## TASKS

- investigates crimes, trading practices and the private affairs of individuals;

- walks or rides near person requiring protection, watches for suspicious occurrences and defends guarded person from attack;

- patrols hotel lobbies, corridors, stores, private and public parks and forests to prevent theft and unauthorised entry;

- checks persons and vehicles entering and leaving premises, establishes their credentials and arranges for escorts for visitors;

- receives duty sheet, time-clock and keys for premises to be visited, checks locks, doors, windows, etc. and reports any suspicious circumstances to security headquarters;

- calls in civil police and gives evidence in court where necessary.

## RELATED JOB TITLES

Doorkeeper
Night watcher
Park ranger
Private detective
Security guard
Security officer
Store detective

## 619 OTHER SECURITY AND PROTECTIVE SERVICE OCCUPATIONS NEC

Workers in this unit group perform a variety of security and protective service occupations not elsewhere classified in MINOR GROUP 61: Security and Protective Service Occupations.

## TYPICAL ENTRY ROUTES AND ASSOCIATED QUALIFICATIONS

These posts have varying entry requirements. Some posts require no academic qualifications whereas others require GCSE/SCE S-grades followed by a training period.

## TASKS

- serves summonses and, on court authority, takes possession of goods to the value of outstanding debt;

- accepts payment on behalf of court and issues receipts;

- ejects persons in illegal occupation of premises;

- patrols beaches to prevent accidents;

- keeps watch for ships in distress, instructs vessels regarding navigation in difficult waters and hoists weather cones;

- watches for illegal fishing or attempted smuggling;

- assists pedestrians trying to cross busy roads by stopping traffic;

- performs other miscellaneous protective service tasks not elsewhere classified including patrolling and dealing with any security difficulties in art galleries and museums, the Houses of Parliament and employers' establishments.

## RELATED JOB TITLES

Coastguard
County court bailiff
Lifeguard
Museum attendant
Road-crossing attendant

# MINOR GROUP 62
## CATERING OCCUPATIONS

Catering workers plan menus, prepare, cook and serve food, beverages and alcoholic drinks in catering, domestic and other establishments.

Occupations in this minor group are classified into the following unit groups:

> 620   CHEFS, COOKS
> 621   WAITERS, WAITRESSES
> 622   BAR STAFF

## 620 CHEFS, COOKS

Chefs and cooks plan menus and prepare, season and cook food in hotels, restaurants, clubs, private households and other establishments.

### TYPICAL ENTRY ROUTES AND ASSOCIATED QUALIFICATIONS

Academic qualifications are not normally required. Training is on-the-job or by City and Guilds course or apprenticeship.

### TASKS

- requisitions or purchases and examines food-stuffs to ensure quality;

- plans meals, prepares, seasons and cooks food-stuffs;

- plans and co-ordinates kitchen work such as fetching, clearing and cleaning of equipment and utensils.

### RELATED JOB TITLES

Chef
Chef de cuisine
Cook
Cook in charge
Head cook
Pastry cook

## 621 WAITERS, WAITRESSES

Waiters and waitresses serve food and beverages in hotels, clubs, restaurants and other establishments.

### TYPICAL ENTRY ROUTES AND ASSOCIATED QUALIFICATIONS

Academic qualifications are not normally required but some employers require GCSE/SCE S-grades. On-the-job training is most common. Some apprenticeships are available.

### TASKS

- sets tables with clean linen, cutlery, crockery and glassware;

- presents menus and wine lists to patrons and may describe dishes and advise on selection of food or wines;

- takes down orders for food and/or drinks and passes order to kitchen;

- serves food and drinks;

- presents bill and accepts payment at end of the meal.

### RELATED JOB TITLES

Head waiter/waitress
Silver service waiter/waitress
Waiter/waitress
Wine waiter/waitress

## 622 BAR STAFF

Bar staff prepare, mix and serve alcoholic and non-alcoholic drinks and beverages at bars in public houses, hotels, clubs and other establishments.

### TYPICAL ENTRY ROUTES AND ASSOCIATED QUALIFICATIONS

Academic qualifications are not normally required. Training is mostly on-the-job. City and Guilds courses are available.

### TASKS

- assists in keeping bar properly stocked;

- washes used glassware and cleans bar area;

- takes customer orders and mixes and serves drinks;

- receives payment for drinks.

### RELATED JOB TITLES

Bar assistant
Bar steward/stewardess
Barman/maid/person

# MINOR GROUP 63
# TRAVEL ATTENDANTS AND RELATED OCCUPATIONS

Travel attendants and related workers attend to the needs and comforts of visitors and travellers on ships, aeroplanes and trains and those in hotels, railway stations and other establishments.

Occupations in this minor group are classified into the following unit groups:

630   TRAVEL AND FLIGHT ATTENDANTS
631   RAILWAY STATION STAFF

## 630  TRAVEL AND FLIGHT ATTENDANTS

Travel and flight attendants conduct tourists on holiday and provide meals and other services for the comfort and safety of passengers in ships, aeroplanes and trains.

### TYPICAL ENTRY ROUTES AND ASSOCIATED QUALIFICATIONS

Academic qualifications may be required. Spoken fluency in a foreign language is essential for some posts. Off- and on-the-job training is provided and professional qualifications are obtainable in some occupations.

### TASKS

- receives passengers and conducts them to a cabin, seat or hotel room;

- serves food and beverages to passengers;

- assists with hand luggage and the loading and unloading of other items;

- helps prepare train, cabin or aeroplane to receive passengers and distributes reading matter, blankets and other material;

- makes announcements to passengers and deals with enquiries;

- deals with local arrangements for transport, food and accommodation of passengers and/or tourists.

### RELATED JOB TITLES

Air host/hostess
Air steward/stewardess
Bus escort
Coach guide
Courier (*tour operator*)
Flight attendant
Guide
Passenger service assistant

## 631  RAILWAY STATION STAFF

Railway station staff collect tickets and perform a variety of duties on railway station platforms in connection with the arrival and departure of trains and the movement of goods and passengers.

### TYPICAL ENTRY ROUTES AND ASSOCIATED QUALIFICATIONS

Entry is possible without specific academic qualifications but a medical examination and normal colour vision are required. Off- and on-the-job training is provided. There are promotion opportunities from these grades to Inspector, Guard, Engine Driver, etc.

### TASKS

- examines and collects tickets at the ticket barrier of a railway station;

- checks train doors are closed before departure and signals to guard when train is ready for departure;

- helps with passenger enquiries and makes announcements over a public address system;

- loads and unloads mail, goods and luggage, operates lifts and hoists and drives small trucks;

- helps to tidy and clean the platform, other areas of the station and train carriages.

## RELATED JOB TITLES

Railman/woman (*railways*)
Stationman/woman (*LRT*)
Ticket collector (*railways*)

# MINOR GROUP 64
# HEALTH AND RELATED OCCUPATIONS

Health and related occupations workers transport patients by ambulance, stretcher, wheelchair or other means and assist health professionals with the care of patients in hospitals, dental surgeries, nursing homes and clinics.

Occupations in this minor group are classified into the following unit groups:

> **640 ASSISTANT NURSES, NURSING AUXILIARIES**
> **641 HOSPITAL WARD ASSISTANTS**
> **642 AMBULANCE STAFF**
> **643 DENTAL NURSES**
> **644 CARE ASSISTANTS AND ATTENDANTS**

## 640 ASSISTANT NURSES, NURSING AUXILIARIES

Assistant nurses and nursing auxiliaries assist doctors, nurses and other health professionals by providing nursing care for the sick and injured and others in need of such care.

### TYPICAL ENTRY ROUTES AND ASSOCIATED QUALIFICATIONS

Academic qualifications are not normally required. All training is in-service.

### TASKS

- dresses, undresses and washes patient;

- prepares, serves and distributes food and feeds helpless patients;

- assists nursing and medical staff as directed.

### RELATED JOB TITLES

Assistant nurse
Nursing assistant
Nursing auxiliary

## 641 HOSPITAL WARD ASSISTANTS

Hospital ward assistants assist in the care of patients and help with light cleaning and food serving in hospitals, nursing homes and clinics.

### TYPICAL ENTRY ROUTES AND ASSOCIATED QUALIFICATIONS

Academic qualifications may not be required. On-the-job training is provided.

### TASKS

- assists with changing bed linen, making beds and tidying wards;

- cleans and sterilizes instruments and utensils;

- takes blood samples as directed;

- assists with preparing patient for examination or treatment;

- assists with serving meals and clearing trays.

### RELATED JOB TITLES

Hospital orderly
Medical assistant (*hospital*)
Phlebotomist

Ward assistant
Ward helper
Ward orderly

## 642  AMBULANCE STAFF

Ambulance staff transport sick, injured and convalescent persons and give first aid treatment in emergencies.

### TYPICAL ENTRY ROUTES AND ASSOCIATED QUALIFICATIONS

Academic qualifications are not normally required. A full clean current driving licence and three years driving experience is required. Candidates will require a minimum of three weeks first aid and patient care training. Further training eventually leads to the Certificate of Proficiency in ambulance aid. Candidates will also be required to undertake a medical and optical test.

### TASKS

- drives ambulance or accompanies driver to transport patients to hospitals or other treatment centres and homes;

- ascertains nature of injuries and provides first aid treatment;

- cleans and disinfects ambulance after use;

- replenishes medical supplies in ambulance as necessary.

### RELATED JOB TITLES

Ambulance attendant
Ambulance driver
Ambulanceman/woman

## 643  DENTAL NURSES

Dental nurses prepare patients for, and assist with, dental examinations, prepare and sterilize instruments and maintain case records.

### TYPICAL ENTRY ROUTES AND ASSOCIATED QUALIFICATIONS

Entry is most common with GCSE/SCE S-grades. Professional qualifications are available.

### TASKS

- prepares patient for examination;

- prepares and sterilizes instruments;

- hands required equipment and medication to dentist during examination;

- assists with minor treatment, such as preparing materials for fillings;

- maintains records, processes and mounts x-ray films and undertakes reception duties.

### RELATED JOB TITLES

Dental nurse
Dental surgery assistant

## 644  CARE ASSISTANTS AND ATTENDANTS

Care assistants and attendants attend to the personal needs and comforts of residents in establishments for the elderly and infirm.

### TYPICAL ENTRY ROUTES AND ASSOCIATED QUALIFICATIONS

No academic qualifications are required. On-the-job training is provided.

### TASKS

- assists residents to dress, undress, wash and bathe;

- serves meals to residents at table or in bed;

- accompanies infirm residents on outings and assists with recreational activities;

- undertakes light cleaning and domestic duties as required.

### RELATED JOB TITLES

Care assistant
Care attendant
Home care assistant
Night care assistant

# MINOR GROUP 65
# CHILDCARE AND RELATED OCCUPATIONS

Childcare and related workers supervise play and other activities for pre-school age children, assist teachers with their non-teaching duties and care for children in day or residential nurseries, children's homes and private households.

Occupations in this minor group are classified into the following unit groups:

> **650  NURSERY NURSES**
>
> **651  PLAYGROUP LEADERS**
>
> **652  EDUCATIONAL ASSISTANTS**
>
> **659  OTHER CHILDCARE AND RELATED OCCUPATIONS NEC**

## 650  NURSERY NURSES

Nursery nurses care for children in day or residential nurseries, children's homes, maternity units and similar establishments.

### TYPICAL ENTRY ROUTES AND ASSOCIATED QUALIFICATIONS

Entry is most common with GCSE/SCE S-grades and the National Nursery Examination Board/Scottish Nursery Nurses Examination Board certificate, but is possible with other academic qualifications and/or professional training.

### TASKS

- baths, dresses, prepares feed for and feeds babies;

- changes babies clothing whenever necessary;

- supervises young children at mealtimes;

- organises games and other activities and supervises children's play.

### RELATED JOB TITLES

Creche attendant
Nursery assistant (*childcare*)
Nursery nurse

## 651  PLAYGROUP LEADERS

Playgroup leaders supervise play and other activities for pre-school age children.

### TYPICAL ENTRY ROUTES AND ASSOCIATED QUALIFICATIONS

Entry does not depend on academic qualifications although some employers require candidates to hold National Nursery Examination Board/Scottish National Nursery Examination Board certificates. Entry is possible with experience alone.

### TASKS

- supervises children's games and encourages the development of physical, social and language skills;

- prepares paints, glue, paper, toys, etc. for children's activities;

- supervises children's activities to ensure safety;

- puts away equipment and cleans premises after use.

### RELATED JOB TITLES

Play leader
Playgroup leader

## 652 EDUCATIONAL ASSISTANTS

Educational assistants assist teachers with, or relieve them of, a variety of non-teaching duties.

### TYPICAL ENTRY ROUTES AND ASSOCIATED QUALIFICATIONS

Academic qualifications may be required but entry is possible with relevant experience alone.

### TASKS

- assists teacher with preparation or clearing up of classroom;

- looks after lesson materials such as paper, pencils and crayons;

- assists children with washing or dressing for outdoor and similar activities;

- assists teachers with other non-teaching duties as required.

### RELATED JOB TITLES

Classroom helper
Educational assistant
School helper

## 659 OTHER CHILDCARE AND RELATED OCCUPATIONS NEC

Workers in this unit group perform a variety of childcare and related occupations not elsewhere classified in MINOR GROUP 65: Childcare and Related Occupations.

### TYPICAL ENTRY ROUTES AND ASSOCIATED QUALIFICATIONS

Entry may not depend on qualifications, though some employers require candidates to hold GCSE/SCE S-grades and the National Nursery Examination Board/Scottish Nursery Nurses Examination Board Certificate or other qualifications.

### TASKS

- assists children to wash and dress;

- prepares and serves children's meals;

- mends, washes and irons children's clothes and tidies their rooms;

- supervises children during meals and keeps order in playground after meals and before classes resume;

- assists playgroup leader with the preparation and supervision of children's games and other activities.

### RELATED JOB TITLES

Au pair
Child minder
Dinner supervisor
Nanny
Playgroup assistant
Playgroup helper

# MINOR GROUP 66
# HAIRDRESSERS, BEAUTICIANS AND RELATED OCCUPATIONS

Hairdressers, beauticians and related workers cut, style and treat hair, apply cosmetics and give various beauty treatments.

Occupations in this minor group are classified into the following unit groups:

**660 HAIRDRESSERS, BARBERS**
**661 BEAUTICIANS AND RELATED OCCUPATIONS**

## 660 HAIRDRESSERS, BARBERS

Hairdressers and barbers shampoo, cut, style and treat hair.

### TYPICAL ENTRY ROUTES AND ASSOCIATED QUALIFICATIONS

No academic qualifications are required but some colleges require candidates to have GCSE/SCE S-grades for entry into courses. Apprenticeships are available and further on-the-job training is provided.

### TASKS

- discusses customer requirements and cuts and trims hair using scissors, clippers, razor and comb;

- washes, bleaches, tints, dyes or waves hair and provides any necessary scalp treatments;

- combs, brushes, blow-dries or sets wet hair in rollers to style or straighten;

- shaves and trims beards and moustaches;

- collects payment, arranges appointments and cleans and tidies salon.

### RELATED JOB TITLES

Barber
Hair stylist
Hairdresser

## 661 BEAUTICIANS AND RELATED OCCUPATIONS

Beauticians and related workers give facial and body beauty treatments, apply cosmetics and dress wigs.

### TYPICAL ENTRY ROUTES AND ASSOCIATED QUALIFICATIONS

No academic qualifications are required but some colleges require candidates to have GCSE/SCE S-grades. Off- and on-the-job training lasts up to three years.

### TASKS

- discusses clients requirements and applies creams or lotions to the face or body;

- massages scalp, face and other parts of the body, shampoos hair and removes any unwanted hair;

- cleans, shapes and polishes finger and/or toe nails;

- prepares and fits masks, wigs or beards and applies make-up to hide blemishes or emphasise facial features;

- cleans, sets and styles wigs and hair pieces;

- advises client on skin care.

## RELATED JOB TITLES

Beautician
Beauty consultant
Beauty therapist
Make-up artist
Manicurist
Pedicurist
Shampooer
Wig dresser

# MINOR GROUP 67
# DOMESTIC STAFF AND RELATED OCCUPATIONS

Domestic staff and related occupations workers supervise, co-ordinate and undertake domestic tasks in private households, hotels, schools, hostels and other residential establishments, take care of schools, churches, offices, flats and other buildings and direct and undertake the washing, dry cleaning, ironing and pressing of clothes, household linen, carpets and other articles.

Occupations in this minor group are classified into the following unit groups:

**670   DOMESTIC HOUSEKEEPERS AND RELATED OCCUPATIONS**
**671   HOUSEKEEPERS (NON-DOMESTIC)**
**672   CARETAKERS**
**673   LAUNDERERS, DRY CLEANERS, PRESSERS**

## 670  DOMESTIC HOUSEKEEPERS AND RELATED OCCUPATIONS

Domestic housekeepers and related workers run private households and perform domestic tasks on behalf of their employer, supervise the activity of dining room and other domestic staff, attend to their employer's personal needs and maintain his/her wardrobe and personal effects in good order.

### TYPICAL ENTRY ROUTES AND ASSOCIATED QUALIFICATIONS

Academic qualifications may be required to commence training.

### TASKS

- purchases food and other household supplies;

- prepares, cooks and serves food;

- washes and irons clothing and linen;

- keeps house clean and tidy;

- sets or supervises the setting of tables and supervises domestic staff;

- controls the ordering, storing and serving of wines and spirits;

- assists employer in washing and dressing and lays out clothes ready for wear;

- maintains employer's wardrobe in good order and packs and unpacks luggage as required.

### RELATED JOB TITLES

Butler
Cook-housekeeper
Housekeeper (*domestic*)
Valet

## 671  HOUSEKEEPERS (NON-DOMESTIC)

Housekeepers (non-domestic) supervise and co-ordinate cleaning and other housekeeping tasks in hotels, schools, hostels and other non-private establishments.

### TYPICAL ENTRY ROUTES AND ASSOCIATED QUALIFICATIONS

Academic qualifications may be required.  Off- and-on-the-job training is provided.

## TASKS

- orders food and other household supplies such as linen and cleaning materials;

- supervises and co-ordinates the activities of cleaners and other housekeeping staff in hotels, schools, hostels or other non-private establishments;

- maintains household records, as required;

- inspects premises to ensure cleanliness;

- ensures that guests and residents are comfortable.

## RELATED JOB TITLES

Housekeeper (*non-domestic*)
School housekeeper

## 672 CARETAKERS

Caretakers supervise and undertake the care and maintenance of church, school, office and other buildings and furnishings.

## TYPICAL ENTRY ROUTES AND ASSOCIATED QUALIFICATIONS

No academic qualifications are required. Training is provided.

## TASKS

- locks and unlocks doors and entrances at appropriate times;

- supervises and/or undertakes the cleaning and maintenance of premises;

- controls heating, lighting and security systems;

- undertakes minor repairs and notifies owner of need for major repairs;

- checks fire and safety equipment for adequate functioning.

## RELATED JOB TITLES

Caretaker
Janitor
School caretaker

## 673 LAUNDERERS, DRY CLEANERS, PRESSERS

Launderers, dry cleaners and pressers supervise and undertake the washing, dry cleaning, ironing and pressing of household and other linen, carpets and other articles.

## TYPICAL ENTRY ROUTES AND ASSOCIATED QUALIFICATIONS

Academic qualifications may be required. Training is mainly on-the-job.

## TASKS

- receives garment or item from customer for cleaning, checks pockets, buttons, zips, etc. and issues receipt;

- sorts articles by fabric, colour and type and determines appropriate cleaning process;

- removes difficult stains using chemicals or steam gun;

- loads articles into washing and dry cleaning machines or electrically operated drum cleaning machine, operates controls to admit cleaning fluids and starts machine;

- sets and operates tumble drying machines and smoothes and shapes washed garments using hand iron or machine press;

- allocates washing machines to customers, ensures correct use of equipment and gives change;

- performs a variety of laundering, dry cleaning and pressing tasks not elsewhere classified, including beating carpets and shaping starched collars, cuffs and hats.

## RELATED JOB TITLES

Carpet cleaner
Dry cleaner
Garment presser
Hoffman presser
Laundry assistant
Laundry worker

# MINOR GROUP 69
# PERSONAL AND PROTECTIVE SERVICE
# OCCUPATIONS NEC

Workers in this minor group perform a variety of personal service occupations not elsewhere classified in MAJOR GROUP 6: Personal and Protective Service Occupations.

Occupations in this minor group are classified into the following unit groups:

**690 UNDERTAKERS**

**691 BOOKMAKERS**

**699 OTHER PERSONAL AND PROTECTIVE SERVICE OCCUPATIONS NEC**

## 690 UNDERTAKERS

Undertakers make funeral arrangements for clients and supervise and help conduct proceedings.

### TYPICAL ENTRY ROUTES AND ASSOCIATED QUALIFICATIONS

Entry does not depend on academic qualifications although some employers require candidates to have GCSE/SCE S-grades. A driving licence is required for some posts. Professional qualifications are available. Training is provided.

### TASKS

- interviews relative or representative of the deceased to discuss their requirements;

- assists with the completion of necessary documents;

- carries out, or arranges for, the laying out of the body;

- liaises with cemetery or crematorium authorities;

- provides hearse and funeral cars and leads funeral procession.

### RELATED JOB TITLES

Funeral director
Undertaker

## 691 BOOKMAKERS

Bookmakers offer odds and accept bets on the result of sporting and other events.

### TYPICAL ENTRY ROUTES AND ASSOCIATED QUALIFICATIONS

Some employers require candidates to have GCSE/SCE S-grades. Training is provided.

### TASKS

- assesses the likely outcome of each event and determines odds, using knowledge of local and national sporting rules;

- accepts and records bets and issues receipts;

- passes bets on to other bookmakers when bet exceeds establishment's safe limit;

- pays out on winning bets;

- directs and co-ordinates the work of other bookmaking staff.

### RELATED JOB TITLES

Bookmaker (*betting*)
Turf accountant

## 699 OTHER PERSONAL AND PROTECTIVE SERVICE OCCUPATIONS NEC

Workers in this unit group perform a variety of personal and protective service occupations not elsewhere classified in MINOR GROUP 69: Personal and Protective Service Occupations n.e.c.

### TYPICAL ENTRY ROUTES AND ASSOCIATED QUALIFICATIONS

Academic qualifications, usually GCSE/SCE S-grades, are required for most posts. Off- and on-the-job training is provided and in some occupations, professional qualifications are available.

### RELATED JOB TITLES

Amusement park attendant
Arcade attendant
Baths attendant
Bingo caller
Carver (*food*)
Commissionaire
Court usher
Croupier
Disinfecting officer
Doorman/woman
Embalmer
Footman/woman
Model
Mortuary attendant
Pest control surveyor
Swimming pool attendant
Taxidermist
Usher/ette

# MAJOR GROUP 7

# SALES OCCUPATIONS

# MAJOR GROUP 7
# SALES OCCUPATIONS

This major group covers occupations whose tasks require the knowledge and experience necessary to buy, sell or demonstrate goods for wholesale or retail consumption.  The main tasks involve a knowledge of sales techniques, including the visual display of goods at the point of sale, familiarity with cash and credit handling procedures and a certain amount of record keeping associated with those tasks.

Most occupations in this major group require a general education and skills in interpersonal communication.  Some occupations require additional specific technical knowledge but are included in this major group because the primary task involves selling.

Occupations in this major group are classified into the following minor groups:

**70   BUYERS, BROKERS AND RELATED AGENTS**

**71   SALES REPRESENTATIVES**

**72   SALES ASSISTANTS AND CHECK-OUT
       OPERATORS**

**73   MOBILE, MARKET AND DOOR-TO-DOOR
       SALESPERSONS AND AGENTS**

**79   SALES OCCUPATIONS NEC**

# MINOR GROUP 70
# BUYERS, BROKERS AND RELATED AGENTS

Buyers, brokers and related agents organise and undertake the buying of merchandise, equipment, services and other goods on behalf of their employers or clients and buy and sell air and shipping cargo space and commodities for import, export and for wholesalers.

Occupations in this minor group are classified into the following unit groups:

700 BUYERS (RETAIL TRADE)
701 BUYERS AND PURCHASING OFFICERS (NOT RETAIL)
702 IMPORTERS AND EXPORTERS
703 AIR, COMMODITY AND SHIP BROKERS

## 700 BUYERS (RETAIL TRADE)

Buyers (retail trade) organise and undertake the buying of merchandise from manufacturers, importers, wholesalers and other sources for resale through retail distribution outlets.

### TYPICAL ENTRY ROUTES AND ASSOCIATED QUALIFICATIONS

Entry is most common with GCSE/SCE S-grades and A-levels/H-grades but is possible with other academic qualifications and/or relevant experience.

### TASKS

- attends trade fairs, shows and displays to examine new product lines;

- assesses budgetary limitations and customer requirements and decides on quantity, type, range and quality of merchandise to be bought;

- orders merchandise, ensures that delivered items comply with order and returns any faulty items;

- prices merchandise, places repeat orders for fast selling goods and arranges for promotions or price reductions for slow selling lines;

- keeps records and writes reports as necessary.

### RELATED JOB TITLES

Assistant buyer (*retail*)
Buyer (*retail*)

## 701 BUYERS AND PURCHASING OFFICERS (NOT RETAIL)

Buyers and purchasing officers (not retail) organise and undertake the buying of raw materials, equipment and merchandise for wholesale distribution and buy advertising space, printed material and other facilities necessary for producing television programmes, films and stage productions.

### TYPICAL ENTRY ROUTES AND ASSOCIATED QUALIFICATIONS

Entry is most common with GCSE/SCE S-grades and A-levels/H-grades but is possible with other academic qualifications and/or relevant experience.

### TASKS

- examines price lists and samples and selects the most suitable supplier or places tenders with suitable firms;

- helps negotiate contract with supplier and specifies details of goods or services required;

- monitors quality of incoming goods and returns unsatisfactory or faulty items;

- undertakes or arranges the expediting of orders when delays occur;

- maintains records and prepares reports as necessary.

**RELATED JOB TITLES**

Buyer (*not retail*)
Media buyer
Properties buyer

## 702  IMPORTERS AND EXPORTERS

Importers and exporters buy commodities from overseas for the home market and sell home-produced commodities to overseas markets.

**TYPICAL ENTRY ROUTES AND ASSOCIATED QUALIFICATIONS**

Entry does not depend on academic qualifications although some employers require candidates to have BTEC/SCOTVEC/degree or equivalent or relevant experience. Some posts require candidates to have knowledge of a foreign language.

**TASKS**

- investigates and evaluates home and overseas demand for particular commodities;

- obtains orders from buyers and arranges payment by bill of exchange, letter of credit or other means;

- arranges for shipment of commodities overseas and ensures that insurance and export licences are in order;

- carries out customs clearance procedures for imports, arranges their storage and delivery and sells them personally or through a commodity broker;

- advises home and overseas producers on the likely future demand for their goods.

**RELATED JOB TITLES**

Export agent
Importer

## 703  AIR, COMMODITY AND SHIP BROKERS

Air, commodity and ship brokers buy and sell commodities in bulk and buy and sell air and shipping freight space.

**TYPICAL ENTRY ROUTES AND ASSOCIATED QUALIFICATIONS**

Entry does not depend on academic qualifications although some employers require candidates to have BTEC/SCOTVEC/degree or relevant experience.

**TASKS**

- discusses buying and/or selling requirements of client and gives advice accordingly;

- arranges for the production of auction catalogues, fixes reserve prices, attends auction and bids on behalf of client;

- negotiates purchase/sale by private treaty of goods not sold at auction;

- obtains cargo space, fixes freight charges and signs and issues bills of loading;

- collects freight charges from client and undertakes all necessary formalities concerning customs and the loading/unloading of cargo;

- obtains information on aircraft/ships and stays abreast of market prices for ship and air freight.

**RELATED JOB TITLES**

Airbroker
Commodity broker
Shipbroker

# MINOR GROUP 71
# SALES REPRESENTATIVES

Sales representatives sell, and seek orders for, equipment, materials, machinery, food, drink, clothing, consumer goods, insurance, security, financial, cleaning and other services.

Occupations in this minor group are classified into the following unit groups:

**710 TECHNICAL AND WHOLESALE SALES REPRESENTATIVES**
**719 OTHER SALES REPRESENTATIVES NEC**

## 710 TECHNICAL AND WHOLESALE SALES REPRESENTATIVES

Technical and wholesale representatives provide technical explanations and advice and seek and receive orders for machinery, equipment, materials and other items and for the wholesale provision of food, drink, and consumer goods.

### TYPICAL ENTRY ROUTES AND ASSOCIATED QUALIFICATIONS

Entry is most common with GCSE/SCE S-grades but is possible with other academic qualifications and/or relevant experience.

### TASKS

- assesses characteristics of product being sold and decides on its main selling points;

- develops and maintains contact with customers;

- discusses customer requirements and advises them on the capabilities and limitations of the goods or services being sold;

- quotes prices, credit details, delivery dates and payment arrangements and arranges for delivery and installation of goods if appropriate;

- makes follow up visits to ensure customer satisfaction and to obtain further orders;

- stays abreast of advances in product/field and suggests possible improvements to product or service.

### RELATED JOB TITLES

Manufacturer's agent
Salesman/woman (*wholesale*)
Technical representative

## 719 OTHER SALES REPRESENTATIVES NEC

Workers in this unit group perform a variety of sales occupations not elsewhere classified in MINOR GROUP 71: Sales Representatives.

### TYPICAL ENTRY ROUTES AND ASSOCIATED QUALIFICATIONS

Entry is most common with GCSE/SCE S-grades but is possible with other academic qualifications and/or relevant experience.

### TASKS

- assesses characteristics of goods/services being sold and decides on main selling points;

- advises vendors and purchasers on market prices of property, accompanies clients to view property and assists with purchasing arrangements;

- makes inventories of items for sale, advises vendor of suitable reserve price, issues catalogues, conducts auction, notes bids and records sale;

- advises clients and agents on insurance related problems, seeks new outlets for business and quotes premiums, bonus rates, tax concessions, etc.;

- obtains orders for data processing, design, advertising, financial, cleaning, laundering, security, maintenance and pest control services;

- keeps abreast of new development in sales fields and performs miscellaneous sales tasks not elsewhere classified including demonstrating goods for sale and negotiating agreements for the passage of supply lines over or under land/property and the siting of supporting structures and other items.

## RELATED JOB TITLES

Auctioneer
Demonstrator
Insurance agent
Insurance inspector
Property negotiator
Sales representative (*retail trade*)

# MINOR GROUP 72
# SALES ASSISTANTS AND CHECK-OUT OPERATORS

Sales assistants and check-out operators sell goods and services in retail or wholesale establishments, accept payments and give change in respect of sales.

Occupations in this minor group are classified into the following unit groups:

> **720 SALES ASSISTANTS**
> **721 RETAIL CASH DESK AND CHECK-OUT OPERATORS**
> **722 PETROL PUMP FORECOURT ATTENDANTS**

## 720 SALES ASSISTANTS

Sales assistants demonstrate and sell a variety of goods and services in shops, showrooms and similar establishments.

### TYPICAL ENTRY ROUTES AND ASSOCIATED QUALIFICATIONS

No academic qualifications are required. Some employers require experience. On-the-job training is provided.

### TASKS

- discusses customer requirements, including type and price range of goods/services desired;

- advises customer on selection, purchase, use and care of merchandise and quotes prices, discounts and delivery times;

- receives full or partial payment, writes bill, receipt or docket and packages merchandise for customer;

- arranges goods on display stands and assists with stock checks.

### RELATED JOB TITLES

Sales assistant
Shop assistant

## 721 RETAIL CASH DESK AND CHECK-OUT OPERATORS

Retail cash desk and check-out operators accept payments from customers and give change in respect of sales or services.

### TYPICAL ENTRY ROUTES AND ASSOCIATED QUALIFICATIONS

No academic qualifications required. Some employers require experience. On-the-job training is provided.

### TASKS

- records cost of each item on cash register or by use of bar code reader;

- totals amount due and receives cash, cheque or credit card payment;

- gives change if necessary and issues receipts for purchase;

- debits customer's account in respect of purchases or services;

- reconciles takings with receipts and till rolls;

- maintains other transaction records as requested.

### RELATED JOB TITLES

Cashier (*restaurant*)
Cashier (*retail trade*)
Check-out operator

## 722 PETROL PUMP FORECOURT ATTENDANTS

Petrol pump forecourt attendants sell petrol, diesel and oil at a petrol service station or garage.

### TYPICAL ENTRY ROUTES AND ASSOCIATED QUALIFICATIONS

No academic qualifications are required. On-the-job training is provided.

### TASKS

- establishes customer requirements and refuels vehicle if requested;

- checks level of engine oil, battery and radiator fluids and tops-up if requested;

- checks and adjusts tyre pressures and washes windscreen if requested;

- accepts payment or records credit transaction;

- monitors fuel taken by self-service customers, ensures correct payment and gives change if necessary.

### RELATED JOB TITLES

Forecourt attendant (*garage*)
Petrol attendant
Petrol pump attendant

# MINOR GROUP 73
# MOBILE, MARKET AND DOOR-TO-DOOR
# SALESPERSONS AND AGENTS

Workers in this minor group visit private households to obtain orders and collect payments, deliver and sell food, drink and other goods in streets and open spaces from portable containers, stalls and vans and collect and deliver customers' articles for laundering, dry cleaning and other service industries.

Occupations in this minor group are classified into the following unit groups:

**730  COLLECTOR SALESPERSONS AND CREDIT AGENTS**
**731  ROUNDSMEN/WOMEN AND VAN SALESPERSONS**
**732  MARKET AND STREET TRADERS AND ASSISTANTS**
**733  SCRAP DEALERS, SCRAP METAL MERCHANTS**

## 730  COLLECTOR SALESPERSONS AND CREDIT AGENTS

Collector salespersons and credit agents visit private households to obtain orders and collect payments for goods and services.

### TYPICAL ENTRY ROUTES AND ASSOCIATED QUALIFICATIONS

No academic qualifications are required. Training is provided.

### TASKS

* calls on household, explains purpose of call and displays or describes goods/services on offer;

* emphasises main selling point of goods/services to stimulate customer interest;

* quotes prices and terms, collects any payments and completes hire purchase or credit arrangements;

* distributes advertising literature and sample goods;

* makes follow up calls to obtain further orders.

### RELATED JOB TITLES

Canvasser
Collector-salesperson
Credit agent
Credit trader
Door-to-door salesman/woman

## 731  ROUNDSMEN/WOMEN AND VAN SALESPERSONS

Roundsmen/women and van salespersons deliver and sell food, drink and other goods by calling on householders or by selling from a mobile shop or van and call on households to collect and receive payment for laundered or similarly serviced articles.

### TYPICAL ENTRY ROUTES AND ASSOCIATED QUALIFICATIONS

No academic qualification are required but candidates should hold a current driving licence. Off- and on-the-job training is provided.

### TASKS

* loads vehicle with food, drink or articles that have been laundered, etc.;

- drives vehicle over established route and parks at recognised stopping places or households;

- calls at customers' premises and delivers ordered goods;

- calls out, rings bell or otherwise attracts attention to the items on sale;

- sells goods, records deliveries, takes further orders or articles requiring servicing and collects cash or prepares bill;

- returns to depot and hands in unsold goods and cash.

### RELATED JOB TITLES

Driver-salesman/woman
Ice cream salesman/woman
Milk roundsman/woman
Milkman/woman (*milk retailing*)
Roundsman/woman
Van salesman/woman

## 732 MARKET AND STREET TRADERS AND ASSISTANTS

Market and street traders and assistants sell goods (other than refreshments) from stalls, barrows and other portable containers in streets and market places.

### TYPICAL ENTRY ROUTES AND ASSOCIATED QUALIFICATIONS

No academic qualifications are required.

### TASKS

- displays products on stall or barrow;

- calls out to attract attention to goods on offer;

- sells goods at fixed price or by bargaining with customer;

- accepts payment and may wrap goods;

- cleans up site on completion of each day's trading.

### RELATED JOB TITLES

Market assistant
Market trader
Stall assistant
Stall holder
Street trader

## 733 SCRAP DEALERS, SCRAP METAL MERCHANTS

Scrap dealers and scrap metal merchants buy and sell scrap metal, rags and waste material.

### TYPICAL ENTRY ROUTES AND ASSOCIATED QUALIFICATIONS

No academic qualifications are required but candidates should hold a current driving licence. Off- and on-the-job training is provided.

### TASKS

- drives established routes and collects rags, scrap metal and other waste from households;

- receives scrap metal from customers and bargains to agree on a price;

- helps customer search through scrap metal yard and sells scrap metal at a fixed price or by bargaining;

- accepts payment for goods.

### RELATED JOB TITLES

Rag and bone merchant
Scrap dealer
Scrap merchant

# MINOR GROUP 79
# SALES OCCUPATIONS NEC

Workers in this minor group perform a variety of sales occupations not elsewhere classified in MAJOR GROUP 7: Sales Occupations.

Occupations in this minor group are classified into the following unit groups:

  790   MERCHANDISERS
  791   WINDOW DRESSERS, FLORAL ARRANGERS
  792   TELEPHONE SALESPERSONS

## 790  MERCHANDISERS

Merchandisers replenish stocks of goods in self service stores and advise retailers on arrangements for making optimum use of material provided for the display of merchandise.

### TYPICAL ENTRY ROUTES AND ASSOCIATED QUALIFICATIONS

No academic qualifications are required. On-the-job training is provided.

### TASKS

- checks stock movements and replenishes goods on shelves as required;
- advises retailers on best use of display materials and possible product promotions, etc.;
- deals with customer enquiries regarding merchandise.

### RELATED JOB TITLES

Merchandiser
Merchandising executive

## 791  WINDOW DRESSERS, FLORAL ARRANGERS

Window dressers and floral arrangers produce artistic and attractive displays of merchandise in shop windows and design and make up floral arrangements.

### TYPICAL ENTRY ROUTES AND ASSOCIATED QUALIFICATIONS

No academic qualifications are required. On-the-job training is provided.

### TASKS

- considers occasion, purpose of display and likely customer requirements;
- arranges clothes, accessories, furnishings, etc. according to plan or own design;
- dresses display dummies, adding accessories as necessary;
- designs wreaths, bouquets, posies and button holes and selects appropriate foliage trimmings;
- wraps flower stems as necessary and selects or makes up suitable frame for flower arrangement;
- secures flowers to frame and adds foliage, ribbons, etc. until the desired effect is achieved.

### RELATED JOB TITLES

Floral arranger
Florist
Window dresser

## 792  TELEPHONE SALESPERSONS

Telephone salespersons obtain, receive and record telephone orders for goods and services.

## TYPICAL ENTRY ROUTES AND ASSOCIATED QUALIFICATIONS

Academic qualifications may be required. Some employers require candidates to have relevant experience.

## TASKS

- assesses the characteristics of product/service being sold and decides on its main selling points;

- telephones potential customers, explains purpose of call, discusses their requirements and advises on the goods/services being offered;

- quotes prices, credit terms and delivery conditions and records details of orders agreed;

- receives orders for goods/services by telephone and records relevant details;

- stays abreast of advances in product/services field.

## RELATED JOB TITLES

Telephone canvasser
Telephone salesperson

# MAJOR GROUP 8

# PLANT AND MACHINE OPERATIVES

# MAJOR GROUP 8
# PLANT AND MACHINE OPERATIVES

This major group covers occupations whose main tasks require the knowledge and experience necessary to operate vehicles and other mobile and stationary machinery, to operate and monitor industrial plant and equipment, to assemble products from component parts according to strict rules and procedures and subject assembled parts to routine tests.

Most occupations in this major group do not specify that a particular standard of education should have been achieved but will usually have an associated period of formal experience-related training.

Occupations in this major group are classified into the following minor groups:

**80 FOOD, DRINK AND TOBACCO PROCESS OPERATIVES**

**81 TEXTILES AND TANNERY PROCESS OPERATIVES**

**82 CHEMICALS, PAPER, PLASTICS AND RELATED PROCESS OPERATIVES**

**83 METAL MAKING AND TREATING PROCESS OPERATIVES**

**84 METAL WORKING PROCESS OPERATIVES**

**85 ASSEMBLERS/LINEWORKERS**

**86 OTHER ROUTINE PROCESS OPERATIVES**

**87 ROAD TRANSPORT OPERATIVES**

**88 OTHER TRANSPORT AND MACHINERY OPERATIVES**

**89 PLANT AND MACHINE OPERATIVES NEC**

# MINOR GROUP 80
# FOOD, DRINK AND TOBACCO PROCESS OPERATIVES

Food, drink and tobacco process operatives bake, freeze, heat, crush, mix, blend and otherwise process foodstuffs, beverages and tobacco leaves.

Occupations in this minor group are classified into the following unit groups:

**800 BAKERY AND CONFECTIONERY PROCESS OPERATIVES**

**801 BREWERY AND VINERY PROCESS OPERATIVES**

**802 TOBACCO PROCESS OPERATIVES**

**809 OTHER FOOD, DRINK AND TOBACCO PROCESS OPERATIVES NEC**

## 800 BAKERY AND CONFECTIONERY PROCESS OPERATIVES

Bakery and confectionery process operatives set, operate and attend machinery to mix, bake and otherwise prepare bread and flour confectionery products.

### TYPICAL ENTRY ROUTES AND ASSOCIATED QUALIFICATIONS

No academic qualifications are required, though some GCSE/SCEs can be an advantage. Training takes place both off- and on-the-job and usually includes technical training for recognised awards.

### TASKS

- sets and operates ovens to bake bread and flour confectionery products;

- operates machinery mixing flour and other baking ingredients;

- sets and operates cutters, rollers, die plates and other baking machinery to prepare or finish bread and flour confectionery products;

- attends equipment which automatically prepares, processes, shapes, or finishes bread or flour confectionery foodstuffs.

### RELATED JOB TITLES

Bakehouse assistant
Bakery worker
Pie maker

## 801 BREWERY AND VINERY PROCESS OPERATIVES

Brewery and vinery process operatives crush, mix, malt, cook and ferment grains and fruits to produce beer, wines, malt liquors, vinegar, yeast and related products.

### TYPICAL ENTRY ROUTES AND ASSOCIATED QUALIFICATIONS

Academic qualifications are not required, but GCSE/SCEs can be an advantage. Training takes place both off- and on-the-job and can include study for recognised awards.

### TASKS

- ripens or dries and then roasts barley and other grain used in making malt;

- heats and mixes crushed malt and water to produce grain wort;

- boils grain wort to produce malt liquor used in beer brewing;

- adds yeast and/or sugar to wort, cider, or wine liquor and controls fermentation;

- operates equipment to filter and carbonate fermented wines, ciders or beers, prior to bottling;

- operates equipment to break down grain to make drink products and to dilute or mix wines, spirits and other ingredients in the manufacture of drinks;

- operates equipment to dry grain or cool wort, liquor or other substances used in the manufacture of drinks.

## RELATED JOB TITLES

Brewery worker
Fermenter
Malt/barley roaster

## 802  TOBACCO PROCESS OPERATIVES

Tobacco processing operatives process tobacco leaf and make cigarettes, cigars, pipe and other tobacco products.

### TYPICAL ENTRY ROUTES AND ASSOCIATED QUALIFICATIONS

No academic qualifications are required. On-the-job training is provided.

### TASKS

- removes stem from tobacco leaf by hand or machine;

- sets machine controls to specify heat or moisture level, depth of cut, printing commands, etc.;

- positions wrapper leaves, paper and filter tips for cigar and cigarette manufacture;

- starts and regulates tobacco flow into drying, moistening, cutting, compressing, spinning, threshing and stemming machines;

- checks processed tobacco and removes any foreign material and rejects or repairs faulty cigarettes and miscut tobacco;

- remedies or reports machine faults.

## RELATED JOB TITLES

Cigarette maker
Cigarette making machinist
Machine feeder (*tobacco*)
Tobacco worker

## 809  OTHER FOOD, DRINK AND TOBACCO PROCESS OPERATIVES NEC

Workers in this unit group perform a variety of food and drink processing occupations not elsewhere classified in MINOR GROUP 80: Food, Drink and Tobacco Process Operatives.

### TYPICAL ENTRY ROUTES AND ASSOCIATED QUALIFICATIONS

Academic qualifications are not normally required. Training is given both off- and on-the-job.

### TASKS

- operates plant and machinery to make jam, toffee, cheese, processed cheese, margarine, syrup, ice, pasta, ice cream, sausages, chocolate, maize starch, edible fats and dextrin;

- operates equipment to cool, heat, dry, roast, blanch, pasteurise, smoke, sterilise, freeze, evaporate and concentrate foodstuffs and liquids used in food processing;

- mixes, pulps, grinds, blends and separates foodstuffs and liquids with churning, pressing, sieving, grinding and filtering equipment;

- performs other processing tasks not elsewhere classified including extracting oil from grain and sugar juice from beet, cubing sugar, coating, cutting and wrapping sugar confectionery, slicing beet, making starch moulds, preserving meat, fish, or vegetables and rolling and softening grain.

## RELATED JOB TITLES

Cheese maker
Confectionery worker (*sugar confectionery mfr*)
Dairy worker (*milk processing*)
Millhand (*food processing*)
Process worker (*food products mfr*)

# MINOR GROUP 81
# TEXTILES AND TANNERY PROCESS OPERATIVES

Textiles and tannery process operatives treat hides, skins and pelts, prepare natural and synthetic fibres to produce yarn and non-woven fabric, dress bristles and fibres for use as brush fillings, spin fibre into thread and yarn, double, twist and wind yarn and thread, wash dry and treat fibres, make braid, plait, line and rope and prepare colouring matter required for printing or dyeing fabrics.

Occupations in this minor group are classified into the following unit groups:

**810 TANNERY PRODUCTION OPERATIVES**
**811 PREPARATORY FIBRE PROCESSORS**
**812 SPINNERS, DOUBLERS, TWISTERS**
**813 WINDERS, REELERS**
**814 OTHER TEXTILES PROCESSING OPERATIVES**

## 810 TANNERY PRODUCTION OPERATIVES

Tannery production operatives treat hides, skins and pelts to prepare them for making up into leather, skin and fur products.

### TYPICAL ENTRY ROUTES AND ASSOCIATED QUALIFICATIONS

Academic qualifications are not normally required. On-the-job training is provided.

### TASKS

- cuts and trims skins and pelts using hand or mechanical cutting device;

- uses hand or machine to coat hides and skins with depilatory substance;

- removes wool from pelts by hand or operates machine to remove unwanted hair, wool, flesh and other waste material from pelts, hides and skins;

- prepares skins for soaking and operates one or more rotary drums to cure, degrease, wash, lime, delime, tan, dye or otherwise treat hides, skins and pelts.

### RELATED JOB TITLES

Currier
Drum room operator
Fellmonger
Leather cutter (*tannery*)
Toggler (*leather dressing*)

## 811 PREPARATORY FIBRE PROCESSORS

Preparatory fibre processors prepare natural, synthetic and reclaimed fibres for spinning into yarn and making into non-woven fabric and dress bristles and fibres for use as brush fillings.

### TYPICAL ENTRY ROUTES AND ASSOCIATED QUALIFICATIONS

Academic qualifications are not normally required. On-the-job training is provided.

### TASKS

- prepares machine for operation by positioning rolls or cans of slivers, feeding loose fibres into machine hopper or belt and setting machine controls;

- starts and monitors the operation of mixing, binding, combing, carding, hacking, drawing, cutting, flagging, severing and fibre opening machines;

- detects and clears blockages, broken slivers, clogged rollers, etc. and replenishes supply of input fibres;

- removes and replaces full output packages and cleans and oils machine.

### RELATED JOB TITLES

Carder (*textile mfr*)
Carding machine operator
Draw frame tenter
Frame attendant (*textile mfr*)

## 812 SPINNERS, DOUBLERS, TWISTERS

Spinners, doublers and twisters operate machines to spin, double and twist fibre into yarn and thread.

### TYPICAL ENTRY ROUTES AND ASSOCIATED QUALIFICATIONS

Academic qualifications are not normally required. On-the-job training is provided.

### TASKS

- prepares machines for operation by setting input packages and feeding thread ends from input packages through guides and rollers and securing them to output packages;

- adjusts machine speed and tension as required;

- starts and monitors the operation of spinning, doubling, twisting and texturing machines;

- detects broken or defective yarn, joins broken ends by hand or mechanical knotting and replenishes supply or input fibres;

- removes and replaces full output packages and cleans and oils machine.

### RELATED JOB TITLES

Doubler (*textile mfr*)
Ring spinner
Textiles spinner
Twister (*textile mfr*)

## 813 WINDERS, REELERS

Winders and reelers operate machines that wind yarn, thread and twine from one package to another package, card or spool.

### TYPICAL ENTRY ROUTES AND ASSOCIATED QUALIFICATIONS

Academic qualifications are not normally required. On-the-job training is provided.

### TASKS

- prepares machines for operation by setting input packages of yarn, thread or twine in machine creel or on spindles or circular frames;

- feeds thread ends through guides, tensioners, conditioning and cleaning devices to output packages, spools or cards;

- starts and monitors the operation of winding, reeling and spooling machines;

- detects yarn or filament breaks, joins broken ends by hand or mechanical knotting and replenishes supply of input fibres;

- removes full output packages, cards and spools;

- cleans and oils machine.

### RELATED JOB TITLES

Cheese winder
Reeler (*textile mfr*)
Winder (*textile mfr*)

## 814 OTHER TEXTILES PROCESSING OPERATIVES

Workers in this unit group wash, rinse, dry carbonise and otherwise treat fibres to remove impurities, make braid, plait, line and rope from natural and synthetic fibre yarn and estimate quantities of colouring matter required for printing and dyeing fabrics.

## TYPICAL ENTRY ROUTES AND ASSOCIATED QUALIFICATIONS

Academic qualifications are not normally required. On-the-job training is provided.

## TASKS

- operates machine to wash, rinse and dry slivers and to carbonise fibres, rags and wool to remove impurities, excess chemicals or vegetable matter;

- loads and operates machines to twist yarn threads or strands into rope, line, twine cord, braid and gimp;

- examines colour cards or specifications, estimates quantity of colouring material needed to print or dye batch of fibre and calculates and mixes ingredients accordingly;

- operates coating, combining, coiling, folding and fibre cleaning machines;

- prepares pattern cards, tapes, chains and harness for use on textile machines;

- interlaces and knots cordage to form nets and joins, repairs and fits attachments to fibre ropes;

- cleans and oils machine.

## RELATED JOB TITLES

Carboniser (*textile mfr*)
Colour matcher (*textile mfr*)
Creeler
Doffer
Scourer (*textile mfr*)

# MINOR GROUP 82
# CHEMICALS, PAPER, PLASTICS AND RELATED PROCESS OPERATIVES

Workers in this minor group operate plant and machinery to produce chemical, paper and related, glass, ceramic, rubber, plastic, synthetic and other products (other than metal) from a variety of raw materials.

Occupations in this minor group are classified into the following unit groups:

**820 CHEMICAL, GAS AND PETROLEUM PROCESS PLANT OPERATIVES**

**821 PAPER, WOOD AND RELATED PROCESS PLANT OPERATIVES**

**822 CUTTING AND SLITTING MACHINE OPERATIVES (PAPER PRODUCTS ETC.)**

**823 GLASS AND CERAMICS FURNACE OPERATIVES, KILNSETTERS**

**824 RUBBER PROCESS OPERATIVES, MOULDING MACHINE OPERATIVES, TYRE BUILDERS**

**825 PLASTICS PROCESS OPERATIVES, MOULDERS AND EXTRUDERS**

**826 SYNTHETIC FIBRE MAKERS**

**829 OTHER CHEMICALS, PAPER, PLASTICS AND RELATED PROCESS OPERATIVES NEC**

## 820 CHEMICAL, GAS AND PETROLEUM PROCESS PLANT OPERATIVES

Chemical, gas and petroleum process plant operatives operate plant to process chemical and related materials by crushing, milling, mixing and separating or by chemical, heat and other treatment.

### TYPICAL ENTRY ROUTES AND ASSOCIATED QUALIFICATIONS

Academic qualifications are not normally required. Training is mostly on-the-job, the amount and extent depending on the equipment, processes and control systems involved. For some jobs training includes study for recognised awards.

### TASKS

- ascertains, weighs and measures necessary ingredients;

- loads or supervises the loading of prescribed quantities of ingredients into plant or regulates flow from feed hoppers and conveyors and starts operational cycle;

- monitors instruments and gauges indicating fluid levels, temperatures, and other conditions affecting the operation of the plant;

- adjusts controls manually or from remote control panel as necessary and periodically withdraws samples for quality control testing;

- removes or regulates discharge of batch material on completion of processing;

- maintains operational log as required and cleans crushing, mixing, blending, milling and filtering plant after use.

## RELATED JOB TITLES

Chemical plant operator
Plant operator (*chemical mfr*)

## 821 PAPER, WOOD AND RELATED PROCESS PLANT OPERATIVES

Workers in this unit group make and combine paper sheets by hand and attend and operate ovens, kilns, crushing, milling, filtering, straining, calendering, coating, drying, finishing, winding, pulp preparing and other machines to produce and/or treat wood, paper, paperboard, leatherboard and plasterboard.

### TYPICAL ENTRY ROUTES AND ASSOCIATED QUALIFICATIONS

Academic qualifications are not normally required. Training is mostly given on-the-job, the amount and extent depending on the equipment and processes involved and the expertise required. For some jobs training includes study for recognised awards.

### TASKS

- ascertains necessary ingredients and loads and operates machines to beat, mix and crush wood, cork and fluid pulp ready for further processing;

- sets vacuum, filtering and rolling controls and operates machines to convert liquid pulp into sheet form;

- operates compressing, laminating, veneering and creosoting equipment;

- lights burners and starts stoker and fans to heat oven/kiln to required temperature, directs loading, ensures that material flows evenly through drier and directs unloading of dried material;

- examines job specifications, sets and adjusts machine controls and operates machines making and treating paper, paperboard, leatherboard and plasterboard;

- moulds pulp stock by hand to produce high quality paper and leatherboard.

## RELATED JOB TITLES

Beater (*paper mill*)
Calenderer (*paper mfr*)
Paper maker
Paper worker (*paper mfr*)
Winder operator (*paper mfr*)

## 822 CUTTING AND SLITTING MACHINE OPERATIVES (PAPER PRODUCTS ETC.)

Cutting and slitting machine operatives operate machines to cut paper and paper patterns, paperboard and abrasive cloth and to cut photographic film or similar material to required size.

### TYPICAL ENTRY ROUTES AND ASSOCIATED QUALIFICATIONS

Academic qualifications are not normally required. Training is mostly on-the-job, the amount and extent depending on the equipment used and operations performed. For some jobs training includes study for recognised awards.

### TASKS

- sets and adjusts edge guides, stops, cutting blade(s) and cutting dies;

- threads paper/film through rollers or loads into machine hopper;

- starts cutting/slitting machine and watches for irregular operation;

- removes product/film/master pattern and clears waste from machine.

## RELATED JOB TITLES

Guillotine cutter (*paper goods mfr*)
Guillotine operator (*paper goods mfr*)

## 823 GLASS AND CERAMICS FURNACE OPERATIVES, KILNSETTERS

Workers in this unit group position articles ready for firing in kilns and operate and attend furnaces and kilns to make and treat glass and ceramic articles.

Academic qualifications are not normally required,
but are an advantage. Training is mostly on-the-job,
the amount and extent depending on the equipment
used and type of operations performed. For some
jobs training includes study for recognised awards.

## TASKS

- directs loading of furnace with prescribed quantities and types of ingredients;

- sets timing and temperature controls, monitors
pressure gauges, adjusts controls as necessary
and regulates level of glass in furnace as required;

- operates controls to rotate rotary furnaces and
create a vacuum in vacuum furnaces, ensures
that static furnaces are correctly positioned and
switches on current;

- monitors temperature of drying and annealing
kilns and reports any significant deviations from
schedule sheet;

- cuts off heat supply after firing/heating/drying
and cleans furnace and kiln areas.

## RELATED JOB TITLES

Glass furnace operator
Kiln burner ( *glass, ceramics mfr* )
Kiln placer
Kilnsetter

## 824 RUBBER PROCESS OPERATIVES, MOULDING MACHINE OPERATIVES, TYRE BUILDERS

Workers in this unit group attend and operate masticating, calendering, mixing, forming, shaping,
moulding, extruding, cutting, trimming and winding machines to make and repair rubber products.

## TYPICAL ENTRY ROUTES AND ASSOCIATED QUALIFICATIONS

Academic qualifications are not normally required.
Training is mostly on-the-job, the amount and extent depending on the equipment and processes
involved and the operations performed. For some
jobs training includes study for recognised awards.

## TASKS

- ascertains ingredients and mixing requirements,
feeds machine or regulates flow from feed conveyors and hoppers;

- regulates speed, temperature and pressure of
masticating, mixing, extruding and vacuum
moulding machinery;

- operates winding machinery to form endless
belts and builds up rubberised material to form
industrial belting and pneumatic tyres;

- prepares surfaces and coats or lines metal or
other products with rubber;

- trims, sandblasts, or manipulates rubber article
against abrasive wheel to finish product;

- locates defects and repairs worn and faulty
sheathing, belting and rubber and pneumatic
tyres.

## RELATED JOB TITLES

Calenderer ( *rubber mfr* )
Extruding machine operator ( *rubber mfr* )
Rubber worker
Tyre builder

## 825 PLASTICS PROCESS OPERATIVES, MOULDERS AND EXTRUDERS

Workers in this unit group attend and operate
moulding, extruding, thermoforming, calendering,
covering, cutting and other machines to make and
repair plastic products.

## TYPICAL ENTRY ROUTES AND ASSOCIATED QUALIFICATIONS

Academic qualifications are not normally required.
Training is mostly on-the-job, the amount and extent depending on the equipment and processes
involved and the operations performed. For some
jobs training includes study for recognised awards.

## TASKS

- prepares machine for operation by affixing any
necessary attachments;

- weighs and mixes ingredients, loads machine with plastic to be worked or regulates flow from feed conveyor or hopper;

- monitors controls regulating temperature, pressure, etc. and operates moulding, extruding, calendering, thermoforming and covering machines;

- makes simple plastic moulds, artificial eyes and contact lens discs and makes and repairs spectacle frames and plastic parts of artificial limbs and other orthopaedic appliances;

- inspects plastic products for defects, takes measurements and repairs plastic belting and sheathing;

- trims, cuts and performs other finishing operations on plastic using hand and machine tools.

## RELATED JOB TITLES

Fibre glass laminator
Injection moulder (*plastic goods mfr*)
Plastic moulder

## 826 SYNTHETIC FIBRE MAKERS

Synthetic fibre makers operate plant in which fibre forming liquid is extruded and wound into packages of continuous filament or cut into short lengths.

### TYPICAL ENTRY ROUTES AND ASSOCIATED QUALIFICATIONS

Academic qualifications are not normally required. Training is mostly on-the-job, the amount and extent depending on the equipment and processes involved. For some jobs training includes study for recognised awards.

### TASKS

- controls chemical reactions to produce synthetic polymers or cellulosic dope;

- regulates input of liquid polymer or feeds polymer chips into hopper of melting unit;

- operates equipment to extrude polymer through holes into evaporating/ cooling chamber or co-agulating bath;

- gathers extruded filaments into strands and feeds strands over or through rolling, cutting and treatment units;

- removes packages of continuous filament and resumes winding on new cores or bobbins;

- checks and replenishes supplies of feedstock and treating solutions.

## RELATED JOB TITLES

Acetate spinner
Nylon spinner
Polyester spinner
Synthetic fibre maker
Viscose spinner

## 829 OTHER CHEMICALS, PAPER, PLASTICS AND RELATED PROCESS OPERATIVES NEC

Workers in this unit group perform a variety of processing occupations not elsewhere classified in MINOR GROUP 82: Chemicals, Paper, Plastics and Related Process Operatives.

### TYPICAL ENTRY ROUTES AND ASSOCIATED QUALIFICATIONS

Academic qualifications are not normally required. Training is mostly on-the-job, the amount and extent depending on the equipment and processes involved. For some jobs training includes study for recognised awards.

### TASKS

- packs products ready for kilnsetting and operates kilns, furnaces and ovens to produce cement clinker, linoleum cement and asphalt, to fire abrasive and carbon products and otherwise cook and heat treat materials and products not elsewhere classified;

- operates machines to mix, blend, crush, wash and separate seeds and other materials not elsewhere classified;

- operates machines to produce flat and corrugated asbestos cement pipes and sheets;

- operates machines to coat film and tape with sensitising material and otherwise impregnate materials by immersion;

- operates plant to split mica and splits and moulds mica by hand;

- performs other chemicals, paper, plastics and related processing tasks not elsewhere classified including colour matching paints and making slips and glazes for ceramic goods.

## RELATED JOB TITLES

Autoclave operator (*glass mfr*)
Calenderer (*asbestos*)
Glaze maker (*ceramics mfr*)
Kiln burner (*cement mfr*)
Kiln operator

# MINOR GROUP 83
# METAL MAKING AND TREATING PROCESS OPERATIVES

Metal making and treating operatives operate furnaces, retorts, ovens and other heating devices, roll hot metal, form and straighten metal rods, bars, tubes and sections, dip, spray, coat, finish, anneal, temper and harden metal articles, help operate forging, hammering, pressing and casting equipment, pour molten metal into moulds and perform other metal processing, forming and treating tasks not elsewhere classified.

Occupations in this minor group are classified into the following unit groups:

830 FURNACE OPERATIVES (METAL)

831 METAL DRAWERS

832 ROLLERS

833 ANNEALERS, HARDENERS, TEMPERERS (METAL)

834 ELECTROPLATERS, GALVANISERS, COLOUR COATERS

839 OTHER METAL MAKING AND TREATING PROCESS OPERATIVES NEC

## 830 FURNACE OPERATIVES (METAL)

Furnace operatives operate furnaces, ovens, retorts and other heating vessels to smelt, reheat, refire and melt metal and metal articles for further working.

### TYPICAL ENTRY ROUTES AND ASSOCIATED QUALIFICATIONS

No academic qualifications are required. Furnace operatives normally start at the lowest operative grade and progress to more skilled furnace jobs on promotion after gaining experience.

### TASKS

- supervises or undertakes charging of furnace with scrap iron and lime;

- operates furnace controls to regulate temperature and the flow of air, gas, oil or oxygen;

- adds oxidising, de-oxidising, alloying and fluxing agents as required;

- withdraws samples of molten metal for laboratory analysis;

- taps slag from surface of molten iron, zinc or other metal and directs flow of molten metal into pouring or casting ladles;

- directs or undertakes removal of product and waste material from furnace lining.

### RELATED JOB TITLES

Blast furnace man
Furnace operator (*metal mfr*)
Metal mixer

## 831 METAL DRAWERS

Metal drawers operate machines to draw metal tubes, rods, bars and wire through dies to reduce the diameter and to obtain finer tolerances and better surface quality.

236

## TYPICAL ENTRY ROUTES AND ASSOCIATED QUALIFICATIONS

No academic qualifications are required. Metal drawers normally start at the lowest operative grade and progress to more skilled jobs on promotion after gaining experience.

## TASKS

- sets machine controls regulating the diameter of the drawing die, drawing speed and quality of finish;

- feeds tube, rod, bar or wire into drawing machine and attaches to drawing block or carriage;

- operates controls to start machine and monitors drawing process;

- joins coils of wire together by welding if continuous drawing is required;

- undertakes routine maintenance of equipment.

## RELATED JOB TITLES

Bar drawer
Metal rod drawer
Wire drawer

## 832 ROLLERS

Rollers operate or direct the operation of hot and cold rolling mills to roll hot metal into slabs, blooms, billets, bars, rods, strip sheet plate or sections and to roll metal to correct temper and finish.

## TYPICAL ENTRY ROUTES AND ASSOCIATED QUALIFICATIONS

No academic qualifications are required. Rollers normally start at the lowest operative grade and progress to become rollers on promotion after gaining experience.

## TASKS

- examines instructions and determines rolling sequence, roll tension, rolling speed, number of passes and required space between rolls;

- sets or directs the setting of rolls' spacing, speed, tension and width of guides;

- guides metal to and from each set of rolls with tongs or using an automatic handling device;

- monitors rolling process to detect and rectify any irregularities;

- ensures that gauge and finish of rolled strip/sheet conform to specifications;

- cleans and changes rolls or directs cleaning and changing operations.

## RELATED JOB TITLES

Pulpit operator (*steel mfr*)
Roller (*metal trades*)
Rolling mill operator

## 833 ANNEALERS, HARDENERS, TEMPERERS (METAL)

Annealers, hardeners and temperers operate equipment to heat, cool and quench metal and metal articles in order to harden, reduce brittleness or stress and restore ductility.

## TYPICAL ENTRY ROUTES AND ASSOCIATED QUALIFICATIONS

No academic qualifications are required. Annealers, hardeners and temperers normally start at the lowest operative grade and progress to annealing, hardening and tempering jobs on promotion after gaining experience.

## TASKS

- examines instructions to determine heating time required;

- sets machine or furnace controls regulating temperature, duration of heating and conveyor or roller speed;

- places salts, lead, charcoal or other material in box or bath in furnace;

- loads articles into equipment or onto conveyor or rollers using tongs or lifting equipment;

- removes articles after specified time and allows articles to cool or quenches them in brine, oil or water.

Hardener (*metal*)
Heat treater (*metal*)
Heat treatment operator (*metal*)

Anodiser
Chrome plater
Colour coater
Electroplater
Galvaniser
Tinner (*metal trades*)

## 834 ELECTROPLATERS, GALVANISERS, COLOUR COATERS

Electroplaters, galvanisers and colour coaters operate continuous plant to coat metal parts and articles electrolytically, form metal articles by electro- and vacuum-deposition, dip and spray articles with another metal, plastic powder or other material and treat articles chemically to produce desired surface finishes.

### TYPICAL ENTRY ROUTES AND ASSOCIATED QUALIFICATIONS

No academic qualifications are required. Training is given in-house and varies according to the work. Electroplaters, galvanisers and colour coaters normally start at the lowest operative grade and progress to electroplating, galvanising and colour coating work on promotion after gaining experience.

### TASKS

- cleans and rinses article or preshaped former to be coated;

- masks area not to be covered with wax, resistant adhesive tape or other material;

- fits appropriate nozzle on spray gun, loads spray gun with appropriate coating material and prepares electrolytic solutions;

- sets machine, plant, or equipment controls to regulate electric current and temperature of molten zinc, tin, chromium, copper or other non-ferrous metal;

- immerses articles in plating solutions or sprays article until required thickness of coating has been deposited;

- removes article from solution and centrifuges, if necessary, to remove excess molten metal before cooling.

## 839 OTHER METAL MAKING AND TREATING PROCESS OPERATIVES NEC

Workers in this unit group perform a variety of metal making and treating occupations not elsewhere classified in MINOR GROUP 83: Metal Making and Treating Process Operatives.

### TYPICAL ENTRY ROUTES AND ASSOCIATED QUALIFICATIONS

No academic qualifications are required. Training is given in-house and varies from one job to another. Metal making and treating operatives normally start at the lowest operative grade and progress to more skilled jobs on promotion after gaining experience.

### TASKS

- sets up, assists with and operates piercing, rolling and extruding equipment to prepare and roll seamless metal tubes and to form and straighten metal tubes, bars and sections;

- assembles plaster mould sections and pours molten metal into moulds, and around bearings;

- assists with the operation of galvanising equipment and forging, power and drop hammers to shape heated metal to requirements;

- operates continuous plant to remove dirt, scale and other surface impurities by immersion in chemical solution;

- operates press and plant to compact and sinter metal;

- performs other metal processing, forming and treating tasks not elsewhere classified including operating machinery to corrugate metal and cut cutlery.

**RELATED JOB TITLES**

Degreaser (*metal trades*)
Extruder operator (*metal trades*)
Forge assistant
Jigger (*metal trades*)
Metal caster
Smith's striker

# MINOR GROUP 84
# METAL WORKING PROCESS OPERATIVES

Metal working process operatives tend and operate previously set up machine tools, presses, drop hammers and grinding and polishing machines to cut, shape, abrade, clean, smooth, sharpen, polish and otherwise machine metal.

Occupations in this minor group are classified into the following unit groups:

**840    MACHINE TOOL OPERATIVES (INCLUDING CNC MACHINE TOOL OPERATIVES)**

**841    PRESS STAMPING AND AUTOMATIC MACHINE OPERATIVES**

**842    METAL POLISHERS**

**843    METAL DRESSING OPERATIVES**

**844    SHOT BLASTERS**

## 840  MACHINE TOOL OPERATIVES (INCLUDING CNC MACHINE TOOL OPERATIVES)

Machine tool operatives operate previously set up drilling, boring, milling planing, grinding, lapping, honing, electrochemical and other shaping machines to cut, shape and otherwise machine metal workpieces.

### TYPICAL ENTRY ROUTES AND ASSOCIATED QUALIFICATIONS

No academic qualifications are required. Skills training takes place at the workbench or in a special training centre. Some operatives also attend college courses for recognised engineering awards.

### TASKS

- secures workpiece in chuck, fixture or machine table according to machining process;

- sets machine controls for simple operations or checks pre-set machine settings;

- starts machine and operates automatic or manual controls to feed tool to workpiece or vice versa;

- repositions workpiece during machining as required;

- withdraws workpiece and examines for accuracy using measuring instruments.

### RELATED JOB TITLES

Lathe operator (*metal trades*)
Machine tool operator
Metal machinist
Tool machinist

## 841  PRESS STAMPING AND AUTOMATIC MACHINE OPERATIVES

Press stamping and automatic machine operatives tend pre-set automatic machines and operate presses and drop hammers equipped with formers and die to shape metal articles and form hollows and relief patterns in metal.

### TYPICAL ENTRY ROUTES AND ASSOCIATED QUALIFICATIONS

No academic qualifications are required. Training is mainly on-the-job and varies according to the job and the machinery used.

## TASKS

- loads metal stock onto press manually or using lifting gear;

- selects and fixes tool in hand or power press;

- operates press by foot or hand control to shape, cut, or bend workpiece and to form springs;

- loads and secures stock and starts automatic metal working, sandblasting, and shot blasting machines to cut, shape, abrade and otherwise machine metal;

- sets and operates drop stampers to form hollow shapes and relief patterns in cold metal;

- removes finished workpiece from press or machine and checks visually or using measuring instruments.

## RELATED JOB TITLES

Hand press operator (*metal trades*)
Power press operator (*metal trades*)
Press bending machine operator
Stamper (*metal trades*)

## 842 METAL POLISHERS

Metal polishers manipulate abrasive materials, polishing heads and other tools to clean and polish metal articles and parts.

## TYPICAL ENTRY ROUTES AND ASSOCIATED QUALIFICATIONS

No academic qualifications are required. Polishers are trained mostly on-the-job and develop skill with experience. Training varies according to the job and in some cases is covered by an apprenticeship.

## TASKS

- selects suitable polishing head and secures and fixes on machine;

- sets controls to regulate speed and angle of polishing head;

- dresses polishing head as necessary with emery, grease or other substance;

- manipulates workpiece against polishing head or applies head to workpiece;

- applies industrial diamond, steel or diamond laps and/or wooden dowel to interior surface of die to obtain semi-smooth and mirror finishes;

- operates barrel polishing machine to clean and polish articles electrolytically or with abrasive materials.

## RELATED JOB TITLES

Die polisher
Jewellery polisher
Metal polisher
Silver polisher

## 843 METAL DRESSING OPERATIVES

Metal dressing operatives use hand and power tools to remove surplus metal and rough surfaces from castings, forgings or other metal parts.

## TYPICAL ENTRY ROUTES AND ASSOCIATED QUALIFICATIONS

No academic qualifications are required. Training varies according to the skill required, but is usually on-the-job.

## TASKS

- operates burning equipment, chipping and grinding equipment to remove defects from steel bars, blooms, ingots, billets or slabs;

- files, chisels, burns and saws off surplus metal;

- smoothes rough surfaces with hand tools and abrasive belts and wheels.

## RELATED JOB TITLES

Deburrer
Fettler (*metal trades*)
Steel dresser
Tyre chipper

## 844 SHOT BLASTERS

Shot blasters clean and smooth metal parts and articles using a jet of vapour or compressed air and abrasive material.

## TYPICAL ENTRY ROUTES AND ASSOCIATED QUALIFICATIONS

No academic qualifications are required. Most training takes place on-the-job by gaining experience.

## TASKS

- removes sand from casting using wire brush;

- charges blasting equipment with shot, grit, or other abrasive material;

- positions workpiece in blasting cabinet or compartment;

- directs jet of vapour or compresses air and abrasive material against workpiece;

- manipulates workpiece in jet until surfaces are evenly abraded;

- examines finished work to ensure a smooth finish.

## RELATED JOB TITLES

Sand blaster (*metal trades*)
Shot blaster

# MINOR GROUP 85
# ASSEMBLERS/LINEWORKERS

Assemblers/lineworkers perform repetitive tasks such as bolting, riveting, and soldering in the batch or mass assembly production of prepared component parts, wire up electronic equipment and make coils and harnesses for electrical and electronic equipment.

Occupations in this minor group are classified into the following unit groups:

**850 ASSEMBLERS/LINEWORKERS (ELECTRICAL/ELECTRONIC GOODS)**

**851 ASSEMBLERS/LINEWORKERS (VEHICLES AND OTHER METAL GOODS)**

**859 OTHER ASSEMBLERS/LINEWORKERS NEC**

## 850 ASSEMBLERS/LINEWORKERS (ELECTRICAL/ELECTRONIC GOODS)

Electrical and electronic assemblers/lineworkers wire up prepared parts and/or sub-assemblies in the manufacture of electrical and electronic equipment, make coils and wiring harnesses and assemble previously prepared parts in the batch or mass production of electrical and electronic goods and components.

### TYPICAL ENTRY ROUTES AND ASSOCIATED QUALIFICATIONS

No academic qualifications are required. In some cases candidates must take aptitude and dexterity tests. Normal colour vision is required for some jobs.

### TASKS

- examines drawings, specifications and wiring diagrams to identify appropriate materials and sequence of operations;

- selects, cuts and connects wire to appropriate terminals by crimping or soldering;

- positions and secures switches, transformers, tags, valve holders or other parts and connects capacitors, resistors, transistors or sub-assemblies to appropriate terminals by soldering;

- lays out and secures wire to make harnesses and operates machine to wind heavy and light coils of wire or copper for transformers, armatures, rotors, stators and light electrical equipment;

- assembles previously prepared electrical or electronic components by winding, bolting, screwing or otherwise fastening using an assembly machine or hand tools.

### RELATED JOB TITLES

Armature winder
Assembler (*electrical / electronic*)
Coil winder
Wireman/woman

## 851 ASSEMBLERS/LINEWORKERS (VEHICLES AND OTHER METAL GOODS)

Vehicles and other metal goods assemblers/lineworkers supervise and undertake the routine assembly of vehicles and other metal goods or components such as frames, axles, wire brushes and wheels.

### TYPICAL ENTRY ROUTES AND ASSOCIATED QUALIFICATIONS

No academic qualifications are required. In some cases candidates must take aptitude and dexterity tests. Normal colour vision is required for some jobs. Training varies according to the complexity of the work.

## TASKS

- follows instructions and drawings and positions components on work bench or in assembly machine;

- assembles prepared components in sequence by soldering, bolting, fastening, spot-welding, screwing and hammering using power and hand tools or assembly machine;

- rejects faulty assembly components;

- inspects finished article for faults, monitors assembly machine operation and reports any faults.

## RELATED JOB TITLES

Assembler (*metal goods*)
Car assembler
Line worker (*vehicle mfr*)

# 859 OTHER ASSEMBLERS/LINEWORKERS NEC

Workers in this unit group perform a variety of assembly occupations not elsewhere classified in MINOR GROUP 85: Assemblers/Lineworkers.

## TYPICAL ENTRY ROUTES AND ASSOCIATED QUALIFICATIONS

No academic qualifications are required. In some cases, candidates must take aptitude and dexterity tests. Normal colour vision is required for some jobs. Training varies according to the complexity of the work.

## TASKS

- follows instructions or drawings and positions prepared parts on work bench or in assembly machine;

- assembles prepared paper, mineral, plastic, rubber, textiles, leather, wood and precision instrument components by soldering, bolting, stapling, clipping and fastening and by using adhesive, nuts, screws and nails, to form chairs, handbags, spectacles, pottery, rubber, footwear, artificial flowers, textiles and other goods using hand or powered tools and assembly machines;

- rejects damaged or faulty components/parts;

- inspects finished article for faults, monitors assembly machine operation and reports any faults.

## RELATED JOB TITLES

Assembler (*leather / rubber goods mfr*)
Cardboard box folder
Carton stitcher
Plastics assembler
Wire stitcher (*paper goods mfr*)

# MINOR GROUP 86
# OTHER ROUTINE PROCESS OPERATIVES

Other routine process operatives inspect, test, examine, view, check, bottle, can, fill, sort, grade, weigh and pack goods, products, parts and materials and perform a variety of painting, coating and routine inspecting tasks not elsewhere classified.

Occupations in this minor group are classified into the following unit groups:

**860 INSPECTORS, VIEWERS AND TESTERS (METAL AND ELECTRICAL GOODS)**

**861 INSPECTORS, VIEWERS, TESTERS AND EXAMINERS (OTHER MANUFACTURED GOODS)**

**862 PACKERS, BOTTLERS, CANNERS, FILLERS**

**863 WEIGHERS, GRADERS, SORTERS**

**864 ROUTINE LABORATORY TESTERS**

**869 OTHER ROUTINE PROCESS OPERATIVES NEC**

## 860 INSPECTORS, VIEWERS AND TESTERS (METAL AND ELECTRICAL GOODS)

Workers in this unit group inspect and/or test metal stock, parts and products, electrical plant, machinery and electronic components, systems and sub-assemblies to detect processing, manufacturing and other defects.

### TYPICAL ENTRY ROUTES AND ASSOCIATED QUALIFICATIONS

Some GCSE/SCE qualifications may be required. Inspectors are recruited directly as assistants or by internal appointment. Training is both off- and on-the-job and may include study for recognised awards.

### TASKS

- examines articles for surface flaws such as cracks, dents, defective sealing or broken wires by visual inspection or using aids such as microscopes or magnifying glasses;

- verifies, from drawings or specifications, dimensions and angles using callipers, micrometers and other instruments;

- checks sequence of assembly operations and checks assemblies and sub-assemblies against parts lists to detect missing items;

- manipulates moving parts of articles to check true running;

- sets up test equipment, connects items/system to power source/pressure outlet, etc. and operates controls to check performance and operation of jet engines, electrical plant and machinery and electronics systems;

- analyses results, prepares reports, recommends improvements and notifies colleagues of any irregularities.

### RELATED JOB TITLES

Examiner (*metal trades*)
Inspector (*metal trades*)
Mechanical inspector
Quality control inspector (*metal trades*)
Test engineer
Viewer (*electrical goods mfr*)

245

## 861 INSPECTORS, VIEWERS, TESTERS AND EXAMINERS (OTHER MANUFACTURED GOODS)

Workers in this unit group inspect, check and view textiles, wood, paper, food, plastics and rubber goods, parts and materials to detect manufacturing and other defects.

### TYPICAL ENTRY ROUTES AND ASSOCIATED QUALIFICATIONS

Some GCSE/SCE qualifications may be required. Inspectors are recruited directly as assistants or by internal appointment. Training is both off- and on-the-job and may include study for recognised awards.

### TASKS

- examines yarn packages, textile fabrics and garments, operates checking equipment to check cord, rope and yarn and straightens and examines dyed yarn;

- examines wood or wood products by sight and touch, checks specifications, marks repairable defects and rejects faulty items;

- examines paper and paperboard for marks, joins, tears, creasing, defective coating, etc., marks repairable defects and rejects faulty items;

- examines plastics and rubber materials or products for blisters, cracks, holes, foreign matter, etc., checks dimensions using gauges and tapes, marks repairable defects and rejects faulty items;

- examines food products, food storage containers, etc., opens food cans and jars, examines contents by sight, smell, colour and taste and removes any faulty products;

- reports any recurrent or major defects and recommends improvements to production methods.

### RELATED JOB TITLES

Inspector (*food products mfr*)
Passer (*textiles mfr*)
Quality control inspector (*paper mfr*)
Textiles examiner
Tyre examiner

## 862 PACKERS, BOTTLERS, CANNERS, FILLERS

Workers in this unit group pack, wrap, fill, label and seal containers by hand or machine.

### TYPICAL ENTRY ROUTES AND ASSOCIATED QUALIFICATIONS

No academic qualifications are required. Training is mostly on-the-job and varies according to the type of packing and product. Formal courses are run for specialist packing.

### TASKS

- selects appropriate cylinder, ensures that there is no corrosion or other damage and fills with gas;

- fills tubes, ampoules, bottles, drums, barrels, bags, sacks, cans, boxes and other containers by hand using measuring/weighing aid or by positioning container under feeder spout;

- packs heavy goods in crates and boxes using hoist, mobile crane or similar lifting equipment;

- loads machine with packaging containers, materials, adhesive, etc., loads hopper with items to be packaged/wrapped, monitors filling, wrapping and packaging, adjusts controls as necessary and clears any blockages;

- examines cans, bottles and seals and rejects any that are faulty;

- labels goods by hand or machine;

- packs specialist items according to specifications and completes necessary documentation.

### RELATED JOB TITLES

Bottle filler
Packer
Packing machine operator
Wrapper

## 863 WEIGHERS, GRADERS, SORTERS

Workers in this unit group weigh, grade and sort materials, goods and products.

Academic qualifications are not normally required. Training is mostly on-the-job and varies according to company training schemes.

## TASKS

- examines hide, skins, leather, fabric, wool, rags, scrap metal, tobacco pipe bowls, fish, fibres, ceramics and other goods;

- assesses product quality visually and by touch and grades according to weight, thickness, colour and other quality criteria;

- ascertains material(s) required from order card, recipe, or specification and weighs and measures prescribed quantities accordingly;

- uses balances, springs weighing platforms, automatic scales and weighbridges to check the weight of goods, products and loaded vehicles;

- records and calculates gross and net weight, checks delivery notes and prepares documents and labels for identification purposes;

- operates machines to measure lengths of rolls of material and irregularly shaped materials such as leather or sheepskin.

## RELATED JOB TITLES

Check weigher
Egg grader
Selector (*plastics mfr*)
Sorter (*textile mfr*)
Weighbridge clerk
Weighbridge operator
Weigher

## 864 ROUTINE LABORATORY TESTERS

Routine laboratory testers perform routine checks, at various stages of production, to verify the physical, chemical and other quality related characteristics of materials and products.

Some GCSE/SCE qualifications may be required. Training is both off- and on-the-job. For some jobs training may include study for recognised awards. Pre-vocational courses are also available.

## TASKS

- examines test card to determine type of test required;

- sets up appropriate testing equipment and prepares item for testing;

- carries out prescribed tests to check acidity, alkalinity, absorption, colour, density, elasticity, solubility, or other physical and chemical characteristics;

- records test data and cleans, maintains and checks equipment for reliability.

## RELATED JOB TITLES

Laboratory assistant
Tester (*paint mfr*)

## 869 OTHER ROUTINE PROCESS OPERATIVES NEC

Workers in this unit group perform a variety of routine process operating occupations not elsewhere classified in MINOR GROUP 86: Other Routine Process Operatives.

## TYPICAL ENTRY ROUTES AND ASSOCIATED QUALIFICATIONS

Academic qualifications are not normally required. Training is mainly on-the-job and varies according to the type of process and company training scheme.

## TASKS

- paints lines on coaches, applies enamel to jewellery and coats, lacquers, dips and touches up articles (other than ceramic);

- sets up and operates machines to apply colour to wallpaper and to coat articles (other than ceramic) with paint, cellulose or other protective/decorative material;

- prepares wood for polishing and vehicle body-work for painting and polishes sprayed surfaces to give desired finish;

- examines leather, tobacco and minerals to detect manufacturing faults and operates checking equipment to test abrasive wheels and asbestos-cement pipes;

- performs miscellaneous painting and coating tasks not elsewhere classified including, staining articles, applying transfers, operating french polishing machines, removing surplus enamel from components and marking design outlines on articles;

- examines, views and checks other products not elsewhere classified including matches, double glazing frames and safety fuses;

- examines and checks optical elements, spectacles, goods vehicles and laundered articles and performs other routine sorting, grading and measuring tasks not elsewhere classified including, preparing cable ends for testing, preparing samples for laboratory analysis, checking contents of drug containers and the cleanliness of casks.

## RELATED JOB TITLES

Dipper (*metal trades*)
Examiner (*tobacco mfr*)
Glass examiner

# MINOR GROUP 87
# ROAD TRANSPORT OPERATIVES

Road transport operatives supervise the activities of drivers and conductors, drive road passenger-carrying vehicles, motor vehicles and articulated and heavy goods vehicles (over three tonnes in weight) and collect fares, issue tickets and control passengers on public service vehicles.

Occupations in this minor group are classified into the following unit groups:

870   BUS INSPECTORS

871   ROAD TRANSPORT DEPOT INSPECTORS AND RELATED OCCUPATIONS

872   DRIVERS OF ROAD GOODS VEHICLES

873   BUS AND COACH DRIVERS

874   TAXI, CAB DRIVERS AND CHAUFFEURS

875   BUS CONDUCTORS


## 870  BUS INSPECTORS

Bus inspectors co-ordinate and supervise the activities of bus drivers and conductors and deal with any operational difficulties on scheduled services.

### TYPICAL ENTRY ROUTES AND ASSOCIATED QUALIFICATIONS

Entry is most common via internal promotion from driver/conductor/operator. No academic qualifications are required as direct entry is rare.

### TASKS

- checks that vehicle is running as scheduled and complying with regulation concerning the number of passengers and items of luggage being carried;

- checks that passengers hold valid tickets;

- organises relief and replacement crews as necessary;

- monitors number of passengers travelling particular routes;

- deals with passenger enquiries;

- submits reports of any irregularities and makes recommendations for improvement of services.

### RELATED JOB TITLES

Bus inspector
Traffic inspector (*road transport*)

## 871  ROAD TRANSPORT DEPOT INSPECTORS AND RELATED OCCUPATIONS

Workers in this unit group co-ordinate and supervise the activities of road transport depot drivers (other than vehicle maintenance workers) and perform other road transport inspecting duties not elsewhere classified.

### TYPICAL ENTRY ROUTES AND ASSOCIATED QUALIFICATIONS

No academic qualifications are required. Entry is most common by internal promotion from driver/conductor/operator.

## TASKS

- checks that goods have been correctly loaded into vehicle;

- arranges for servicing, refuelling, cleaning and repair of depot vehicles;

- performs other road transport inspecting duties n.e.c.

## RELATED JOB TITLES

Depot inspector (*transport*)
Transport depot foreman/woman

# 872 DRIVERS OF ROAD GOODS VEHICLES

Drivers of road goods vehicles drive heavy goods vehicles (over three tonnes), light goods vehicles (less than three tonnes) and articulated vehicles to transport goods and animals.

## TYPICAL ENTRY ROUTES AND ASSOCIATED QUALIFICATIONS

No academic qualifications are required. There is a lower age limit of 21, a medical test is mandatory and a current, clean Class A full or provisional driving licence is required. Off- and on-the-job training is provided.

## TASKS

- checks tyres, brakes, lights, oil, water and fuel levels and general condition of the vehicle;

- drives vehicle from depot to loading/unloading point;

- assists with loading/unloading and ensures that load is evenly distributed and safely secured;

- drives vehicle to destination in accordance with schedule;

- maintains records of journey times, mileage and hours worked;

- undertakes minor repairs and notifies supervisor of any mechanical faults.

## RELATED JOB TITLES

Delivery driver
Dray man/woman
Goods driver
Haulage contractor
HGV driver
Lorry driver
Motor driver
Tanker driver
Van driver

# 873 BUS AND COACH DRIVERS

Bus and coach drivers drive road passenger-carrying vehicles such as buses, coaches, trams and mini-buses.

## TYPICAL ENTRY ROUTES AND ASSOCIATED QUALIFICATIONS

No academic qualifications are required but candidates are usually over 21 years old, between 5'4" and 6'2" tall and in possession of a current clean driving licence. Off- and on-the-job training is provided including training to obtain a Public Service Vehicle driving licence.

## TASKS

- checks tyres, brakes, lights, oil, water and fuel levels and general condition of the vehicle before start of journey;

- drives single- and double-decked vehicle over pre-determined route, complying with traffic regulations and keeping to time schedule;

- stops and opens and closes doors at pre-arranged places to allow passengers to board and alight, observing regulations concerning the number of passengers carried;

- may collect fares from passengers and issue tickets or ensure that they use a ticket machine;

- may plan routes in conjunction with private hirer and assist with loading and unloading of luggage;

- balances cash taken with tickets sold and may be responsible for cleanliness of vehicle.

Bus driver
Coach driver

# 874 TAXI, CAB DRIVERS AND CHAUFFEURS

Taxi, cab drivers and chauffeurs drive motor cars for private individuals, government departments and industrial organisations, drive taxis for public hire, drive new cars to delivery points and drive motorcycles and other motor vehicles.

## TYPICAL ENTRY ROUTES AND ASSOCIATED QUALIFICATIONS

No academic qualifications are required but most posts require a clean, current driving licence and a medical examination. Taxi drivers require at least three years training before being licensed.

## TASKS

- checks tyres, brakes, lights, oil, water and fuel levels and general condition of vehicle before start of journey;

- drives passenger-carrying motor cars, taxis and other motor cars and motorcycles, complying with road and traffic regulations;

- collects passengers when hailed or in response to telephone/radio message and helps them to secure their luggage;

- conveys passenger to destination and helps unload luggage;

- cleans, services and maintains vehicle or motorcycle;

- drives other motor vehicles including road sweeping vehicles.

## RELATED JOB TITLES

Cab driver
Chauffeur
Taxi driver

# 875 BUS CONDUCTORS

Bus conductors collect fares, issue tickets and control passengers on a public service vehicle.

## TYPICAL ENTRY ROUTES AND ASSOCIATED QUALIFICATIONS

No academic qualifications are required but candidates are usually over 18 and between 5'4" and 6'2" tall. Off- and on-the-job training is provided.

## TASKS

- observes regulations concerning the carrying capacity of vehicles and controls the boarding of passengers accordingly;

- signals to driver when to stop and start bus;

- collects fares from passengers and issues tickets;

- changes destination indicators as necessary;

- completes way-bill at scheduled points on route and balances cash taken with tickets issued;

- takes charge of property found on vehicle.

## RELATED JOB TITLES

Bus conductor

# MINOR GROUP 88
# OTHER TRANSPORT AND MACHINERY OPERATIVES

Other transport and machinery operatives perform a variety of dock duties and maintain mechanical equipment on board ships, organise and effect the safe movement of passenger and goods trains, drive and operate earth moving and surfacing equipment and cranes, trucks, hoists, winches, loading machines and conveyor belts, to load, unload and move goods and materials in factories, warehouses and on site and perform other transport and materials handling tasks not elsewhere classified.

Occupations in this minor group are classified into the following unit groups:

880    **SEAFARERS (MERCHANT NAVY); BARGE, LIGHTER AND BOAT OPERATIVES**

881    **RAIL TRANSPORT INSPECTORS, SUPERVISORS AND GUARDS**

882    **RAIL ENGINE DRIVERS AND ASSISTANTS**

883    **RAIL SIGNAL OPERATIVES AND CROSSING KEEPERS**

884    **SHUNTERS AND POINTS OPERATIVES**

885    **MECHANICAL PLANT DRIVERS AND OPERATIVES (EARTH MOVING AND CIVIL ENGINEERING)**

886    **CRANE DRIVERS**

887    **FORK LIFT AND MECHANICAL TRUCK DRIVERS**

889    **OTHER TRANSPORT AND MACHINERY OPERATIVES NEC**

## 880   SEAFARERS (MERCHANT NAVY); BARGE, LIGHTER AND BOAT OPERATIVES

Workers in this minor group supervise and carry out a variety of deck duties and operate and maintain engines, boilers and mechanical equipment on board ships.

### TYPICAL ENTRY ROUTES AND ASSOCIATED QUALIFICATIONS

Academic qualifications may be required for some posts. Off- and on-the-job training of between 10 and 14 weeks is provided. A medical examination is usually required.

### TASKS

- ensures that necessary fuel supplies are on board and inspects engine, boilers and other mechanisms for correct functioning;

- removes and repairs or replaces damaged or worn parts of plant and machinery and ensures that engine and plant machinery are well lubricated;

- stows cargo, assists passengers to embark and disembark, watches for hazards and moors or casts off mooring ropes as required;

- steers ship, under the supervision of a Duty Officer, checks navigational aids and keeps bridge, wheel and chartroom clean and tidy;

- performs other deck duties, including servicing and maintaining deck gear and rigging, splicing wire and fibre ropes, greasing winches and derricks opening up and battening down hatches, securing gangways and ladders and lowering and raising lifeboats.

## RELATED JOB TITLES

Boatman/woman
Deckhand (*shipping*)
Lighterman/woman
Merchant seaman/woman
Seaman/woman

# 881 RAIL TRANSPORT INSPECTORS, SUPERVISORS AND GUARDS

Rail transport inspectors, supervisors and guards direct, co-ordinate and undertake charge of safeguarding passenger and goods trains on surface and underground railways and investigate the work practices of train drivers, guards and signal operatives.

## TYPICAL ENTRY ROUTES AND ASSOCIATED QUALIFICATIONS

Entry is only available by internal promotion. No academic qualifications are required.

## TASKS

- provides crews for breakdown trains, allocates relief and replacement crews as necessary and keeps crews informed of any line repairs or restrictions;

- checks train running times for punctuality, visits and checks signal boxes and tests staff knowledge of signalling rules and regulations;

- couples tubs, carriages and locomotive to make up train and checks loading of tubs and carriages and security of couplings;

- informs driver of load distribution and any special features of the route and signals driver by whistle or light signal when to start or stop the train;

- checks control panel operation before the start of journey and operates push button controls to open and close doors on underground trains;

- inspects and collects tickets, collects excess fares, deals with passenger enquiries and takes charge of goods such as parcels, livestock and passenger's luggage.

## RELATED JOB TITLES

Goods guard
Guard (*railways*)
Railway guard
Railway inspector
Train guard

# 882 RAIL ENGINE DRIVERS AND ASSISTANTS

Rail engine drivers and assistants drive and assist with the driving of diesel, diesel-electric, electric and steam locomotives and multiple unit passenger trains on surface and underground railways.

## TYPICAL ENTRY ROUTES AND ASSOCIATED QUALIFICATIONS

Perfect colour vision (without spectacles or contact lenses) is required. There is an upper age limit of 23 for entry into training, which is only by internal promotion. No academic qualifications are required.

## TASKS

- checks controls, gauges, brakes and lights before start of journey and studies route, timetable and track information;

- starts train when directed and operates controls to regulate speed;

- watches for track hazards, observes signals and temperature, pressure and other gauges;

- stops as directed to allow passengers to embark/disembark, the loading and unloading of freight and coupling/uncoupling of carriages and tubs;

- checks safety equipment, regulates the heating of passenger compartments and records engine defects or unusual incidents on the journey.

Diesel engine driver
Locomotive driver
Train driver

## 883 RAIL SIGNAL OPERATIVES AND CROSSING KEEPERS

Rail signal operatives and crossing keepers supervise and undertake the operation of signals and the opening and closing of gates and barriers at level crossings to control the movement of rail traffic and safeguard passengers and pedestrians.

### TYPICAL ENTRY ROUTES AND ASSOCIATED QUALIFICATIONS

Entry is only available by internal promotion. No academic qualifications are required.

### TASKS

- examines instructions and time schedules of trains entering and leaving line and decides priority of movement of trains;

- receives and sends messages of train movements from or to signal operatives of neighbouring line sections;

- monitors panel indicating the movement of trains and issues instructions to drivers;

- opens and closes gates and barriers at level crossings as required;

- records time of trains passing through line section.

### RELATED JOB TITLES

Level crossing keeper
Signalman/woman (*railways*)

## 884 SHUNTERS AND POINTS OPERATIVES

Shunters and points operatives supervise and undertake the changing of points and guiding of wagons and coaches in marshalling yards and railway sidings to make up trains.

### TYPICAL ENTRY ROUTES AND ASSOCIATED QUALIFICATIONS

Entry is only available by internal promotion. No academic qualifications are required.

### TASKS

- examines instructions and signals to driver the lines to which train should be shunted;

- indicates to shunters which wagons and coaches should be uncoupled and where they should be moved to;

- disconnects brake and heating systems, uncouples wagons and coaches and guides them onto different lines as directed;

- operates manual points and wagon brakes to control their movement;

- links up wagons and coaches and reconnects brake and heating systems;

- maintains contact with signal operative throughout shunting operations.

### RELATED JOB TITLES

Points operator (*railways*)
Shunter

## 885 MECHANICAL PLANT DRIVERS AND OPERATIVES (EARTH MOVING AND CIVIL ENGINEERING)

Workers in this unit group supervise and undertake the operation of machines to excavate, grade, level and compact sand, earth, gravel and similar materials, drive piles into the ground and lay surfaces of asphalt, concrete and chippings.

### TYPICAL ENTRY ROUTES AND ASSOCIATED QUALIFICATIONS

No academic qualifications are required. On-the-job training is provided. The appropriate current driving licence will be required for driving on public highways.

**TASKS**

- determines job requirements from instructions or site plans;

- fixes any necessary extensions onto machine and loads machine with asphalt, concrete, bitumen, tar, stone chippings or any other required materials;

- manipulates levers, pedals and switches to manoeuvre vehicle, regulate angle and height of blades, buckets and hammers and starts conveyor, suction or water spraying system;

- watches operation and removes any likely obstacle or obstructions;

- directs refilling of machine hopper and repeats operations as necessary;

- cleans, oils and greases machine and carries out minor repairs.

**RELATED JOB TITLES**

Digger driver
Excavator driver
JCB operator
Plant operator (*building and contracting*)

## 886 CRANE DRIVERS

Crane drivers supervise and undertake the operation of cranes, jib cranes, power driven hoisting machinery and power driven stationary engine to raise and lower mine and other cages, lift and move equipment, materials, machinery and containers and to wind cables round drum(s) to haul objects.

**TYPICAL ENTRY ROUTES AND ASSOCIATED QUALIFICATIONS**

No academic qualifications are required. On-the-job training is provided. The appropriate current driving licence will be required for driving on public highways.

**TASKS**

- gives signals for movement of cage carrying workers/equipment;

- starts crane or engine motor and checks that cables run freely and that brakes and drum(s) are working;

- manipulates levers, switches and pedals to rotate jibs into position and turns winding drum to raise or lower hook, bucket or other holding equipment;

- lifts load or cage, or hauls object into required position and lowers or positions for ground workers to detach, unload or load;

- watches control panel for warning lights and indications of wind speed and direction and carrying capacity of crane;

- oils and greases machine and checks ropes.

**RELATED JOB TITLES**

Crane driver/operator
Winding engine operator

## 887 FORK LIFT AND MECHANICAL TRUCK DRIVERS

Fork lift and mechanical truck drivers supervise and undertake the driving and operation of fork lift and mechanical trucks in factories, warehouses, storerooms and other areas to transfer goods and materials.

**TYPICAL ENTRY ROUTES AND ASSOCIATED QUALIFICATIONS**

No academic qualifications are required. Some employers require a medical examination.

**TASKS**

- drives truck to load and operates controls to pick up load on forks or in hopper;

- drives truck to unloading point and lowers forks or hopper to correct position on stack or ground;

- ensures that truck is connected to charger or is correctly refuelled for use;

- may keep records of work undertaken;

- cleans, oils and greases machine.

Dumper driver
Fork lift driver
Fork lift truck driver
Stacker truck driver
Truck driver

## 889 OTHER TRANSPORT AND MACHINERY OPERATIVES NEC

Workers in this unit group perform a variety of transport and machinery operating occupations not elsewhere classified in MINOR GROUP 88: Other Transport and Machinery Operatives.

### TYPICAL ENTRY ROUTES AND ASSOCIATED QUALIFICATIONS

No academic qualifications are required.

### TASKS

- operates lighthouses and locks, opens and closes moving bridge across inland waterways and docks, assists in mooring craft, measures depth of water in canals, rivers, etc. to determine possible dumping or dredging sites and performs other miscellaneous water transport operating and related tasks;

- refuels aircraft from mobile tanker, fills road and rail tankers with liquids and gases and directs the movement of aircraft in aerodromes;

- drives horses or ponies and horse drawn vehicles to transport goods and passengers;

- controls the operation of equipment to transfer materials from underground and surface conveyors to bunkers, tubs and rail trucks and to load road/rail trucks with other materials;

- operates machinery to charge and discharge furnaces, position and transport hot billets, remove and replace coke oven doors and to hoist, winch and convey material and empty blast furnaces, coke ovens and similar industrial equipment not elsewhere classified;

- conveys goods and materials to and from work areas, loads and unloads wagons, tubs, mine cars and kilns, operates mechanism to invert loaded containers and changes ropes on haulage systems;

- performs other transport and materials handling tasks not elsewhere classified including supervising dock workers and crane and hoist operators, maintaining navigational lights in harbours, operating aerial ropeways and ingot cars, patrolling conveyor belts and clearing blockages and operating gates to release coke onto conveyor belts for screening plant or blast furnace.

### RELATED JOB TITLES

Airport hand
Belt attendant
Conveyor attendant
Conveyor operator
Lighthouse keeper
Material handler
Rope runner

# MINOR GROUP 89
# PLANT AND MACHINE OPERATIVES NEC

Workers in this minor group perform a variety of plant and machine operating occupations not elsewhere classified in MAJOR GROUP 8: Plant and Machine Operatives.

Occupations in this minor group are classified into the following unit groups:

**890 WASHERS, SCREENERS AND CRUSHERS IN MINES AND QUARRIES**

**891 PRINTING MACHINE MINDERS AND ASSISTANTS**

**892 WATER AND SEWERAGE PLANT ATTENDANTS**

**893 ELECTRICAL, ENERGY, BOILER AND RELATED PLANT OPERATIVES AND ATTENDANTS**

**894 OILERS, GREASERS, LUBRICATORS**

**895 MAINS AND SERVICE PIPE LAYERS, PIPE JOINTERS**

**896 CONSTRUCTION AND RELATED OPERATIVES**

**897 WOODWORKING MACHINE OPERATIVES**

**898 MINE (EXCLUDING COAL) AND QUARRY WORKERS**

**899 OTHER PLANT AND MACHINE OPERATIVES NEC**

## 890 WASHERS, SCREENERS AND CRUSHERS IN MINES AND QUARRIES

Workers in this unit group attend and operate crushing, grinding, milling, washing, sieving and other mechanical separating plant and machinery to wash, crush or separate coal, stone or ores.

### TYPICAL ENTRY ROUTES AND ASSOCIATED QUALIFICATIONS

No academic qualifications are required. On-the-job training is provided.

### TASKS

- prepares plant for operation by fixing grading screens or any other attachments;

- regulates flow of materials from conveyors and feed pipes and clears any blockages;

- tests solution for specific gravity and adds sand or shale as necessary;

- starts agitators/vibrators to separate minerals and monitors separation to ensure that light constituents remain in suspension whilst heavy constituents sink;

- ensures that screened, filtered, crushed and separated material is discharged to appropriate chutes or conveyors;

- cleans equipment after use.

### RELATED JOB TITLES

Clay processing operator
Crusher operator (*mine*)
Filter press operator (*coal mine*)
Magnetic separator operator
Washery attendant (*coal mine*)
Washery operator

## 891 PRINTING MACHINE MINDERS AND ASSISTANTS

Printing machine minders and assistants set and operate letter press, platen or cylinder, lithographic and photogravure printing machines.

### TYPICAL ENTRY ROUTES AND ASSOCIATED QUALIFICATIONS

No academic qualifications are required. Off- and on-the-job training is provided.

### TASKS

- installs printing cylinders in press and positions and fixes printing plates or blocks of composed type (formes);

- fills ink ducts and water tank and operates controls to regulate ink supply and imposition of colours;

- packs impression cylinder with paper or sets machine controls to ensure that all parts of work receive even pressure;

- loads paper rolls or sheets into press and adjusts feeding mechanism;

- prints and examines proof copies and makes any necessary adjustments;

- replenishes ink and material supplies, cleans and oils press and otherwise assists machine minder.

### RELATED JOB TITLES

Letterpress printer
Lithographic machine operator
Printer's assistant
Printing machine operator

## 892 WATER AND SEWERAGE PLANT ATTENDANTS

Water and sewerage plant attendants operate valves to control water supplies in mains and pipelines, attend screening, filtering, water purifying and sedimentation plant, clear any blockages and patrol and maintain sewerage systems.

### TYPICAL ENTRY ROUTES AND ASSOCIATED QUALIFICATIONS

No academic qualifications are required. Off- and on-the-job training is provided.

### TASKS

- attends water filtration and purification plant, monitors chemical treatment, regulates treatment of water supply within strict guidelines;

- opens and closes valves to regulate quantity and pressure of water and reports defective valves or abnormal water pressure, stops water supply in an emergency and informs consumers likely to be affected;

- regulates flow of raw sewage into screening plant, releases screened sewage and regulates its flow into detritus pits, sedimentation tanks and filtration beds;

- cleans out screen compartments, sedimentation tanks and filtration beds manually or using mechanical scraper;

- patrols sections of sewer, examines for any blockages or gas releases and clears blockages by flushing or by using boring rods;

- digs trenches and assists pipelayers to lay, renew or repair sewerage pipes.

### RELATED JOB TITLES

Sewage plant attendant
Sewage worker
Sewage works operator
Turncock
Water treatment plant operator

## 893 ELECTRICAL, ENERGY, BOILER AND RELATED PLANT OPERATIVES AND ATTENDANTS

Workers in this unit group operate boilers to produce hot water or steam and attend and operate compressors, turbines, electrical substations, switchboards and auxiliary plant and machinery to fuel nuclear reactors, drive blowers and pumps, electricity generators and other equipment.

## TYPICAL ENTRY ROUTES AND ASSOCIATED QUALIFICATIONS

Some academic qualifications or relevant experience may be required. Training is either by related apprenticeship (electrical) or off- and on-the-job.

## TASKS

- determines job requirements from switchboard attendant or operating instructions;

- opens valves and operates controls to regulate the flow of fuel to boiler or generating equipment;

- operates remote control panel to load fuel and remove discharged fuel elements from nuclear reactors;

- adjusts controls to maintain correct running speed of turbine or generator and monitors temperature and pressure controls on boilers;

- records instrument readings periodically and shuts down turbine/generator or boiler as demand decreases;

- carries out minor maintenance tasks and prescribed tests and reports any faults.

## RELATED JOB TITLES

Auxiliary plant attendant
Boiler attendant
Boiler operator
Compressor attendant
Stoker
Substation attendant (*electricity board*)
Turbine operator

## 894 OILERS, GREASERS, LUBRICATORS

Oilers, greasers and lubricators lubricate moving parts of stationary engines, rolling stock, machinery and similar equipment.

## TYPICAL ENTRY ROUTES AND ASSOCIATED QUALIFICATIONS

No academic qualifications are required.

## TASKS

- examines lubricant charts and other instructions to determine job requirements;

- fills grease gun with grease of appropriate grade;

- applies grease or oil to grease points or lubrication holes in machinery or equipment and over bearings, axles and other similar parts by hand;

- ensures that rollers in rope haulage system are well greased and running freely;

- inspects machines, equipment and haulage ropes visually and reports any faults;

- performs other oiling, greasing and lubricating tasks not elsewhere classified.

## RELATED JOB TITLES

Greaser
Lubricator
Oiler

## 895 MAINS AND SERVICE PIPE LAYERS, PIPE JOINTERS

Workers in this unit group lay, joint and examine pipe sections for drainage, gas, water or similar piping systems.

## TYPICAL ENTRY ROUTES AND ASSOCIATED QUALIFICATIONS

No academic qualifications are required. Some employers require candidates to have relevant experience or CITB approved training. Off- and on-the-job training is provided.

## TASKS

- examines drawings and specifications to determine job requirements;

- adds/removes sand or gravel in trench bottom to obtain required gradient;

- selects appropriate asbestos, clay, concrete, plastic or metal pipe sections and lowers them into prepared trenches using hoisting equipment;

- joints pipe by sealing with rubber, cement, lead, etc. connects piping to manholes and attaches pipe junctions as required;

- tests joints by filling piping with water, smoke or compressed air;

- uses electronic test equipment to detect leaks in pipes, hydrants or valves;

- visits consumers' premises to examine leaks, cases of contamination and unauthorised uses of water, gas or electricity.

**RELATED JOB TITLES**

Drain layer
Mains layer
Pipe jointer
Pipe layer
Service layer

## 896 CONSTRUCTION AND RELATED OPERATIVES

Construction and related operatives operate insulating equipment, fix plasterboard or dry linings to ceilings and walls, help construct, maintain, repair and demolish buildings and clean and resurface eroded stonework.

### TYPICAL ENTRY ROUTES AND ASSOCIATED QUALIFICATIONS

No academic qualifications are required. Training is either by apprenticeship or on-the-job.

### TASKS

- fills machine with insulating mixture, positions hose, drills access hole and fills cavities or coats surfaces to prevent loss or absorption of heat and provide fire protection;

- examines specifications and selects appropriate plasterboard or dry lining panels, cuts them to required size and fixes them to ceilings and walls;

- cuts, shapes and fits wood, lays bricks and tiles and performs other tasks in the construction, alteration and repair of buildings;

- cleans exterior surfaces of buildings and resurfaces eroded stone or brickwork with plastic compound;

- erects suspended ceilings and installs window blinds and roller shutters on windows, doors and shop fronts;

- demolishes buildings using hand or powered hand tools.

**RELATED JOB TITLES**

Ceiling fixer
Demolition worker
General handyman/woman
Loft insulator
Thermal insulator

## 897 WOODWORKING MACHINE OPERATIVES

Woodworking machine operatives operate or set up and operate machines to cut, turn, smooth and otherwise shape wood.

### TYPICAL ENTRY ROUTES AND ASSOCIATED QUALIFICATIONS

No academic qualifications are required. Training is by apprenticeship or off- and on-the-job.

### TASKS

- examines drawings and specifications to determine method and sequence of operations;

- selects and fixes jigs, templates and appropriate machining tools and adjusts table stops and guides to requirements;

- operates sawing equipment to cut logs, timber baulks, rough planks or boards and to slice veneers;

- sets cutting angle and rotation speed of blade and operates cutting, boring, dovetailing, planing, routing, tenoning, spindle cutting and wood turning machines;

- operates powered shears and sanding and automatic woodworking machines to smooth wood.

**RELATED JOB TITLES**

Cross cut sawyer
Saw operator (*sawmilling*)
Sawyer (*wood*)
Wood machine operator
Wood turner
Woodcutting machinist

# 898 MINE (EXCLUDING COAL) AND QUARRY WORKERS

Mine (excluding coal) and quarry workers extract minerals (other than coal) from underground workings, drill holes for blasting, erect supports, set and detonate explosives to loosen rocks, set up and operate drilling equipment and may perform offshore work.

## TYPICAL ENTRY ROUTES AND ASSOCIATED QUALIFICATIONS

No academic qualifications are required to commence training which is both off- and on-the-job. There is a lower age limit of 18 for underground work.

## TASKS

- determines work priorities and procedures and assigns duties to workers;

- assists in erecting derrick and installing hoisting equipment and assembles drilling and cutting tools;

- operates controls to start drill or cutting machine and regulates the speed and pressure of cutting and drilling;

- inspects blasting area, drills shot holes, inserts explosives and detonates charges to loosen large pieces of rock/ore;

- breaks material from rock face using powered drill, spade and/or shovel and lifts material into wagons;

- erects timber or metal supports to shore up tunnel and assists tunnel miner with the excavation of vertical shafts and underground tunnels;

- performs other mining and quarrying tasks not elsewhere classified including digging clay from open pits, operating high pressure hoses to wash china clay from open pit faces and otherwise assisting miners.

**RELATED JOB TITLES**

Miner (*excluding coal*)
Pit operative
Quarry worker
Roughneck
Well driller

# 899 OTHER PLANT AND MACHINE OPERATIVES NEC

Other plant and machine operatives n.e.c. operate a variety of plant and machinery not elsewhere classified in MINOR GROUP 89: Plant and Machine Operatives n.e.c.

## TYPICAL ENTRY ROUTES AND ASSOCIATED QUALIFICATIONS

No academic qualifications are required. Training is on-the-job.

## RELATED JOB TITLES

Barrel straightener
Frame setter
Duct erector
Guillotine operator (*metal trades*)
Pencil maker
Pipe moulder
Saw doctor
Saw smith
Shearing machine operator (*metal trades*)
Television aerial erector
Woollen fettler

# MAJOR GROUP 9

## OTHER
## OCCUPATIONS

# MAJOR GROUP 9
## OTHER OCCUPATIONS

This major group covers occupations which require the knowledge and experience necessary to perform mostly routine tasks, often involving the use of simple hand-held tools and, in some cases, requiring a degree of physical effort.

Most occupations in this major group do not require formal educational qualifications but will usually have an associated short period of formal experience-related training. All non-managerial agricultural occupations are also included in this major group, primarily because of the difficulty of distinguishing between those occupations which require only a limited knowledge of agricultural techniques, animal husbandry, etc., from those which require specific training and experience in these areas. These occupations are defined in a separate minor group.

Occupations in this major group are classified into the following minor groups:

**90   OTHER OCCUPATIONS IN AGRICULTURE, FORESTRY AND FISHING**

**91   OTHER OCCUPATIONS IN MINING AND MANUFACTURING**

**92   OTHER OCCUPATIONS IN CONSTRUCTION**

**93   OTHER OCCUPATIONS IN TRANSPORT**

**94   OTHER OCCUPATIONS IN COMMUNICATION**

**95   OTHER OCCUPATIONS IN SALES AND SERVICES**

**99   OTHER OCCUPATIONS NEC**

# MINOR GROUP 90
# OTHER OCCUPATIONS IN AGRICULTURE, FORESTRY AND FISHING

Workers in this minor group cultivate and harvest crops, breed, tend and train animals, catch and breed fish and other aquatic creatures and perform forestry and related tasks.

Occupations in this minor group are classified into the following unit groups:

**900 FARM WORKERS**
**901 AGRICULTURAL MACHINERY DRIVERS AND OPERATIVES**
**902 ALL OTHER OCCUPATIONS IN FARMING AND RELATED**
**903 FISHING AND RELATED WORKERS**
**904 FORESTRY WORKERS**

## 900 FARM WORKERS

Farm workers perform a variety of tasks, by hand and machine, to produce and harvest crops and to breed and rear cattle, sheep, pigs and poultry.

### TYPICAL ENTRY ROUTES AND ASSOCIATED QUALIFICATIONS

No academic qualifications are required to obtain an apprenticeship or Craft Training Scheme place from the Agricultural Training Board. To take either the National Certificate in Agriculture or the Certificate in General Agriculture will require one year of practical experience and GCSE/SCE S-grades.

### TASKS

- operates farm machinery to prepare soil, fertilize and treat crops;

- cultivates growing crops by hoeing, spraying and thinning as necessary;

- weighs and measures feedstuffs, feeds animals and checks them for any signs of disease;

- cleans barns, sheds, pens, yards, incubators and breeding units and sterilizes milking and other equipment as necessary;

- treats minor ailments and assists veterinary surgeon as required;

- tends flock of sheep and is responsible for their welfare;

- implements breeding policy, mates animals and tends them during birth of young.

### RELATED JOB TITLES

Agricultural worker
Dairyman/woman (*farming*)
Farm hand
Farm worker
Herdsman/woman
Pigman/woman
Poultry worker
Shepherd
Stockman/woman (*farming*)

## 901 AGRICULTURAL MACHINERY DRIVERS AND OPERATIVES

Workers in this unit group operate and drive tractor-drawn or other machinery to clear and cultivate land and to sow and harvest plants and crops.

### TYPICAL ENTRY ROUTES AND ASSOCIATED QUALIFICATIONS

No academic qualifications are required. Candidates will require the relevant driving licence to operate vehicles on public roads.

## TASKS

- attaches plough, cultivator, distributor, mower, baler or other implement to tractor;

- adjusts depth, speed and height of attached implement according to requirements;

- drives and operates machinery to plough, fertilize, plant, cultivate or harvest crops;

- services and maintains equipment and carries out any minor repairs.

## RELATED JOB TITLES

Agricultural tractor driver
Tractor driver (*agriculture*)

## 902  ALL OTHER OCCUPATIONS IN FARMING AND RELATED

Workers in this unit group perform a variety of tasks in the breeding, rearing and care of domestic and wild animals, horses, game animals, bees and mink, inseminate animals by artificial means, assist in the picking and lifting of crops, plant and maintain hedges, oversee the incubation and hatching of eggs and perform other farming and related tasks not elsewhere classified.

### TYPICAL ENTRY ROUTES AND ASSOCIATED QUALIFICATIONS

Some academic qualifications and/or relevant experience may be required. Training is provided.

## TASKS

- feeds, grooms, trims and exercises animals;

- cleans animals' quarters and renews bedding as necessary;

- extracts semen for storage, selects appropriate semen from store, injects recipient animal and issues certificate giving pedigree and date of insemination;

- incubates eggs in hatchery and supplies chicks for meat and egg production and game birds for reserves;

- plants cuttings or shrubs and maintains hedges by clipping, pruning and re-planting;

- picks soft and hard fruits, vegetables, hops and flowers;

- performs other farming and related tasks not elsewhere classified including sorting and marking livestock, catching rabbits, cutting peat, trimming dogs, shearing sheep and sexing chickens.

## RELATED JOB TITLES

Artificial inseminator
Dog handler
Gamekeeper
Groom
Kennelman/maid
Mushroom picker
Stablehand

## 903  FISHING AND RELATED WORKERS

Fishing and related workers catch fish at sea, breed and rear fish in captivity and cultivate shellfish and mussels, gather seaweed and perform other fishing and related tasks not elsewhere classified.

### TYPICAL ENTRY ROUTES AND ASSOCIATED QUALIFICATIONS

For sea-going posts, pre-sea training is required for all candidates. Training lasts 12 months and is both off- and on-the-job. Candidates with four years experience can apply for further training leading to Department of Trade Certificates of Competency as Mate and Skipper. For land based posts, some academic qualifications or relevant experience may be required.

## TASKS

- undertakes watchkeeping, bridge control and navigation duties on fishing vessels;

- assists with the shooting, hauling and repairing of nets and operates winches and lifting gear;

- guts, sorts and stows fish and washes deck;

- prepares, lays and empties baited pots at intervals;

- cultivates and harvests oysters, mussels and clams on natural or artificial beds and controls predators;

- nets river fish and feeds and maintains them in spawning pens, assists with feeding, water treatment and disease experiments and empties and cleans outdoor tanks;

- performs other fishing and related tasks not elsewhere classified including gathering seaweed and mussels, dredging for oysters and harpooning whales.

## RELATED JOB TITLES

Fisherman/woman
Trawlerman/woman

## 904 FORESTRY WORKERS

Forestry workers perform a variety of tasks related to the planting, cultivation and protection of trees.

### TYPICAL ENTRY ROUTES AND ASSOCIATED QUALIFICATIONS

No academic qualifications are required. Two years off- and on-the-job training is provided.

### TASKS

- prepares ground for planting by clearing vegetation and other debris;

- drains and ploughs land and erects and maintains fences as necessary;

- collects seeds, plants and prunes trees and selects and marks trees for felling;

- fells trees using axe or power saw and saws wood into required lengths;

- removes tops of standing trees and lops branches as necessary;

- assists in the control of harmful diseases, pests or forms of wildlife;

- maintains watch for fires and operates firefighting equipment.

## RELATED JOB TITLES

Forestry worker
Lumberjack
Timber feller
Woodman/woman

# MINOR GROUP 91
# OTHER OCCUPATIONS IN MINING AND MANUFACTURING

Workers in this minor group assist metal, electrical and electronic crafts workers and perform a variety of heavy and light manual tasks in coal mines and foundries and in engineering, chemical, gas, textiles, glass ceramics and other making and processing establishments.

Occupations in this minor group are classified into the following unit groups:

910 COAL MINE LABOURERS

911 LABOURERS IN FOUNDRIES

912 LABOURERS IN ENGINEERING AND ALLIED TRADES

913 MATES TO METAL/ELECTRICAL AND RELATED FITTERS

919 OTHER LABOURERS IN MAKING AND PROCESSING INDUSTRIES NEC

## 910 COAL MINE LABOURERS

Workers in this unit group perform a variety of manual tasks in coal mines.

### TYPICAL ENTRY ROUTES AND ASSOCIATED QUALIFICATIONS

No academic qualifications are required. Training is provided. There is a lower age limit of 18 for underground work.

### TASKS

- loads and unloads, stacks and stores materials;

- assists in setting up drilling and other mining machinery;

- washes and cleans machinery, equipment and tools and clears waste and any spillages from work area;

- otherwise assists coalmining workers as directed.

### RELATED JOB TITLES

Coalmining labourer
Labourer (*coal mine*)
Underground worker (*coal mine*)

## 911 LABOURERS IN FOUNDRIES

Workers in this unit group perform various manual tasks in foundries in engineering and allied trades.

### TYPICAL ENTRY ROUTES AND ASSOCIATED QUALIFICATIONS

No academic qualifications are required. On-the-job training is provided.

### TASKS

- assists with the charging of furnaces and keeps furnace area or casting bay clean;

- supplies moulders with sand and/or molten metal, assists with pouring molten metal into moulds, removes castings from moulds and conveys them to dresser;

- assists in setting up attachments on plant and machinery, helps load metal billets and operates saws, shears or other equipment;

- removes scale and scrap metal from work area, cleans scale from shears, roll and water channels and assist with the cleaning and changing of rolls and otherwise assist blast furnace, teeming, rolling, tube making, moulding and casting crews as directed.

## RELATED JOB TITLES

Foundry labourer
Foundry worker

## 912 LABOURERS IN ENGINEERING AND ALLIED TRADES

Workers in this unit group assist galvanizers and tinners and perform other manual tasks in engineering and allied industries.

## TYPICAL ENTRY ROUTES AND ASSOCIATED QUALIFICATIONS

No academic qualifications are required. On-the-job training is provided.

## TASKS

- dries articles in drying machine after coating;

- loads wire or sheets for galvanizing and feeds wire through galvanizing plant;

- stacks coated sheets for removal;

- cleans machinery, equipment and tools, keeps work area tidy and clears waste and any spillages;

- otherwise assists engineering and allied trades workers as directed.

## RELATED JOB TITLES

Factory hand (*engineering*)
Labourer (*engineering*)
Labourer (*galvanizing, tinning*)

## 913 MATES TO METAL/ELECTRICAL AND RELATED FITTERS

Workers in this unit group directly assist pipe, sheet and structural metal workers and electrical and electronics fitters in the performance of their tasks.

## TYPICAL ENTRY ROUTES AND ASSOCIATED QUALIFICATIONS

No academic qualifications are required. Some posts require certificates of competence or relevant experience. On-the-job training is provided.

## TASKS

- conveys tools and materials to work area and assists with the erection of ladders and scaffolding, the rigging of cradles of hoisting equipment and the attaching of slings, hooks and guide ropes;

- cuts or drills holes in walls, floors and ceilings and cuts conduit tubing and screw threads;

- assists in positioning and securing pipework, ducting, fittings and appliances;

- joins lengths of conduit tubing, strips insulation from wires and heats lead or pitch to molten state in ladles;

- assists plater to mark out, bend, drill and otherwise machine metal;

- otherwise assists metal/electrical/electronic fitters as directed.

## RELATED JOB TITLES

Electrician's mate
Fitter's mate
Jointer's mate (*cable*)
Plater's helper
Plumber's mate

## 919 OTHER LABOURERS IN MAKING AND PROCESSING INDUSTRIES NEC

Workers in this unit group perform a variety of manual tasks in making and processing industries not elsewhere classified in MINOR GROUP 91: Other Occupations in Mining and Manufacturing.

## TYPICAL ENTRY ROUTES AND
## ASSOCIATED QUALIFICATIONS

No academic qualifications are required. On-the-job training is provided.

## TASKS

- conveys goods, materials, equipment, etc. to work area, assists in setting up machinery and equipment and prepares tools, lamps and other equipment for use;

- clears machine blockages and cleans machinery, equipment and tools;

- loads and unloads vehicles, trucks and trolleys;

- paints or fixes identification labels or markers on products or containers;

- keeps work area tidy and clears waste or any spillages.

## RELATED JOB TITLES

Factory worker (*other manufacturing industries*)
Production labourer

# MINOR GROUP 92
# OTHER OCCUPATIONS IN CONSTRUCTION

Workers in this minor group lay, maintain and repair rail track, roads, paving slabs, kerb stones and pipes, assist woodworking and building craftsmen/women and perform miscellaneous building and civil engineering tasks not elsewhere classified.

Occupations in this minor group are classified into the following unit groups:

- **920 MATES TO WOODWORKING TRADES WORKERS**
- **921 MATES TO BUILDING TRADES WORKERS**
- **922 RAIL CONSTRUCTION AND MAINTENANCE WORKERS**
- **923 ROAD CONSTRUCTION AND MAINTENANCE WORKERS**
- **924 PAVIORS, KERB LAYERS**
- **929 OTHER BUILDING AND CIVIL ENGINEERING LABOURERS NEC**

## 920 MATES TO WOODWORKING TRADES WORKERS

Workers in this unit group assist woodworking trades workers and machine operators with the performance of their tasks.

### TYPICAL ENTRY ROUTES AND ASSOCIATED QUALIFICATIONS

No academic qualifications are required. On-the-job training is provided.

### TASKS

- carries logs, planks, baulks of wood, tools, nails, screws and other material and equipment to work area;

- stacks wood for craftsmen/women or machinist and assists with the placing of wood on saw or machine carriage using lifting equipment if necessary;

- removes and stacks machined wood and loads wood onto truck or conveyor;

- cleans equipment and work area and otherwise assists woodworking trades workers as directed.

### RELATED JOB TITLES

Joiner's labourer
Joiner's mate
Sawyer's assistant
Sawyer's mate

## 921 MATES TO BUILDING TRADES WORKERS

Workers in this unit group assist building trades workers with the performance of their tasks.

### TYPICAL ENTRY ROUTES AND ASSOCIATED QUALIFICATIONS

No academic qualifications are required. On-the-job training is provided.

### TASKS

- mixes mortar, grouting material, cement screed, plaster and terrazzo manually or using machine;

- conveys blocks, bricks, stone, mortar, roofing, felt, slates or other materials to work area;

- assists, under supervision, with the erection of scaffolding and working platforms and attaches ladders to spikes in stone or brickwork;

- removes old or damaged tiles from floors, walls and ceilings and brushes, dries, roughens and otherwise prepares surface for tiling;

- cuts holes in brickwork, dresses used bricks, cuts away damaged stonework and cleans facing or finished stonework;

- cleans equipment, tools and work area and otherwise assists building trades workers as directed.

## RELATED JOB TITLES

Bricklayer's labourer
Bricklayer's mate
Hod carrier
Plasterer's labourer
Plasterer's mate
Scaffolder's mate

## 922 RAIL CONSTRUCTION AND MAINTENANCE WORKERS

Workers in this unit group lay, re-lay, repair and examine railway track.

## TYPICAL ENTRY ROUTES AND ASSOCIATED QUALIFICATIONS

No academic qualifications are required. On-the-job training is provided.

## TASKS

- patrols length of track and visually inspects rails, bolts, fishplates and chairs for distortion or fracture;

- checks tightness of bolts and wedges, replaces damaged rail chairs and repacks ballast under sleepers if necessary;

- lubricates points, examines fences, drains, culverts and embankments and carries out any necessary maintenance;

- spreads ballast and lays sleepers or metal plates at specified intervals;

- positions lengths of rail, sets of points and crossovers and secures rail with bolts, wooden wedges or clips;

- fastens together sections of rail by bolting fishplates to rails.

## RELATED JOB TITLES

Leading trackman/woman (*railways*)
Platelayer
Trackman/woman (*railways*)

## 923 ROAD CONSTRUCTION AND MAINTENANCE WORKERS

Workers in this unit group construct, repair and maintain roads and erect prefabricated concrete structures.

## TYPICAL ENTRY ROUTES AND ASSOCIATED QUALIFICATIONS

No academic qualifications are required. On-the-job training is provided.

## TASKS

- inspects road surfaces for hazards or signs of deterioration, clears mud, weeds and debris from road and spreads grit or salt as required;

- cuts away broken road surface with pick or pneumatic drill;

- heats bitumen in bucket, applies it to newly laid asphalt and beats or draws tamper head on asphalt to close joints;

- spreads bitumen, tar or asphalt and compacts surface using roller;

- spreads aggregate over road surfaces using shovel and lays markings on road surface;

- selects appropriate prefabricated units and positions and joints units to form structures.

## RELATED JOB TITLES

Asphalt raker
Asphalter
Concrete erector
Road worker
Roadman/woman (*building and contracting*)
Tarmac layer

## 924 PAVIORS, KERB LAYERS

Paviors and kerblayers lay paving slabs and kerb stones on prepared foundations to form pavement and street gutters.

**TYPICAL ENTRY ROUTES AND
ASSOCIATED QUALIFICATIONS**

No academic qualifications are required. On-the-job training is provided.

**TASKS**

- marks out work area with guidelines;

- lays bedding of sand, concrete or mortar on prepared foundation;

- cuts slabs or stones to required size as necessary;

- fills joints with mortar;

- removes and replaces damaged paving slabs and kerb stones.

**RELATED JOB TITLES**

Flagger
Kerb layer
Pavior

# 929 OTHER BUILDING AND CIVIL ENGINEERING LABOURERS NEC

Workers in this unit group perform a variety of labouring occupations in building and civil engineering not elsewhere classified in MINOR GROUP 92: Other Occupations in Construction.

**TYPICAL ENTRY ROUTES AND
ASSOCIATED QUALIFICATIONS**

No academic qualifications are required. On-the-job training is provided.

**TASKS**

- covers ceilings, floors, walls and exposed surfaces of boilers, pipes and plant with insulating material;

- lights oil, coal or other heating vessel and breaks up blocks of asphalt, bitumen or tar;

- stirs melting mixture, adds aggregate if required, pours mixture into buckets and turns off heating;

- measures and fixes timber and other structures to support excavations, cables or other rail, signal and telecommunications equipment;

- erects and repairs fencing, excavates, constructs and maintains land drainage systems and prepares graves for burial;

- operates, cleans and lubricates valves and sluices, removes weeds, dead animals and other debris from water and carries out minor repairs to banks and footbridges.

**RELATED JOB TITLES**

Drainage worker
Fence erector
Grave digger
Loft insulator
Pipe insulator
Reservoir attendant

# MINOR GROUP 93
# OTHER OCCUPATIONS IN TRANSPORT

Workers in this minor group accompany motor vehicle and other road vehicle drivers, carry, load and unload furniture and other items, load and unload aircraft and ships' cargoes, carry baggage for passengers at docks and at terminals, attach loads to be lifted to lifting equipment and collect refuse from business and private premises.

Occupations in this minor group are classified into the following unit groups:

**930  STEVEDORES, DOCKERS**

**931  GOODS PORTERS**

**932  SLINGERS**

**933  REFUSE AND SALVAGE COLLECTORS**

**934  DRIVER'S MATES**

## 930  STEVEDORES, DOCKERS

Stevedores and dockers co-ordinate and undertake the loading and unloading of cargo from ships, boats and barges and supply berthed ships with water.

### TYPICAL ENTRY ROUTES AND ASSOCIATED QUALIFICATIONS

No academic qualifications are required. Off- and on-the-job training is provided.

### TASKS

- arranges cargo on quayside or in hold for loading or unloading;

- attaches winch or crane hooks, slings, ropes or clamps to load and hoses to ship's flow connections;

- operates winch or derrick to lift cargo, or signals to crane driver to commence lifting;

- starts pump to transfer oil, petroleum or water to and from a ship and uncouples hose system when loading/discharging is complete;

- removes slings, hooks, clamps or ropes from cargo and stows cargo in hold or loads cargo onto lorries, railway wagons or into warehouses.

### RELATED JOB TITLES

Dock labourer
Dock worker
Docker (*docks*)
Stevedore

## 931  GOODS PORTERS

Goods porters direct and undertake the loading, unloading and moving of household and office furniture and goods and equipment in or near warehouses, slaughterhouses, shops, goods depots, etc., load and unload baggage and equipment onto aircraft and attend to passengers' luggage at airports and docks.

### TYPICAL ENTRY ROUTES AND ASSOCIATED QUALIFICATIONS

No academic qualifications are required. On-the-job training is provided.

### TASKS

- packs furniture and household goods into crates and cartons, lifts floor coverings and may remove and replace structural fittings;

273

- loads furniture, household and other goods, materials and equipment into vehicles, removal vans and aircraft either manually or using lifting equipment;

- unloads contents of removal van, placing furniture in rooms or storage as required;

- conveys furniture and goods about storage areas or into removal van manually or using hand trucks;

- conveys passengers' baggage to check-in area at airport or dock and then to loading point or to outside transport.

## RELATED JOB TITLES

Baggage handler (*air transport*)
Furniture porter
Furniture remover
Loader
Market porter
Porter (*goods*)

## 932  SLINGERS

Slingers attach chains, hooks, slings and other grappling attachments to loads and/or lifting equipment and signal to crane drivers when to lift, move and lower load.

## TYPICAL ENTRY ROUTES AND ASSOCIATED QUALIFICATIONS

No academic qualifications are required. On-the-job training is provided.

## TASKS

- examines type and weight of load to be moved and inspects and selects appropriate hook, chain, rope, sling or other grappling attachment;

- attaches hook, chain, rope, sling or other grappling attachment to load;

- signals to crane driver when to lift, move and lower load;

- visually checks that load is balanced and ensures that route is clear for movement;

- releases grappling attachment when load has been lowered.

## RELATED JOB TITLES

Crane slinger
Slinger

## 933  REFUSE AND SALVAGE COLLECTORS

Refuse and salvage collectors direct and undertake the collection of refuse from household, commercial and industrial premises and load it into refuse vehicles.

## TYPICAL ENTRY ROUTES AND ASSOCIATED QUALIFICATIONS

No academic qualifications are required. On-the-job training is provided.

## TASKS

- rides in or on refuse vehicle and alights to pick up refuse;

- carries waste material in dustbins or other containers from premises to refuse vehicle;

- carries waste material in dustbins or other containers from premises to refuse vehicle;

- empties refuse into vehicle manually or using an electronic tipping device;

- returns dustbins or other containers to premises.

## RELATED JOB TITLES

Binman/woman (*refuse collection*)
Dustman/woman
Refuse collector

## 934  DRIVER'S MATES

Driver's mates accompany drivers of motorised and other road vehicles and assist with the loading and unloading of vehicles.

## TYPICAL ENTRY ROUTES AND ASSOCIATED QUALIFICATIONS

Academic qualifications may not be required. Off- and on-the-job training is provided. Some posts require a current driving licence.

## TASKS

- accompanies driver on journey and assists him/her with manoeuvres such as reversing;

- assists driver to load and unload vehicle;

- secures goods to prevent movement or damage during journey;

- assists driver with cleaning and maintenance of vehicle;

- performs other tasks as directed by driver.

## RELATED JOB TITLES

Driver's assistant (*road transport*)
Driver's mate
Lorry driver's mate

# MINOR GROUP 94
# OTHER OCCUPATIONS IN COMMUNICATION

Workers in this minor group receive, sort and deliver mail, parcels and other messages.

Occupations in this minor group are classified into the following unit groups:

### 940  POSTAL WORKERS, MAIL SORTERS
### 941  MESSENGERS, COURIERS

## 940  POSTAL WORKERS, MAIL SORTERS

Postal workers and mail sorters collect and receive mail, sort it into specified divisions and then deliver it.

### TYPICAL ENTRY ROUTES AND ASSOCIATED QUALIFICATIONS

Entry is most common with GCSE/SCE S-grades but is possible with no formal academic qualifications.

### TASKS

- collects mail from post boxes;

- sorts mail or parcels into specified divisions and then into delivery order;

- completes delivery forms, collects charges and obtains signatures for delivery of registered or recorded mail;

- maintains records of mail received and despatched;

- delivers mail and parcels following a specified route;

- may transport mail and parcels to railway stations, docks and airports.

### RELATED JOB TITLES

Mail sorter
Postal worker
Postman/woman

## 941  MESSENGERS, COURIERS

Messengers and couriers collect and deliver messages, documents, correspondence and other material within, or on behalf of, an establishment.

### TYPICAL ENTRY ROUTES AND ASSOCIATED QUALIFICATIONS

Academic qualifications may not be required.

### TASKS

- collects correspondence, documents and other material from, and delivers to, individuals, offices or other premises as directed;

- sorts incoming and outgoing material;

- collects charges and/or signatures from customers;

- gives and receives receipts for pick-up and delivery items;

- may assist and direct callers as required.

### RELATED JOB TITLES

Bank messenger
Courier
Despatch rider
Messenger

# MINOR GROUP 95
# OTHER OCCUPATIONS IN SALES AND SERVICES

Workers in this minor group perform a variety of cleaning, fetching, serving and carrying tasks in kitchens, operate passenger and goods lifts and control the parking of vehicles, clean interiors of buildings, aircraft, road vehicles, ships and trains, clean windows and chimneys, sweep streets, wash down vehicle exteriors and perform a variety of manual tasks in shops, hotels and hospitals.

Occupations in this minor group are classified into the following unit groups:

950 HOSPITAL PORTERS
951 HOTEL PORTERS
952 KITCHEN PORTERS, HANDS
953 COUNTERHANDS, CATERING ASSISTANTS
954 SHELF FILLERS
955 LIFT AND CAR PARK ATTENDANTS
956 WINDOW CLEANERS
957 ROAD SWEEPERS
958 CLEANERS, DOMESTICS
959 OTHER OCCUPATIONS IN SALES AND
      SERVICES NEC

## 950 HOSPITAL PORTERS

Hospital porters perform various manual tasks in hospitals to assist nursing and domestic staff with the care of patients.

### TYPICAL ENTRY ROUTES AND ASSOCIATED QUALIFICATIONS

Academic qualifications are not normally required. Training is mainly on-the-job. A medical examination may be required.

### TASKS

- lifts, escorts and wheels patients between hospital wards;

- assists with the delivery of meals, laundry, medical supplies and post to the wards or theatres;

- collects and disposes of refuse from wards and other departments;

- assists with unloading and delivery of supplies.

### RELATED JOB TITLES

Hospital porter

## 951 HOTEL PORTERS

Hotel porters meet guests, assist with their luggage and direct them to an appropriate room in an hotel or similar establishment.

### TYPICAL ENTRY ROUTES AND ASSOCIATED QUALIFICATIONS

No academic qualifications are required. On-the-job training is provided.

## TASKS

- meets guests on arrival and assists with their luggage;

- assists in tidying entrance hall;

- collects room keys from departing guests and arranges transport where necessary;

- deals with enquiries regarding hotel services and local amenities.

## RELATED JOB TITLES

Hall porter
Hotel porter
House Porter

## 952  KITCHEN PORTERS, HANDS

Kitchen porters and hands assist other kitchen and service staff in the preparation of food and perform various cleaning, fetching and carrying tasks.

## TYPICAL ENTRY ROUTES AND ASSOCIATED QUALIFICATIONS

No academic qualifications are required but on-the-job training is provided.

## TASKS

- cleans or prepares food for cooks by hand or machine;

- carries meat, vegetables and other foodstuffs from delivery van to storeroom and from storeroom to kitchen;

- washes crockery, cutlery, glassware and kitchen utensils;

- washes and cleans kitchen surfaces and areas and disposes of refuse.

## RELATED JOB TITLES

Kitchen assistant
Kitchen hand
Kitchen help
Kitchen porter

## 953  COUNTER HANDS, CATERING ASSISTANTS

Counter hands and catering assistants serve food and beverages from counters of self-service restaurants, cafes and other eating establishments.

## TYPICAL ENTRY ROUTES AND ASSOCIATED QUALIFICATIONS

No academic qualifications are required.  Some on-the-job training is provided.

## TASKS

- prepares and serves beverages and light refreshments;

- cleans service area, crockery, cutlery and other utensils;

- accepts payment and gives change;

- may check stocks and keep service area well stocked;

- may serve some customers at their tables.

## RELATED JOB TITLES

Cafeteria assistant
Canteen assistant
Catering assistant
Counter hand (*catering*)
Snack bar attendant

## 954  SHELF FILLERS

Shelf fillers receive incoming goods from storage, check them for damage and place them on the appropriate shelves in the store.

## TYPICAL ENTRY ROUTES AND ASSOCIATED QUALIFICATIONS

No academic qualifications are required.  Some on-the-job training is provided.

## TASKS

- selects goods from storeroom and checks for any damage;

- checks store layout or written instructions to determine the appropriate shelf location for the goods;

- prices goods by machine and fills shelves with goods;

- monitors depletion of stocks and re-fills shelves as required.

## RELATED JOB TITLES

Shelf filler (*retail trade*)
Stock handler (*retail trade*)

# 955  LIFT AND CAR PARK ATTENDANTS

Lift and car park attendants operate passenger and goods lifts in commercial, industrial, residential and other establishments and control the parking of vehicles in public and private car parks.

## TYPICAL ENTRY ROUTES AND ASSOCIATED QUALIFICATIONS

No academic qualifications are required. On-the-job training is provided.

## TASKS

- operates push-button or hand controls to raise and lower lifts to required floor;

- ensures safety of goods and passengers carried in lift;

- regulates entry/exit of vehicles to and from car parks and may park cars;

- issues and examines tickets in car parks, collects charges and gives change.

## RELATED JOB TITLES

Car park attendant
Lift attendant
Parking attendant

# 956  WINDOW CLEANERS

Window cleaners wash and polish windows and other glass fittings.

## TYPICAL ENTRY ROUTES AND ASSOCIATED QUALIFICATIONS

No academic qualifications are required. Some on-the-job training is provided.

## TASKS

- secures ladders and other equipment to gain access to glass;

- selects appropriate cleaning or polishing implement;

- washes and polishes glass with brushes, cloths, water, solvents and squeegees.

## RELATED JOB TITLES

Window cleaner

# 957  ROAD SWEEPERS

Workers in this unit group sweep and remove refuse from public thoroughfares and clean soot and deposits from flues and chimneys.

## TYPICAL ENTRY ROUTES AND ASSOCIATED QUALIFICATIONS

No academic qualifications are required. On-the-job training is provided.

## TASKS

- sweeps pavements, gutters and roadways with hand broom;

- shovels refuse into containers and empties public litter bins into containers;

- selects appropriate brush head and pushes it through flue or chimney, collects soot and other dislodged material with brush or vacuum equipment.

279

**RELATED JOB TITLES**

Chimney sweep
Road sweeper
Street cleaner

## 958  CLEANERS, DOMESTICS

Cleaners and domestics clean interiors of private houses, shops, hotels, schools, offices, other buildings, ships, aircraft, trains and road vehicles and wash and polish vehicle exteriors.

### TYPICAL ENTRY ROUTES AND ASSOCIATED QUALIFICATIONS

No academic qualifications are required. Some on-the-job training is provided.

### TASKS

- scrubs, washes, sweeps and polishes floors, corridors and stairs;

- dusts and polishes furniture and fittings;

- cleans toilets and bathrooms;

- washes down walls and ceilings;

- empties ashtrays, waste bins and removes rubbish.

### RELATED JOB TITLES

Car cleaner
Cleaner
Chambermaid
Domestic
Domestic cleaner
Industrial cleaner
Office cleaner
School cleaner

## 959  OTHER OCCUPATIONS IN SALES AND SERVICES NEC

Workers in this unit group perform a variety of other occupations in services not elsewhere classified in MINOR GROUP 95: Other Occupations in Sales and Services.

### TYPICAL ENTRY ROUTES AND ASSOCIATED QUALIFICATIONS

No academic qualifications are required. On-the-job training is provided.

### TASKS

- removes used crockery, cutlery, glassware and rubbish from tables, cleans and wipes tables, stacks used crockery for washing and refills water jugs, condiment containers, etc.;

- washes and prepares vegetables for cooking and cleans glasses in licensed bars;

- receives clothing, luggage and other articles, collects fee and issues ticket and returns item to depositor on presentation of receipt;

- cleans toilets and washrooms, replenishes supplies of soap, paper and towels and reports any defects in lavatory equipment;

- strips old posters from hoardings and fits new posters using brushes and working from a ladder if necessary;

- examines and collects tickets at harbours, piers and similar thoroughfares or establishments not elsewhere classified;

- performs a variety of attending and service tasks not elsewhere classified including attending bathing huts and deck chairs.

### RELATED JOB TITLES

Billposter
Cloakroom attendant
Deck chair attendant
Toilet attendant

# MINOR GROUP 99
# OTHER OCCUPATIONS NEC

Workers in this minor group perform a variety of manual tasks not elsewhere classified in MAJOR GROUP 9: Other Occupations.

Occupations in this minor group are classified into the following unit groups:

**990 ALL OTHER LABOURERS AND RELATED WORKERS**
**999 ALL OTHERS IN MISCELLANEOUS OCCUPATIONS NEC**

## 990 ALL OTHER LABOURERS AND RELATED WORKERS

Other labourers and related workers perform heavy and light manual tasks in industries (other than making and processing) not elsewhere classified.

### TYPICAL ENTRY ROUTES AND ASSOCIATED QUALIFICATIONS

No academic qualifications are required. On-the-job training is provided.

### TASKS

- conveys goods, materials, equipment, etc. about work areas and stacks goods and materials;

- washes and cleans parts, components and finished articles and keeps work area clean and clears waste material and any spillages;

- loads and unloads vehicles, trucks, trolleys, etc.;

- disposes of waste by baling, tipping on waste heap and burning;

- sweeps and cleans paths, roadways, etc. and performs routine maintenance tasks.

### RELATED JOB TITLES

General hand
Labourer

## 999 ALL OTHERS IN MISCELLANEOUS OCCUPATIONS NEC

Workers in this unit group perform a variety of miscellaneous tasks not elsewhere classified in MINOR GROUP 99: Other Occupations n.e.c.

### TYPICAL ENTRY ROUTES AND ASSOCIATED QUALIFICATIONS

No academic qualifications are required. On-the-job training is provided.

### RELATED JOB TITLES

Incinerator operator
Pump attendant
Stage hand (*entertainment*)
Washbay attendant

Printed in the United Kingdom for HMSO
Dd 292631, 3/90, C95, 3385/2, 16268.